SATSANG
WITH THE
ABBOT

SATSANG WITH THE ABBOT

Questions and Answers About Life, Spiritual Liberty, and the Pursuit of Ultimate Happiness

ABBOT GEORGE BURKE
(SWAMI NIRMALANANDA GIRI)

LIGHT OF THE SPIRIT
PRESS
CEDAR CREST, NEW MEXICO

Published by

    Light of the Spirit Press

    lightofthespiritpress.com

    Light of the Spirit Monastery

    P. O. Box 1370

    Cedar Crest, New Mexico 87008

    www.ocoy.org

ISBN-13: 978-0-9985998-5-4
ISBN-10: 0-9985998-5-9

Library of Congress Control Number: 2018936959
Light of the Spirit Press, Cedar Crest, New Mexico

1. OCC010000 BODY, MIND & SPIRIT / Mindfulness & Meditation
2. OCC021000 BODY, MIND & SPIRIT / Reference
3. REL062000 RELIGION / Spirituality

First edition, April 2018

07022019

CONTENTS

About the Author vii

Satsang with the Abbot 1

Did You Enjoy This Book? 346

Get Your Free Meditation Guide 347

Glossary 348

Index 370

Light of the Spirit Monastery 377

Reading for Awakening 378

ABOUT THE AUTHOR

Abbot George Burke (Swami Nirmalananda Giri) is the founder and director of the Light of the Spirit Monastery (Atma Jyoti Ashram) in Cedar Crest, New Mexico, USA.

In his many pilgrimages to India, he had the opportunity of meeting some of India's greatest spiritual figures, including Swami Sivananda of Rishikesh and Anandamayi Ma. During his first trip to India he was made a member of the ancient Swami Order by Swami Vidyananda Giri, a direct disciple of Paramhansa Yogananda, who had himself been given sannyas by the Shankaracharya of Puri, Jagadguru Bharati Krishna Tirtha.

In the United States he also encountered various Christian saints, including Saint John Maximovich of San Francisco and Saint Philaret Voznesensky of New York. He was ordained in the Liberal Catholic Church (International) to the priesthood on January 25, 1974, and consecrated a bishop on August 23, 1975.

For many years Abbot George has researched the identity of Jesus Christ and his teachings with India and Sanatana Dharma, including Yoga. It is his conclusion that Jesus lived in India for most of his life, and was a yogi and Sanatana Dharma missionary to the West. After his resurrection he returned to India and lived the rest of his life in the Himalayas. He has written about this in *The Christ of India*.

He is the author of numerous books on practical spiritual life, including *Om Yoga Meditation: Its Theory and Practice, Dwelling In The Mirror: A Study of Illusions Produced By Delusive Meditation And How to Be Free from Them*, and the Dharma for Awakening series, commentaries on important spiritual writings such as the Dhammapada, the Gospel of Thomas, the Bhagavad Gita and other scriptures.

All of his books, in addition to being available in print and as ebooks, are also available for reading for free on our website, OCOY.org, as well as are his other writings.

NOTE:

You can find out more about many of the books mentioned in these questions and answers in the Reading for Awakening section at the end of this book.

SATSANG WITH THE ABBOT

One of the most valuable spiritual activities in East or West is satsang: a gathering of spiritual aspirants for spiritual study, discussion and inspiration. A satsang is especially beneficial when there is someone with many years of practice and experience who answers the questions asked by the aspirants. Over the years, and especially after the advent of the internet, people have written to me with questions that I have answered according to my understanding. This book is a collection of those questions and my answers. I hope they will be interesting and helpful to others.

I am interested in climbing the stairs that may lead to samadhi. Please guide.

Samadhi is a natural consequence of meditation—in Buddhism profound meditation is considered samadhi—and there need be no special attention placed on it. Rather, your attention should be on making sure your practice is correct, of sufficient time, and that nothing in your life is working against it.

1

Swami Vivekananda told M (Mahendranath Gupta) that Sri Ramakrishna once asked him: "What do you want?" He answered, "I want to remain absorbed in samadhi." Whereupon Sri Ramakrishna responded: "What a poor understanding you have! Get beyond samadhi. Samadhi is a petty thing."

Sri Ramakrishna also said: "The seed of his Name has great Power. It destroys ignorance. A seed is so soft, a sprout is so soft. Yet they pierce the hard earth. The earth cracks." Success is assured.

Four years back one of my friends made the following statement: "Nothing is Everything. Everything is Nothing and there is Nothing called Nothing." Is this is a statement to explain Brahman?

Your friend's statement is just nonsensical gibberish by someone who thinks he can express Advaitic ideas by spouting contradictory jargon. The truth is expressed fully in the Bhagavad Gita. That should be your major focus of study.

The mantra beginning "Purnamidah" is the nearest to a perfect Advaitic statement there is:

> *Purnamidah, purnamidam,*
> *purnat purnamudachyate;*
> *Purnasya purnamadaya,*
> *purnam ewawashishyate.*

Purna means "total, full, complete," which is what our English term "perfect" used to mean, rather than just "without fault." In this verse, the word "complete" (purna) refers to God. Here, as best I can, is a translation into English:

This is the Complete; That is the Complete.
The Complete has come out of the Complete.
If we take the Complete away from the Complete,
Only the Complete remains.

We could also say:

This is the Totality; That is the Totality.
The Totality has come out of the Totality.
If we take the Totality away from the Totality,
Only the Totality remains.

Fools discuss philosophy and excuse themselves from practical application. The wise engage in sadhana and come to know the Truth.

I am extremely interested in pursuing a path wherein I can realize God, yet as any other ordinary mortal I am being pulled down by negative forces. But I truly want to be away from this because once I feed my hunger for these forces I see pain and sorrow immediately following me. I have experienced this many times. Moreover the more I want to go away from these bad elements the more I am going towards them in reality. Is there a way for me to come out of these negative forces and become good?

Goodness is your nature. You are realizing this through your spiritual intuition, and that is why the elements of ignorance in your life are unsettling to you. This is a sign of being well along the path; be assured of this.

Meditation is the only remedy for the ills of life. It may take time, but those who persevere will emerge fully into the Light. You will find meditation instruction on our website that we hope will prove helpful to you. The book *Soham Yoga* is available in both PDF, Kindle and print editions. Also please see the article: The Foundations of Yoga.

It will be most beneficial for you to daily read from the Bhagavad Gita, as it is completely practical, and not just abstract philosophy. The best translation is *The Song of God* by Swami Prabhavananda.

Please remember this: a diamond is a piece of coal that never gave up.

The following is a reply to an inquirer who described an experience in consciousness and asked what was its nature and if it was enlightenment:

Along the way many doors swing open, giving us unexpected insights. But we must just keep moving on. On occasion we enter into profound states of consciousness, some of which begin to fade away since they are messages from our Self (Atman) to seek and become established in them, and others are plateaus from which we do not regress. Whichever they are, in the words of Sri Ramakrishna: "Go forward." Infinity lies ahead.

How does one know if one is meant to live a monastic life versus a householder's life? I have been going over this in my mind for some years now and I am still uncertain of my calling to one or the other. Anything you might be able to say in regards to discerning if one has a monastic calling would be most appreciated and very helpful.

Since we are not external beings, the external mode of life is not "the thing." Rather, it is the interior development–sadhana–that matters.

Two people once asked Sri Ma Anandamayi if they should some day become monastics (they were married, but living a celibate life). Her reply was: "Those who do sadhana automatically become sadhus."

Once a young man came to Sri Ramana Maharshi and asked if he should become a monk. Immediately Sri Ramana responded: "No." Taken aback the young man protested: "But *you* did!" "Yes, but I did not need to ask anyone if I should," replied Ramana.

Please focus on your sadhana, making sure that it is going right. Then everything will unfold as it should. As Jesus assures us: "Seek ye first the kingdom of God, and his righteousness; and all these things shall be added unto you" (Matthew 6:33).

Nothing is more miserable than a monk without a genuine interior life–India is filled with them.

I have a question about gurus and their supposed infallibility. I do not mean to be disrespectful, but guru infallibility is just a mite suspect. Any thoughts that can help me out here?

If we look at the scriptures which form the basis of Sanatana Dharma– the eleven major Upanishads, the Bhagavad Gita, and the Yoga Sutras–we do not find the exaggerated view of the guru that has arisen and gripped Hinduism in its degeneracy, and is a major source of its continuing degeneracy. A true teacher is, in the simile of Buddha, a finger pointing to the Supreme. He is of great value and benefit, but he is never the Supreme Itself. The tendency in India for popular gurus to be declared avatars is irresponsible and ultimately destructive.

In the Taittiriya Upanishad (1:2:2) it is said: "Let your mother be a god to you; let your father be a god to you; let your teacher be a god to you; let your guest also be a god to you." The word here translated "god" is "deva," which means "a shining one." A deva is a semi-divine or celestial being with great powers, and therefore a "god"—sometimes called a demigod. (In Christianity they would be called angels.) So we are being told to look upon mother, father, teacher (acharya) and even guests as sacred, as angelic beings worthy of great respect. That is all. They are never God.

To look upon any human being as God or infallible like God is utterly foolish and self-deceiving. (I ought to know; I did it for years.) It is also foolish to consider that the records of their teachings are infallible. That is why we seek within ourselves for the Truth.

The foregoing is not the opinion of most Hindus, but it is consistent with real Dharma. And consistent with good sense.

Can you advise me as to a daily spiritual routine?

The yogi's life and experience is his laboratory. It is good to experiment and try out various routines to come up with the one that fits you best, keeping in mind that what will be relevant to you at one point in your development will have little relevance at another time, and vice-versa. Like you yourself, your routine should evolve.

Certainly routines are very beneficial, but there can be a pitfall. Some people get so occupied with routines that they mistakenly think they have a spiritual life. A classic example is that of the Western Christian monastics who attend Mass and hours of the Divine Office daily, but have no interior life at all.

What is needed is a spiritual routine as the nucleus around which spiritual realization can result. Spirit is consciousness, so dealing with that is the only really spiritual activity. For us, meditation on Soham and continual repetition of Soham throughout the day is the preferred nucleus. (See *Soham Yoga*.) Our spiritual study, etc., is necessary yet definitely secondary.

I would like to receive a mantra for healing _____.

A physical problem should be cared for by physical means. However japa and meditation of a sacred mantra, being divine vibration, definitely affects the health. Sri Ma Sarada Devi said that if a person is faithful and constant in japa and meditation his karma becomes attenuated or mitigated. If it was his karma to be sick for months he may only be sick for weeks. If his karma was to break his leg he might only be struck in the leg or sprain his ankle. In the beginning of my sadhana it was my experience that repeating my mantra when I was sick would make me feel worse, but I understood that my karma was being sped up and the illness would pass. And it always did. But I did not hesitate to use external remedies at the same time.

I am married and have two children. How can I lead a spiritual life in this situation?

All the Vedic Rishis were married with families, as were all the ancient sages of India including Janaka and even Sri Rama and Sri Krishna. Therefore marriage cannot be an impediment to spiritual life if it is a dharmic marriage. My sannyasa guru, Sri Swami Vidyananda Giri, once said to me: "There are many dharmic households that are more spiritual than some ashrams." I have lived in such households myself and know that to be true.

Spiritual life is in the heart. Please practice meditation daily. This is the prime necessity. Every day read from the Bhagavad Gita. This is a supreme help in spiritual life. Read *Sri Sri Ramakrishna Kathamrita* (*The Gospel of Sri Ramakrishna*) to find practical advice to married men on how to lead a spiritual life. Also, please obtain and read *Meditation and Spiritual Life* by Swami Yatiswarananda of the Ramakrishna Mission. It is published by the Ramakrishna Mission in Bangalore but should be available at the Ramakrishna Mission center (in America: Vedanta Society) nearest you.

In reply to a person who believed he was being invaded and oppressed by negative spirits and was suffering in a variety of physical and mental ways.

It would not be possible—or responsible—for me to give an assured "diagnosis" and prescribe a "treatment" for your situation, knowing only what is in your brief communication.

However, I can tell you this: negative entities cannot stand the supremely high and holy vibrations of the sacred syllable Om. Therefore I urge you to continually repeat Om mentally in a careful and relaxed manner, without strain. It may be helpful to sometimes intone It aloud, as the entering of the sacred sound into the ears has often proved effective against obsessing or possessing entities.

This may seem easy for me to say and hard for you to do, but smile and laugh as much as you can. Negative entities hate happiness and joy and flee from them. This is why negative human beings are stern and morose and bark at those who laugh or make a joke.

There is no telling how long the trouble will persist if you follow these suggestions, but it should not be too long. If you do not feel completely free from your problem after a week or so, I suggest you obtain and read *Psychic Self-defense* by Dion Fortune. It is available from Amazon.com. And I certainly recommend our own publication, *Soham Yoga*, which uses another approach you may want to consider.

I have read "Christian Insights into Reincarnation." How is a Christian to believe in a continuous cycle of death and rebirth until spiritual immortality is achieved when Jesus and the Bible mention hell as a place of eternal suffering for God's enemies?

First, you should also read *May a Christian Believe in Reincarnation?* as that contains more information that relates to your question.

Let's talk about hell. (Most religions like to.)

In the Bible there are three words translated "hell." They are: *Sheol, Gehenna, and Hades.*

Sheol is Hebrew, and merely means the grave–sometimes "pit." It is therefore a matter of interpretation as to whether it means a realm where the spirit is conscious after death. In the places throughout the Old Testament where sheol is used, it seems to always be a synonym for death itself.

In the New Testament we have the two words translated hell: Gehenna and Hades.

Gehenna, the term used by Matthew and Mark, means "Valley of Hinnom," which at the time of Jesus referred to the valley outside Jerusalem which was the garbage dump, in smell and appearance very like the infamous (and usually never mentioned) "Delhi sewer," the area on the west side of Delhi where all kinds of refuse are continually smoking and smoldering–and smelling terrible. This was used by Jesus as a symbol of *samsara*–the continuous cycle of birth and death. Orthodox Judaism uses the term *gilgal* or *ha'atakah* to convey the same idea. (This is discussed in *May a Christian Believe in Reincarnation?*) Although the fires burned and smoked continually in the Valley of Hinnom, the maggots were not destroyed, but kept "working" in the muck. Jesus was referring to this when he spoke of Gehenna as a place "where their worm dieth not, and the fire is not quenched" (Mark 9:44). And Revelation speaks of how "the smoke of their torment ascendeth up for ever and ever: and they have no rest day nor night" (Revelation 14:11).

Luke uses the Greek word hades, which merely means "the unseen world." In Greek mythology hades was in the depths of the earth, so "hell"–a word meaning "the nether regions" was used in English translations. Holland is really Hella-land, the Low Land, and so is also called the Netherlands.

As to "hell" lasting forever, this is based on incorrect understanding of *aionios*, which means "pertaining to the aeon." Greek cosmology, like Christian cosmology (John 14:2) believed in many levels or "worlds" within creation, and referred to them as aeons (or eons). Christianity, like Hinduism and Buddhism, originally believed in many worlds, including both heavens and hells. So in a world of fiery torment the fire would be aionion. Since these worlds last a long time (but none last forever), aionios could also mean lasting a long time.

It is a matter of personal interpretation as to whether in a particular New Testament passage aionios means a long time or a condition proper to a particular world, but there is no doubt as to its meaning only a limited span of time, for Jesus said: "Lo, I am with you alway, even unto the end of the world [aion–aeon]" (Matthew 28:20). Here we see that the King James editors considered aeon could mean a world. Aionios, then, could mean something lasting the lifespan of a world.

I have a question about something I have been trying to find for a year now. The exact location of the Rig Veda verse that begins *Prajapati vai idam*, and is the original of the first verse of the Gospel of John.

I understand your dilemma. I found the quotation (without exact reference) in writings by Indian scholars whose integrity I trusted, so

I passed on the misinformation about the source being the Rig Veda. Fortunately, an internet friend supplied us with the correct sources and the exact text: "In the beginning was Prajapati. With him was the Word" (*Prajapati vai idam agra asit. Tasya vak dvitiya asit*). This verse is found in the following places: 1) Krishna Yajurveda, Kathaka Samhita, 12.5, 27.1; 2) Krishna Yajurveda, Kathakapisthala Samhita, 42.1; 3) Jaiminiya Brahmana II, Sameveda, 2244. Prajapati refers to God as Creator.

I was able to visit the cave of Jesus near Vashishtha Guha with friends twice in the past six months! It is a powerful and vibrant cave. No one was near when we engaged ourselves in meditation. I thank you again and again. Would you please tell me of some more places in India visited by Jesus and directions to visit there.

There are two places in the holy city of Kankhal which I usually do not speak about as most people would think I was being over-imaginative, but I will describe them to you.

The first is the Ganga channel that you cross when going from Hardwar to Kankhal. You reach this by turning to the right (east) at the Mrityunjaya fountain as you are entering the main part of Hardwar. Stand in the middle of the bridge and you may feel a very definite spiritual atmosphere. I always do. The canal was made less than twenty years after independence, so apparently Jesus stayed and meditated here when it was solid land.

To reach the second place, just keep on going east across the bridge into Kankhal—not very far. As you proceed, you will come to several old ashrams on your right hand (south). After a bit you will come to a large area enclosed by iron fencing in the middle of which there is a small but ornate Shiva temple of carved stone (really a roof on supports rather than an enclosed building). Meditate there and you may feel the presence of Jesus.

Whenever I have been in Hardwar I always visited these two places. Sometimes I have made flower offerings into the Ganga from the bridge.

Two other places where Jesus lived are Varanasi and Jagannath Puri. We have no idea where he lived in Varanasi, but in Puri he lived in the Govardhan Math of Sri Shankaracharya–so said Jagadguru Bharati Krishna Tirtha, a former Shankaracharya and my param-sannyasa-guru. He claimed there were records of Jesus having lived there, but his research was thrown out by a servant while he was visiting America, and he did not live long enough to rewrite it.

It is also said that somewhere in Puri there is a small shrine containing nothing but a plain wooden cross, and that every day for many centuries a Brahmin priest has done some kind of worship there. Unfortunately this is all I know.

I hope this will be helpful for you and that you will be able to visit these places. I hope that you will also visit Rudra Prayag (Allahabad) and take a bath in the sacred Triveni. Also that you will visit Varanasi (Kashi) and its many temples, especially those of Vishwanath and Annapurna. Sri Brindaban is a spiritual paradise (not so appealing outwardly) with many temples filled with spiritual power. Please have darshan of the living Krishna murti at the Bankey Bihari temple.

I would like to know whether the departed soul gets our prayers and the love we express. Also, how do those prayers help the departed soul?

Certainly the departed receive the effects of our prayers and the love we send them. All viable religions have rituals for the benefit of the departed that are effective. Japa done while holding the departed person in mind is very beneficial for them. But the best rule is this: Show love and care for those dear to you while they live. Help them to keep their mind on higher things, to worship and meditate on God every day. Then they will carry with them the blessing and knowledge of your love and will need no further help, but will ascend to higher worlds as Sri Krishna assures us in the Gita.

How can I understand the teachings of Jesus better?

First, be sure you distinguish between the teachings of Jesus and the doctrines of contemporary Christianity, including the English translations of the Bible.

Here are five things I feel will be of assistance to you:

1. That you obtain a computer Bible program that enables you to go through the text word-by-word and see the various meanings of the Greek terms. Online Bible is extremely good. It is integrated with many Bible versions, but I prefer the New King James version.

2. *Strong's Exhaustive Concordance* is very helpful as it has a very good dictionary of the Greek words in the New Testament.

3. That you consider purchasing a copy of *The Emphatic Diaglott* of Benjamin Wilson. This is now published by the Jehovah's Witnesses, but was originally published in the early part of the twentieth century by Ludgate and Hill in England. The Witnesses bought the rights, but have not changed the text at all except to put capital Thetas on the word *Theos* in the Greek text. It contains both an interlinear Greek-English text and Wilson's translation.

4. That you obtain a copy of *The Aquarian Gospel of Jesus the Christ* published by DeVorss Publications. This is not a "channeled" book as some claim. Levi Dowling, a Disciples of Christ (Christian Church)

minister, developed his ability to look into the past and spoke out his impressions as his wife wrote them down. He did not claim his records were infallible or of divine authority–only psychic perceptions. Yet this book is a marvel of spiritual philosophy and is truer to the facts than the four canonical Gospels that have been edited to conform to official doctrine.

5. I have saved the best for last. I recommend that you look into the writings of Paramhansa Yogananda, especially *The Second Coming of Christ*, which has a scripture index so you can see his commentary on specific verses. His *Autobiography of a Yogi* contains a great deal of material on the Bible, as do the three volumes of his talks. We feel that Yogananda had a spiritual comprehension of the teachings of Jesus that was unique, and that there is no better source for understanding the message of Jesus.

A Saint Thomas Christian priest of south India once said to me: "You cannot understand the teachings of Jesus if you do not know the scriptures of India." He was right. The teachings of Jesus are the teaching of the Indian scriptures–not something different.

I do not understand why it is all right to kill and eat plants but not all right to kill and eat animals. It feels like the Consciousness is the same in both. I am not asking this so I can eat meat. I am a vegetarian because my mind, memory and meditation are sharper when I eat only vegetables. I am asking because I hope to understand better.

Here is a relevant paragraph from *The Four Soul Killers*:

"Often the objection is raised that we are killing plants to eat them. But this is not accurate, either. When we harvest vegetables, we do so at the *end* of their growth cycle; otherwise they just wither and decay. Animals, however, are slaughtered long before their natural lifespan is finished. We must also distinguish between the fruit and the plant. When we pick, say a tomato, we do not kill the plant, but it continues to grow–no life is taken. As for root vegetables such as carrots or potatoes, the root that we harvest is the final stage in the plant's growth; if it were not harvested, the plant would merely rot in the earth. Furthermore, in plants the sensory mind is only *potential,* it is 'asleep.' They do not feel pain. Although they do have a rudimentary nervous system that responds to injury, the conscious mind that would receive the message of pain in animal organisms is not functional."

The bottom line, however, is obvious. We can live a better and healthier life by not eating animals. But if we do not eat plants we will die. Philosophy really does not come into this. Things are as they are.

How can I not kill pests? If I do not discourage ants and rats, they tend to move into my house. If I do not spray my garden with some kind of pesticide, the harvest is attacked. Also, when we bathe, thousands of bacteria on the skin probably drown.

There are many ways to avoid killing "pests"–usually by repelling them. Ants, for example, work through smell. Spraying ant trails with something like Lysol makes them go away. Mice you can catch with "live traps" and take them some distance away and set them free. Things that come in the attic and rumble around in the walls can be repelled with mothballs. (It apparently smells like cat urine to them.) We have a large rabbit population. By spraying around the susceptible plants we ensure the rabbits leave them alone.

Involuntary taking of life has no karmic result. As Swami Sri Yukteswar pointed out to Yogananda, it is the intention or desire to take life that violates ahimsa. Buddha considered this very intently and even declared that involuntary manslaughter creates no negative karma.

Is it possible for an ordinary person who has wasted his or her energy for years to make up their lost energy by practicing brahmacharya when in their thirties or forties?

Certainly it is possible to do so by observing brahmacharya in thought, word, and deed. Please be aware that diet has a strong influence on brahmacharya, that Gandhi recommended not only abstention from meat, fish, and eggs, but also from dairy.

Prayer, japa and meditation are the sure foundations of brahmacharya, and indeed of all virtues.

I would like to ask two questions: 1. What is the purpose of human life? There must be a defined purpose of human life, as all human beings appear to be suffering from the same cause–desires. So there must be only one solution to end human suffering. 2. Why are there are so many religious variations? Don't you think this confuses an already confused mortal in choosing what is the right way of leading a right life?

If you study the Bhagavad Gita carefully and sincerely–and daily–you will find all the answers to any relevant questions about life and the removal of suffering. The Gita is the pinnacle of practical spiritual knowledge.

In the Bhagavad Gita Krishna tells Arjuna to meditate with his eyes half-shut, focused on the point of his nose. I read other articles that say to focus the eyes upwards. Can you explain this disparity?

The confusion comes from faulty translation. Krishna says to fix the eyes on the *nasikagram*, which means "origin of the nose." So it depends on where you think the nose "begins"! Actually, your eyes will turn up and down spontaneously in meditation, so the best and most relaxing thing to do at the beginning of meditation is to turn them slightly downward and then forget all about them. Your practice will do the rest.

The Gita says nothing about half-closed eyes–that is an interpolation of translators.

These words from *Advice to Sannyasins–Part 2* by Swami Sivananda Saraswati, found on your website are cruel and hurtful:

"Woman is more venomous than the cobra. Cobra kills a man by a bite; but woman kills him by even a mere sight, and not only one life, but thousands of lives will be lost by contact with woman. Be ever vigilant. Maya is so very powerful. Be far away from women. Even if you have to serve women, mentally you must be far away from them. You should just do your duty (service) and run away."

When read by Indian men and women, in the spiritual and cultural context in which they were written, Sivananda's counsel to monks is not at all either cruel or hurtful. It is true that Westerners, without that context, may misconstrue them and think they are defamatory.

It should be noted that Sivananda speaks of "Woman" as an abstract concept–not of female human beings. He is speaking of the delusive image within the mind of the male human–an image that has been reinforced by many lifetimes of ignorance and lust, even if in this life a man inclines to purity and on the conscious level seems free from lustful attitudes toward women. He quite rightly tells monks to avoid casual and personal contact with women, lest their own subconscious (and often conscious!) negativity arises and harms both them and the women.

In contemporary India women are much too trusting toward monks and associate with them as freely and openly as though they were close members of their own family. Terrible grief is often the result of this. Recently an American monk on pilgrimage wrote to us from India saying that he was not able to stay in the home of a devout family in the Himalayas because a short time before an Indian monk had been invited into that home only to run away with a daughter of the house after a few days.

Sri Ramakrishna, whose respect for women was a marked characteristic, often warned his male visitors against the destructive possibilities of "Woman and Gold." He did not say "women," but "Woman"–meaning it in the psychological sense of men's mental corruption. Furthermore, the specific term he used was *kamini*, which means a woman as an object of lust–kama. But when he spoke with women he warned them about "Man and Gold."

Sri Ma Sarada Devi, the virgin wife of Sri Ramakrishna, continually advised her women disciples to never trust men, and she advised her male disciples to never trust women. She meant this in the sense of those of the opposite sex who would not observe a respectful reserve in regard to them. Sri Ma would not allow her female devotees to be present when male devotees came to see her, nor would she allow men in her house when women devotees were with her.

Readers in the lust-ridden West may find this distasteful, but serious sadhakas are not offended. It has been my observation for many decades that people who rave on about how the sexes should be considered "the same" and who shriek that it is "unspiritual" to observe a distance between male and female sadhakas because we are all "atmas" are usually sex slaves—or enslavers—angered at the suggestion they should distance themselves from the objects of their addiction. A truly spiritual man or woman understands well the potential dangers of association with the opposite sex, though blaming only the ignorance and delusion that produces such dangers—in themselves.

The twelfth chapter of *Autobiography of Yogi* has this instructive passage:

> "My guru mixed freely with men and women disciples, treating all as his children. Perceiving their soul equality, he showed no distinction or partiality.
>
> "'In sleep, you do not know whether you are a man or a woman,' he said. 'Just as a man, impersonating a woman, does not become one, so the soul, impersonating both man and woman, has no sex. The soul is the pure, changeless image of God.'
>
> "Sri Yukteswar never avoided or blamed women as objects of seduction. Men, he said, were also a temptation to women. I once inquired of my guru why a great ancient saint had called women 'the door to hell.'
>
> "'A girl must have proved very troublesome to his peace of mind in his early life,' my guru answered caustically. 'Otherwise he would have denounced, not woman, but some imperfection in his own self-control.'
>
> "If a visitor dared to relate a suggestive story in the hermitage, Master would maintain an unresponsive silence. 'Do not allow yourself to be thrashed by the provoking whip of a beautiful face,' he told the disciples. 'How can sense slaves enjoy the world? Its subtle flavors escape them while they grovel in primal mud. All nice discriminations are lost to the man of elemental lusts.'"

It should be noted that Yogananda, though having both men and women living in his American ashram, demanded strict segregation of the sexes–a segregation that is rightly observed even now over half a century after his physical departure.

I had the inestimable blessing of living for a while in the Sivanandashram and being with Sivananda himself at least twice a day, and I can assure you that he had no dislike of women. The female monastics and sadhakas of the ashram were as respected as the males. However, a respectful and proper distance was observed on both sides. At the same time there was a remarkable familial feeling pervading the ashram.

Sivananda's advice was for male monastics–sannyasis. If he had written something for women monastics–sannyasinis–he would have told them that Man was more venomous than the cobra!

Wise are those who are aware of their actual and potential weaknesses and act accordingly, not blaming the objects of their delusions, but their delusion itself. Those who do not guard themselves–and others–intend to fall into the snares of ignorance.

Have you ever heard of anyone refusing to reincarnate–and succeeding? If we have free will we must surely be able to make such a decision. Otherwise, in my opinion, we are nothing but slaves.

First we must realize that reincarnation is determined exclusively by the individual spirit, or atman. God has nothing to do with it, although God has manifested the worlds in which reincarnation can occur. Nor are there any "Lords of Karma" that decide when spirits reincarnate. Even more important, we must understand that karma is not some blind, omnipotent and inescapable force that drags or impels us into incarnation after incarnation. The belief in these three "causes" of reincarnation arises from a miscomprehension of what karma actually is, and an ignorance of the sole purpose of rebirth.

Karma is not some kind of subtle energy accumulation of merit ("good karma") or demerit ("bad karma"), but rather is the psychic conditioning (positive or negative) resulting from the states of mind and will that produced our past actions. Karma is a kind of kink or whorl in the mind (which is a field of ever-moving energy) and the other subtle energy bodies which at present make us "human." The atman is consciously—and intelligently—working its way toward the state of perfection we call Liberation. It is the atman alone that determines when and where we shall reincarnate and exactly which kinks we will be working on in each life. If the will of the atman is not carried out then evolution stops and we stagnate.

The spiritual intelligence of the atman is often called the "higher mind." In contrast to this is the "lower mind" that is the egocentric bundle of attraction/aversion impulses that are rooted in complete ignorance and selfishness. This lower mind is always in conflict with the higher mind, for its basis is ignorance and distortion of perception. This mind is indeed a slave, and has no possibility of free will, for it not only functions only in the world of bondage, it has no existence independent of the Self. It is a mirage, an illusion. It does not really "exist" in the ultimate sense. Naturally, it claims to be the only mind we have, and insists that it possesses and exercises free will.

Although the lower mind is not a conscious entity unto itself, nevertheless it is energy-force and therefore can produce effects, including influencing our incarnate and discarnate states.

On occasion the higher mind stands aside and lets the lower mind have its way so the folly and impotence of the lower mind can be revealed—even to itself. This results in suffering as the only possible consequence, something the lower mind—being psychopathic—insists comes from God, the Lords of Karma, or even karma itself. Rarely does it admit the truth of its own responsibility, and when it does we know that its dissolution is beginning and freedom is dawning.

Deluded people often refuse to incarnate. Usually this results in nothing more than their being rebellious and embittered for the entire time of a particular birth. But it can also be the cause of continual bouts of life-threatening illnesses. The individual bounces between nearly dying and being cured—often suddenly. The lower mind is trying to escape through death, but it also possesses a clinging to life that militates against its attempts. This psychic schizophrenia grips a lot of human beings.

On occasion the individual tries to avoid rebirth by preventing the subtle bodies from entering the physical body at birth (for there is a separation during the mother's labor). If he succeeds, then the body remains inert, often paralyzed, and observers assume the person is a hopeless idiot. (See *The Secrets of Doctor Taverner* by Dion Fortune for a true account of this phenomenon.) At other times the refusal results in the production of a horribly defective body—oftentimes not even of human configuration. Whichever occurs, the foolish person has to spend the span of an entire incarnation standing next to the body it has refused to incarnate—hardly an enjoyable consequence.

Other deluded people refuse to die and so they remain earthbound, attached to their physical body. This awful bondage can last for hundreds and even thousands of years. This is horrific slavery.

Nevertheless, in time the futility of such pain-bearing refusals become evident to even the most stubborn individuals and they stop such stupid attempts at thwarting the true free will, the free will of the divine Self. Then evolution proceeds, and in time they are free from the necessity for rebirth. This alone is freedom.

Please give me some practical advice to achieve progress in the practice of brahmacharya.

The prime key to success in cultivating the great spiritual gem of brahmacharya is perseverance. Persevere and you will attain perfection in this virtue.

Please be aware that meditation is the cornerstone of brahmacharya.

Besides the material to be found on our website, we recommend that you obtain the book *Meditation and Spiritual Life* by Swami Yatiswarananda. This book covers every aspect of spiritual life, including very good instructions on brahmacharya. You can order it from: amazon.com.

May the blessings of God be with you in your endeavors.

I am writing to you because I am very puzzled about some yogic masters' view that every religion is the infinite God expressing himself in different ways, that every religion teaches the same fundamental truth. I think that this is very naive. Isn't it only logical that some religions grow and spread because a man lusting for power deceives those around him by the claim that he is sent from God–threatening hell to those disobeying him and promising heaven to those obeying him? And what about Satanism... is that really a religion bearing God's light? It is also very illogical from another point of view: many religious texts claim that their religion is the only true religion, thereby banning every other religion.

Please help me understand why the great realized masters claim that a religion spreading violent messages should be a religion from God. Please help me–I really don't understand it at all.... The masters may be filled with peace, silence and happiness, but how much is that worth if they lose the simple truth and their common sense in the process? Then their realization is nothing but a psychological state of peace and naïveté. The thing is, I don't want to be realized if it's only a psychological state including peace, but excluding truth. Every time I see a swami or other claiming that all religions are true I think: "Oh no, not again–does the truth really not matter at all when one gets 'realized'?" Or are they really claiming that it is godly to kill, torture and hate, exactly as some religions teach?

I really hope for your help. Please make me understand why the masters make that claim about "all religions." Or please let me know why the things I have pointed out are the way God really wants it. Please help me to clarity.

You do not need me to help you to clarity–you have it, and I congratulate you for it. You are absolutely right: it is foolish and irresponsible to say that every religion–or form of a religion–is valid, and that all religions are equal.

In the West, the assertion that all religions are good and equally valid was taken up only in the latter part of the twentieth century for purely cosmetic effect by those opportunists who wanted to appear "open" and "positive"–as well as by the "make nice" people to whom reality is always sacrificed to make them look and feel good. (We also have the groups that publicly say all religions are true and then privately rant on about how *their* "revelation" is the only presently valid one.)

This view originated, however, in India where it was put forth by two classes of people: 1) belly-crawling cowards who wanted to lick the hands and feet of their sadistic, barbarian conquerors–first the Moslems and then the British, and 2) genuine yogis who met and recognized truly spiritually awakened people–in other words, mystics–among the differing sects of modern Hinduism and occasionally among the adherents of Buddhism, Christianity and Islam.

We must also not confuse a religion with those in whose names those religions are being perpetrated. Yogananda used to point out that if all the founders of the world's major religions were assembled in the same room it would be heaven on earth, but if their followers are put in the same place there is a war! What has Jesus to do with Christianity? And frankly, how much has Krishna or Buddha to do with a great deal of contemporary Hinduism and Buddhism? A great deal in the world's religion is indefensible superstition and perversity. Most religionists worship their ego, not God. As Yogananda also said: "No one religion has an exclusive franchise on spiritual ignorance." We can also add that none has an exclusive franchise on Truth, either.

It is not religion which is valid–rather it is the seeking of God. It is the awakened spirit that gives validity to a spiritual path–not the other way round. The religion of the ignorant is ignorance; the religion of the wise is wisdom. Therefore it is not the religion we should take into consideration but the individual spiritual aspirant. Sri Ramakrishna said that devotees of God form a caste or religion of their own. This is the only true religion, the only truly universal faith: the seeking of God.

In the *Unknown Life of Jesus Christ* Jesus says that we should not worship images of God or deities. Is this worship really wrong?

There is a great difference between worshipping a material image itself and worshipping God through or within that image. A primitive person having never before seen a telephone would assume that someone using it is talking to the phone receiver, but we would know that he was speaking through the receiver to the person on the other end. It is the same with spiritual imagery. We who understand that God is at the heart of all existence are aware that we can relate to him and even communicate with him through a material image. It will be according to our understanding and intention.

It is very easy to think that the problem lies with an object rather than the user of the object. What is needed, however, is a spiritual perspective on our part. Then no matter how involved we are with imagery we will never be "idolators." After all, we know that a person is only spirit (atman) and not the body. But we speak to their body, give gifts to the body, embrace and even love that body, and no one accuses us of materiality. We are relating to the essential spirit by means of their body vehicle. It is the same with the use of religious imagery. It is a matter of spiritual intelligence. Those who lack that intelligence will never get the idea. Jesus was speaking to those whose ignorance made them idolators.

How is yoga just the stopping of thoughts in the mind? Is that all there is to it?

No. Yoga is much more sophisticated than that. It is also pretty technical, but there is no avoiding that.

"Yoga is the suppression of the modifications of the chitta," is the beginning statement of the Yoga Sutras as well as being Patanjali's definition of yoga. Meditation establishes our consciousness in the true Self and renders the chitta (mental energy, mind substance) free from outer-caused modifications or vrittis (waves). We should look at this further.

"To the purusha the chitta is the sole object in the form of its modifications. And chitta with its modifications [vrittis] inhibited [suppressed] would no longer be an object," according to Shankara. The spirit, whose nature is consciousness alone, experiences the modifications of the mind (chitta) and mistakenly identifies with them. Though it seems to see many things, the only thing it ever really does see is the chitta as it dances before it in the form of ever-changing waves (vrittis). It is this objective consciousness that is the root of bondage—actually *is* the state of bondage. For Vyasa comments on Yoga Sutra 4:22: "Though unmoving and unchanging, the purusha-experiencer has as it were entered into the changing object [of the chitta and its many forms or objects] and conformed itself to its function" by false identification with it. Shankara, considering the same sutra, says: "A wave in the mind, by merely arising, becomes an object for the purusha,...[although] its true nature is pure awareness." Therefore, over-simple as it may seem, it is the removal of such objective consciousness that is liberation. And meditation is the direct means to remove such a binding consciousness.

By the resulting direct experience of our spirit-self, "ignorance comes to an end, and when that ceases there are none of the taints. With no taints, there is no karma-fruition. In that state the gunas have finished with their involvement and no longer arise before the purusha as perceived objects. That is the liberation of the spirit when the spirit stands alone in its true nature as pure light. So it is." This is the conclusion of Vyasa.

I hope you will help me with a long-standing question: Can a person realize Brahman just by spiritual activities such as meditation, without ritualistic worship and prayers or devotion to personal gods?

If ritualistic worship and devotion to various deity forms assist the sadhaka, they should be used. But they are not necessary. However the Gita indicates that we should cultivate devotion to the Infinite Being, Brahman, who was speaking through Sri Krishna.

The Bhagavad Gita gives complete instruction on how to realize Brahman. Please take the Gita as your most authoritative teacher and read a chapter from it each day. You will succeed in spiritual life if you follow its teachings. And you will surely have the living blessing of Sri Vyasa, the author, as well as Sri Krishna.

Isn't Advaita the same as Monism?

Advaita should never be equated with monism. Advaita simply means Not Two and is not the same as the simplistic idea "All is One," of monism. Certainly Advaita postulates an eternal unity, but again not in the simplistic sense of monism. The Gita and the Upanishads are the authoritative sources of authentic Advaita. Even a brief perusal will reveal the vast difference between their real advaitic teachings and the popular contemporary understanding of non-dualism.

Also, it should not be forgotten that advaita, vishishtadvaita, and dvaita–the teachings of Shankara, Ramanuja, and Madhvacharya–are all said to be orthodox Sanatana Dharma. In other words, all three are true. It is when we limit ourselves to only one that we get confused.

For some reason the West, especially, just cannot grasp the fact that One is not merely a numerical term, but is also a quality of essential being. The Christians killed each other over this when some said Jesus had only one nature (*monophysis*) and others said he had two natures (*duophysis*). The dualists just could not get the idea that One could be taken in a metaphysical sense, not just a mathematical one.

Never did it occur to the ancient sages of India that someone would try to reduce their teachings to mere intellection. Being themselves adept yogis, they were writing to assist other yogis along the way to enlightenment. This is why the Gita and Upanishads are filled with practical instruction on how to reach the true vision of Reality.

There is a question I have been posing to various sadhus and pundits recently. I wonder if you might care to address it. It concerns "Ekam sad vipra bahudha vadantikam Sat..." Why is it said

that the "wise" call the same truth by different names? Why are the wise singled out in this regard? Don't regular people call it by different names, too? I'm sorry if the question sounds too elementary, but this is such a basic tenet of the Perennial Philosophy that I don't want to simply pretend to understand just because it's elementary.

The words you quote come from the sixty-fourth verse of the one hundred and sixty-fourth hymn of the first section of the Rig Veda (Rig Veda 1.164.46). There is really no problem at all in discerning its meaning provided it is translated honestly and completely.

First the honest translation: "The Real/True [Sat] is One [ekam]. The twice-born [vipra] call It [vadanti] variously [bahudha]."

In modern times "vipra" is usually applied to the Brahmins—those who have been invested with the yajnopavita (sacred thread) and initiated into the Gayatri mantra. (In earlier times the Kshatriyas and Vaishyas also did this.) Of course it has a higher meaning: one who has been "born" into the consciousness of Spirit as well as physically. Each of us has to decide which (or both) is meant in the Vedic text.

Second, the complete translation: "The Real/True [Sat] is One [ekam]. The twice-born [vipra] call It [vadanti] variously [bahudha]: Agni, Yama, Matarisvan, Indra, Mitra, Varuna, Garutman."

There you have it. The illumined sages of India have called the One Reality, the Ekam Evam Advityam Brahman, by the many names found in the Veda. Even though many names are used, the Reality spoken about in the Veda is one. There is not a thought of other religions. The question of their validity or invalidity just does not come into this matter.

Certainly there are parts of the Gita that affirm the validity of the various paths by which human beings seek God. But to quote these Vedic words in support of that view is simply indefensible. *Satyam Eva Jayate!* Truth Alone is Victorious.

Sex (thought and act) was part of my life while I was in college but I repent for having done that. Recently someone told me that if you commit a mistake it can never be erased, and that is the end to me becoming a brahmachari because the guilt will always be there in my mind. Does this mean that even if I try now to improve myself and follow a strict life, I will never be blessed?

A person who has lied can reform and practice truthfulness (satya). A person who has stolen can reform and practice non-stealing (asteya). A person who has done harm (himsa) can reform and practice ahimsa. It only follows to reason, then, that someone who has engaged in sexual acts can reform and practice brahmacharya.

Some of the greatest sannyasis (and therefore brahmacharis) in modern times had been married and begotten children. Yet, when they took up a new order of life they attained liberation and uplifted many others and inspired them to purity of life. Among the great monastic disciples of Sri Ramakrishna, Swami Brahmananda—the first president of Ramakrishna Mission—had been married and had one child. The great Swami Sivananda of Rishikesh, founder of the Divine Life Society, was married and had two children. When his wife and children were killed in a fire he took sannyas and became one of the greatest yogis of our times, even writing a book on brahmacharya. The beloved Swami (Papa) Ramdas of Anandashram, the embodiment of purity, had been married and also had children.

In the Gita Sri Krishna tells us: "And though you were the foulest of sinners, this knowledge alone would carry you like a raft, over all your sin. The blazing fire turns wood to ashes: the fire of knowledge turns all karmas to ashes." (Bhagavad Gita 4:36, 37) "Though a man be soiled with the sins of a lifetime, let him but love me, rightly resolved, in utter devotion: I see no sinner, that man is holy. Holiness soon shall refashion his nature to peace eternal; O son of Kunti, of this be certain: the man that loves me, he shall not perish" (Bhagavad Gita 9:30-31).

In *Autobiography of a Yogi*, we find this: "A new student occasionally expressed doubts regarding his own worthiness to engage in yoga practice. 'Forget the past,' Sri Yukteswar would console him. 'The vanished lives of all men are dark with many shames. Human conduct is ever unreliable until anchored in the Divine. Everything in future will improve if you are making a spiritual effort now.'"

This is the truth of the matter. Trust in God and in your divine Self.

To a friend who sent us an email asking whether scriptures claiming to be the teachings of a great teacher can be fully trusted.

The really relevant question at all times is: WHO AM I? Knowing that John Rockefeller was the richest man in the world does not put a penny in anyone's pocket. Knowing who was or was not a true prophet does not affect our spiritual life in the least. Remember: Krishna, Buddha, and Jesus wrote no books of teachings. We really have no way of knowing if the Buddhist sutras or the Four Gospels contain the pure or complete teachings of Buddha or Jesus.

No scripture is perfect because it is a product of a human mind and has been copied by fallible (and sometimes unreliable and even dishonest) scribes through centuries—even millennia. Things get even worse when we have only a translation! Silly and outright incorrect things can be found mixed in with wisdom. The wise take the wisdom and leave the unwisdom, the way an ant upon finding a heap of white sand and sugar takes the sugar and leaves the sand.

The wisest advice in all this is given in the Bhagavad Gita: "Great is that yogi who seeks to be with Brahman, greater than those who mortify the body, greater than the learned, greater than the doers of good works: therefore, Arjuna, become a yogi." (Bhagavad Gita 6:46)

Does God pay personal attention to our needs as most people think? If our sole purpose is to reunite with God, I get the idea that it is kind of one-sided. We do all the work and He sits there waiting for us to figure it out.

If that is what we need, that is the way it will be. The sum of it all is this: God is everything. There is a single, unitary field of conscious, intelligent Being. It is One. Yet in this Unity there is an eternal diversity–that is where "we" come in. God (Brahman) being Pure Awareness, It cannot but be aware of us in totality. The cosmos is also Divine–whether we see it as real or as a dream of God. And remember: we are thoroughly one with creation and Creator. There is no point at which we leave off and That begins. So we are also the universe and one with the God of the Universe which responds to us. Separation is completely impossible. Therefore, when we decide to evolve everything begins to move toward that–even the things that seem to oppose it. God is in the mix right there with us. The Gita explains this, saying that God is in the heart of all beings. And since Brahman is the sole power, It is working right along with us. Is God "He" or "It"? Both, since he embraces all modes of being. Let me tell you, God is no simplistic bore!

Do I have this right? The atman is the part of God that is within each of us (like a drop of water in the ocean) and Brahman is the entire ocean?

That is correct. We are in God and God is in us. He is the Whole and we are the parts. But this is just the way we have to speak about it. In reality there is only the Divine Unity which we see variously–and not necessarily erroneously. Few things are more tiresome than those who seek to tell God and us what he and we cannot do. It is beyond all thought and concept, but not beyond experiencing. "Therefore, Arjuna, become a yogi." (Bhagavad Gita 6:46)

Sometimes I am overwhelmed by how little I know and how much I have to learn.

Don't worry. You have an infinite capacity for knowing (which is much better than "knowledge") and eternity in which to gain it.

Can we really pray for another and affect their life or health? Is it right to try to intervene in another's life through prayer?

Actually, when we pray for another person we are simply supplying them with the positive energies needed to help them. If their inner mind is receptive and agreeable, they are benefited. If not, the blessing energy comes back to the senders and *we* are helped! This is why prayers are not answered for a long time and then suddenly they seem to work. The decisive factor was the inner will of the one prayed for. Keep in mind that karma is both absolute and flexible, however our inner minds are reacting to or projecting it.

What is your opinion of suicide?

As you can imagine, Sanatana Dharma views suicide differently from other religions, since its fundamental principle is the divinity of the individual. Here is how the Sanatana Dharmis see it:

Suicide is the most destructive thing a person can do because it takes such a tremendous act of will, and in future lives this can cause the person to be born wanting to die and—even worse—create the habit of suicide. For the situation that drove him to suicide will come up again and again until he works through it—in the sense of understanding and dealing with it.

In India it is commonly believed that a suicide goes into a kind of void, an astral version of solitary confinement. As a consequence, no prayers are offered for the suicide until a year has gone by. Many feel that a person stays "in solitary" until their normal lifespan has gone by, that a twenty-year-old destined to live for eighty will pass sixty years in that terrible condition.

I expect this is right as far as the immediate consequences, but since there are no cookie-cutter "divine legislative" rules about anyone's life (or death) it only makes sense to pray for and send healing vibrations to the person from the time of their death. After all, they may have sometime before the final moment realized their folly and wished that they had not made that mistake. That alone could turn them back from experiencing the void and enable them to have the astral experiences of someone who died because of foolish self-neglect. As Jesus said: "Blessed are the merciful."

We have long believed in the Yogic powers of our ancient Rishis and Siddhas. We have even heard of spiritually elevated Rishis walking on water or levitating from the ground. Do we have any concrete references to this in any ancient text (Veda/Upanishad, etc.)?

The authentic scriptures of Sanatana Dharma are concerned with one thing only: the liberation of the individual spirit (atman). The "siddhis" are mere psychic technology and of no spiritual value–quite the opposite: all the spiritual adepts of India have warned seekers against their exercise. Patanjali (4:1) takes pains to point out that these powers are purely psychic and can even be induced by drugs (*aushadhi*). Though real, they are in essence mere psychic tricks with no practical value at all except to the earth-oriented ego, which their exercise strengthens to a potentially dangerous degree.

Can others really help us, or do we have to do it all ourselves?

Each of us is eternally perfect by nature. Therefore any improvement occurs only because that perfection is being uncovered–never is it a matter of being "made better." This is so important to realize, because we tend to think of needing to become something or have someone else (including God) change us. Rather, external factors (including books and teachers) are catalysts for the revelation of our inner perfection. They are valuable and in many instances necessary, but it is erroneous to attribute to them any power to make us something we are not already. They are worthy of respect, but our Self is worthy of reverence! As my beloved friend, Swami Sivananda, used to sing: "Know your Self and be free."

We must "give permission" for improvement to take place on any level of our existence. No external factors really "do it"—they only trigger our own realization. Sri Ramakrishna often said: "The mind is everything."

And we never really affect others—they respond to us. That is why if we wrong an ordinary person they will hate us and if we wrong a saint they will forgive us. They respond according to their nature. "Even a wise man acts according to the tendencies of his own nature. All living creatures follow their tendencies" (Bhagavad Gita 3:33).

It is possible to help others through prayer?

The best prayer is for someone's perfection. That is going to take place eventually and is part of the divine plan. The rest can be left to their own higher mind.

Did Jesus learn much of what he taught in India?

Jesus learned in India EVERYTHING he taught.

What do you say to the idea that Krishna, Buddha, and Jesus were only myths?

Everything we believe is nothing but a myth until we know it for ourselves. Even what we think is "us" is mostly a silly mythology. Yogananda points out in the last sentence of the thirty-fifth chapter of his autobiography that through meditation "persons who cannot bring themselves to believe in the divinity of any man will behold at last the full divinity of their own selves."

What if I have no faith in yoga?

Yoga is wonderful. It requires no faith, but proves its own premises.

What are visions?

The subject of visions is vast. Anyone who gives you a simple/simplistic definition or analysis is either very ignorant or putting you on. (This is true of just about any simple answer to anything.)

Some visions are seeing subtle levels of existence that normally are not seen. Some are projections of our inner (higher and lower) mind—usually for communication with us. Some are messages from other intelligences, using visual rather than verbal symbols. Some are exactly what they seem to be while others are totally symbolic. Some are incomplete; others are not. Visions are true, false, or mixed.

So how can we figure them out? Often we cannot. The best advice is that given by Sri Ramana Maharshi: "Visions do occur. To know how you look you must look into a mirror, but do not take that reflection to be yourself. What is perceived by our senses and the mind is never the truth. [He means this in the ultimate sense. Even hallucinations are "real" mental phenomena.] All visions are mere mental creations, and if you believe in them, your progress ceases. Enquire to whom the visions occur. Find out who is their witness. Stay in pure awareness, free from all thoughts. Do not move out of that state."

As someone who grew up with visionaries and as a yogi has had visions beyond number myself, I assure you this is the best attitude.

Would you say more about visions?

Visions may be true or false, positive or negative. How do we judge? Many times we cannot, and that is why the masters of wisdom counsel us to basically ignore them altogether.

Higher intelligences, God, and our own Self communicate through a kind of *knowing* that arises in us. This is trustworthy. Even Saint Teresa of Avila, the great mystic, wrote that visions are chancy and of much less value than inner knowing or spiritual intuition–which she called "intellectual visions."

Once we begin accepting visual "revelations" we are on a very dangerous path indeed. I have seen many people either trivialized or ruined by accepting everything they saw as truth. Some have even come to think that their every dream is a spiritual vision. I knew one woman who dreamed her husband was cheating on her, so when she woke up she starting beating and cursing him!

Many times people have visions that prove to be true, so they begin to trust everything. Then they have a very serious "message" which they follow and fall into disaster. It is as though they are being led along and trapped, like when gamblers let a victim win a few times and then wipe him out.

It is when the senses–even the inner ones–get involved that we must be wary and avoid trouble. Intuition or clairsentience is another matter. That comes from the intellect, not the lower, sensory mind. That is much more trustworthy. But even there we must be careful. That which arises from within, from our Self–and from God who is the core of our Self–is the only absolutely sure thing. Still, we work with what we get, but work discriminatingly.

What about miracles?

The more supernatural or miraculous a thing may be, the more normal it is—in the sense of being closer to the Source.

Is it necessary for me to be married or unmarried to succeed in yoga?

Both married and unmarried people have been great yogis. It is the yoga *life* that matters, not marital status. There is no need to be married or to be unmarried. What is needed is to be a real yogi.

What does the Bhagavad Gita mean by "devil"?

Swami Prabhavananda, whose translation is mostly used in my writings, used "devil" as the translation of the word *asura*. Sargeant prefers "demon" or "demoniacal" and so do I. "Asura" literally means "without the light," and is a term applied to negative people, especially those who are willfully (and contentedly) evil. The entire sixteenth chapter of the Gita is devoted to both "devas" ("shining ones") and asuras ("dark ones")—those who dwell in the light and those who dwell in darkness. An asura can be either a negative human being or a disembodied spirit.

Are there really demons and angels?

Yes. There are dwellers in the dark (asuras—without light) and devas (shining ones, light-filled ones). A great many human beings fall into these categories.

When the human asuras and devas leave the body they usually go to astral worlds that reflect their consciousness until they are reborn. As you can imagine, the worlds of the asuras are hells and the worlds of the devas are heavens.

Some asuras have such unfortunate karma that they cannot make the transition from earth to the astral, but remain earthbound. They wander around, often influencing (obsessing) those still in the body and even sometimes invading their bodies and minds in possession. They do great harm in this way.

Some devas return from the heavenly realms in their astral bodies and do just the opposite: they bless and uplift human beings as much as they can, even bringing them mental and physical healing. They especially work to awaken and expand spiritual consciousness. We call them angels and saints.

The rest of humanity are "grays" mentally wandering in the misty flats referred to in the following poem by John Oxenham which is very wise and to be taken seriously:

> To every man there openeth
> A Way, and Ways, and a Way,
> And the High Soul climbs the High Way,
> And the Low Soul gropes the Low,
> And in between, on the misty flats,
> The rest drift to and fro.
> But to every man there openeth

A High Way, and a Low.
And every man decideth
The way his soul shall go.

What about Satan–the Devil?

There is no malevolent, evil counterpart to God, some kind of inverted Deity. There are, as already explained, earthbound spirits that work evil. Some are very powerful, but still not "the Devil."

However–a big however–there is a force of cosmic evil, a great field of negative energy that is produced by negative thought and action, the result of ages of evil intent on the part of intelligent (?) beings. It is a reservoir of negativity. Since all things are inherently conscious to some degree, this dark field has a kind of lumbering, robotic sentience that does become attracted to negative emanations from sentient beings–responds to and influences and affects them. It does, in a magnetic sense, impel and even dominate them. It is very real, and has a definite effect on humanity. Since it is not really natural it is expended, like the power in a battery, but continual evil on the part of human beings keeps feeding and recharging it. Widespread wars and mass suffering (as in concentrations camps and oppressed countries) vastly increase its strength. Paramhansa Yogananda called this entity "Satan," not to be confused with Lucifer, a fallen archangel that many people mistakenly think is "the Devil."

Can demons and Satan harm me?

Not unless you are attuned to negativity by your thoughts, words, and deeds. If you stay tuned to God through spiritual life–which includes spiritual practice–Satan and demons cannot come near you, much less harm you. Also, your positive vibrations will lessen their power. So you protect and benefit the cosmos as well as yourself by your spiritual cultivation.

What is "Self-realization"?

It is the full knowledge–by direct and permanent experience–of the Self (Atman), our eternal, immortal Spirit. Since our Self (jivatman) and the Supreme Self (Paramatman) are essentially one, even though distinct, it is also knowledge of God. The result of self-realization is perfection in consciousness and freedom from all conditionings and karmas, and total liberation from the cycle of birth and death. It is absolute freedom (moksha). A self-realized person is truly a "god" within the greater Being of God.

What is the difference between the air and ether elements?

Ether–akasha–is the substance within which all the other elements exist. It is space, but not in the ordinary idea of emptiness. It is an actual substance–a substratum containing all that exists. Think of it as the canvas and the other four elements as the paints.

Since it is all a matter of our personal development, why do Masters come into the world at all?

The presence of a perfected being enables those who are ready to experience a more open state of spiritual awareness. Actually, such a person does in a sense awaken those who are capable of awakening. People are changed by encountering them if they are so inclined. Those who truly awake then listen to the teachings being given and follow them. The teachings of a real master are only minimally philosophical and theoretical. Most are practical ways for their hearers to gain realization for themselves. The last thing they want to do is start a religion.

All master-teachers are yogis and so are their disciples. Theologians and "believers" are those that move into the station and live there, never ever taking the train. "Why, the kingdom of God has come on earth!" they say. And never get anywhere. But, as Jesus said: "They have their reward." And to them he inquires: "Why call ye me, Lord, Lord, and do not the things which I say?" It is in the doing, not the "believing," "trusting," "hoping," "obeying," "dedicating"–no, not even "loving"–that we truly follow a Great One.

In my yoga practice I have not yet reached the thoughtless state, so is it really meditation?

In their commentaries on the Yoga Sutras both Vyasa and Shankara define meditation as a continuous stream of identical thoughts. So if your mantra japa is continuous you are definitely meditating though sometimes distracted. It is only natural that in the beginning extraneous thoughts will be arising during meditation. But through diligent practice you will find that after some time in meditation the thoughts will cease and only the japa will remain.

The statement in the Yoga Sutras that yoga is the non-arising (nirodha) of waves (vrittis) in the mind-substance (chitta) is not a reference to mere thoughts, but to the much more profound state in which the mind cannot be influenced or conditioned by external experiences. So please be assured that the presence of thoughts does not indicate failure in meditation.

How should I go about "entering the stream" of Sanatana Dharma, so to speak? What do I need to do to accomplish this?

You—and every single particle of every atom in the cosmos—are already in the stream of Eternal Dharma. It only needs to be recognized, and your inquiry shows that for you this has already happened.

Since I knew many people who wished to "officially" adopt Sanatana Dharma, I once asked Sri Ma Anandamayi about what they should do. Her answer was exactly this: "There is no need for anyone to do any special procedure or anushthana. All they need do to adopt our dharma is to take it up and begin to practice it." This is logical, for dharma is in the living of a philosophy. (Please note that Ma said "*our* dharma," indicating that she identified with Sanatana Dharma, though it is often said that she did not identify with any one religion.)

"Anushthana" is the Sanskrit word for any kind of special spiritual observance or religious exercise undertaken for a special purpose or benefit. To express Sanatana Dharma in thought, word, and deed is the only "anushthana" we need.

The philosophical principles of Sanatana Dharma are to be found in their pristine purity in the eleven major Upanishads: the Isha, Kena, Katha, Prashna, Mundaka, Mandukya, Taittiriya, Aitareya, Chandogya,

Brihadaranyaka, and Svetasvatara Upanishads. Two other texts tell us how to perfectly act upon the upanishadic philosophy and attain self-realization/liberation: the Bhagavad Gita, which is a digest and exposition of the upanishadic philosophy with emphasis on its practical application, and the Yoga Sutras (Yoga Darshan) of Patanjali.

Study and apply what you learn in these thirteen sources and you will be a true Sanatana Dharmi—one who embodies the Sanatana Dharma.

Wouldn't a "virgin birth" be against natural laws? What would be the purpose, anyway?

Nothing is more natural than the supernatural! God is the only "natural" thing there is.

Just as there are many strata in the earth and in the sea, so there are many levels of existence with their own laws. The higher supersede the lower. Until humans discovered the laws of aerodynamics they could not fly—it seemed impossible, even miraculous.

Once a spirit has attained to Supreme Consciousness the rules are completely different. Remember, our bodies are in exact correspondence to our level of consciousness. A human body is for human consciousness. How, then, can Divine Consciousness totally manifest through a human body? It cannot. So a kind of "hybrid" body, human-yet-divine, is needed. Otherwise the body will be electrocuted or blown apart by the incredible force that is normal for an avatar. It seems that such a great one can have a mother, but not a father. The elements of a body can be drawn from a human mother, but that which is usually "supplied" by the father must be created or manifested in a special form. These women experience a great light entering into them and pervading them, when the supernatural conception occurs. It was this way with the mothers of Buddha and Jesus. This was seen by several people in the case of Sri Ramakrishna's mother. All the ins and outs are incomprehensible to us.

What really matters is the teaching of such sacred persons, for by following their words we also come into spiritual alignment with them and receive great blessings and upliftment. They really are "saviors," but not in the lazy way supposed by most religionists.

An avatar is a perfectly liberated spirit returning to the world for the upliftment and liberation–salvation–of others. Such a one is a "divine incarnation," though not Brahman or Ishwara, of whom an incarnation is impossible. However, God can take on an illusory form that is not a real "incarnation." Such a form appears and disappears at the direct will of God.

Why is it considered unfortunate to die in a state of unconsciousness?

To be unconscious at the time of death is not fortunate because a yogi should consciously by an act of will leave the body. Being able to do so can be the difference between having to come back and being freed from (at least earthly) rebirth. How are we able to consciously leave the body? This ability is developed by meditation itself, for meditation enables us to even now begin separating our consciousness from materiality. Not that we can die from meditation! Nor do we need to work on some technique of consciously leaving the body, either. Meditation takes care of everything.

During one of my trips to India I met a disciple of a great Master in the Kriya Yoga tradition. (Later I met the Master, and he certainly was one.) He told me that although he was a Raja yogi practicing elaborate sadhana, he had personally known several illiterate village women whom he had seen leave the body at will. They were adept meditators, practicers of mantra japa. At the end of their life they cooked a feast for all the inhabitants of their villages. When the feast was over they bade everyone farewell, then went into their huts, lay upon the floor and left this world—no doubt forever.

At the conclusion of his narrative to me he laughed and said: "Just two weeks ago gurudeva was speaking to a few disciples, including me. He explained that our form of yoga was necessary for over-educated and degreed men such as ourselves who have to 'know' and 'understand' sadhana practice as a 'science.' But for all the rest mantra japa does the needful as it has for thousand of years in India—often better than our practices do for us."

What is the value of "holy company" (satsang)?

One tuning fork can make another vibrate at the same rate if they are brought close to one another. The same is true of holy people—their physical proximity or the simple sight of them makes our innate holiness wake up and emerge.

Does meditation affect dreams?

Yes, meditation definitely affects the dreams, because it is restructuring the entire mind and consciousness. Meditation makes the subconscious conscious.

Odd dreams may occur, some even unpleasant, but it is all part of the clearing out and ordering process. There is usually little value in trying to figure them out. The purpose of the dream was accomplished while you were centered in the subconscious and often has no relevance to the conscious mind. Some dreams are significant, but it is best to let them be.

Life itself is a message from the inmost Self.

Could you recommend a Gita translation or commentary that I could purchase?

The absolute best translation is *The Song of God: Bhagavad Gita*, by Swami Prabhavananda and Christopher Isherwood. It conveys the spirit of the Gita as no other translation does. It is, though, an interpretive translation. But the interpretations are according to the great commentators such as Adi Shankaracharya. The supplementary material, including an essay by Aldous Huxley, is extremely valuable in understanding the Gita's subtle philosophy.

However, in time you need to engage in a deeper study of the Gita, and for that you need translations that will give you the original Sanskrit text, a word-by-word translation, and some commentary. Among the best of these are the translations of Swami Sivananda, Swami Swarupananda, and Winthrop Sargeant.

All four of these translations can be bought from Amazon.com.

The Gita is a lifetime study which you will find continually reveals new insights and inspiration.

Since the Gita is a digest of the Upanishads, I also recommend that you get *The Upanishads: Breath of the Eternal* by Swami Prabhavananda. This is also available from Amazon.

When you are ready for the graduate course I recommend you get the two-volume translation and commentary of Paramhansa Yogananda entitled: *God Talks With Arjuna*. That is a treasure beyond price for those who want the most complete understanding of the Gita.

And there is always my endeavor, *The Bhagavad Gita, the Song of God*.

≈

Just what is a "Master"?

There are many ideas about what constitutes a Master. I will give you mine so you will know what I mean by it in my writings.

Essentially, a Master is a liberated being. Such a one is a master of himself–not of others. And a real Master wants others to become Masters–not his disciples. As the great Master, Neem Karoli Baba, would say: "I do not make disciples–I make devotees of God."

There are three major benefits of being with a Master: 1) His presence awakens spiritual consciousness. 2) His presence arouses inner spiritual energy (shaktipat). 3) He can teach you the way to attain what he has attained and advise you as you apply what he has taught you. A true Master does virtually nothing but these three things. And for the qualified seeker that is enough.

A Master will not guide your thoughts, direct your life, claim to be taking on your karma, or tell you he knows a shortcut to God realization. (Whether a yogi runs or walks he still has to go through the full length of the path. There are faster and slower ways of traveling the path, but no short ways.) Often he will answer philosophical questions, but will let you know that only practice matters–not philosophizing.

Furthermore, he will not manipulate or blackmail you with talk of "unconditional love" or either offer or demand it. You do not need love. You need *God* who is love. That is what a Master wants you to have.

No true Master will create or cultivate a "relationship" with you, because it cannot be done. You can only relate to the One. And when you do, then you will be one with everyone and everything. You will yourself be a Master.

A Master will never ask you to make promises or commitments, knowing that you will do what you will do–and not a bit more. A Master never makes, accepts, or demands a vow. In fact, a Master will reject such things.

Beside the three I listed there is a fourth and wonderful benefit: A Master will help you to become free; an adult, not a child; independent, not dependent. If your childish ego demands anything less, a true Master will truthfully tell you to look elsewhere. (There is a lot of "elsewhere" for you to find what you want.)

What should you do? Listen; Learn; Practice; Experience; Know. That is it. Anything more is impossible, and anything less is worthless.

You can be with a Master, though your bodies are not in the same place. The Master Yogi Shyama Charan Lahiri (known in *Autobiography of a Yogi* as Lahiri Mahasaya) would tell his students: "Why come to view my bones and flesh, when I am ever within range of your kutastha (spiritual sight)?" Those who do what I have outlined above will ever be in contact with the Master every step of their life. The worthy student is never alone.

I have a CD of spiritual chants. Is it helpful to listen to this as I meditate?

It is best to meditate in silence. Even beginners should do so lest they become conditioned by any artificial sound. But outside meditation such a recording can be very helpful in reminding us to keep our mind on God. A lot of Indian devotional music sounds more like a raucous hillbilly hoedown than praise of God. I recommend that you obtain recordings of Paramhansa Yogananda's spiritualized chants, both those issued by Self-Realization Fellowship and Crystal Clarity Publishers.

One recording I can recommend for use outside meditation to help you to remember to do japa, no matter what mantra you use, is *The Eternal Om* by Robert Slap, issued by Valley of the Sun Publishing. You should play it very softly, so it is almost subliminal, for you want to be intent on the sound of your inner intonations of a mantra, not an external sound. The recording is very soothing, as well, and is good to listen to during day and night when it is appropriate or practical. If it helps you to go to sleep, use it at night.

My parents expect me to marry, but I am interested in the monastic life. What should I do?

Pay attention only to the Real Parent: God and your own Self. You have had billions of parents in the past, beginning with when you were a plant and on up till now. Does any pair of them have more claim on you than another? Just being the latest link in your chain of rebirths does not give anyone a priority of influence.

Krishna says that we must follow our own dharma (swadharma). "Better is one's own dharma done imperfectly than the dharma of another well-performed. Better is death in one's own dharma. [Doing] the dharma of another invites danger." (Bhagavad Gita 3:35)

The wise thing is to meditate and get in touch with your own divine Self (Atman) and intuit what your dharma is for this lifetime. Both married people and monastics have been great saints, and both married people and monastics have been pathetic failures as human beings. The key is in following our swadharma. This can only be revealed to us from within—not by another.

Yogananda is frequently mentioned in your articles. Do you recommend certain of his writings?

I certainly do. *Autobiography of a Yogi* should be read through carefully many times, giving very close attention to the footnotes. It is the most perfect presentation of Indian philosophy and spirituality that I know, though Swami Yatiswarananda's *Meditation and Spiritual Life*, which I recommend also, is a close second.

Here is the order I recommend for the study of Yogananda's writings:

Autobiography of a Yogi (First Edition–Crystal Clarity Publishers)
Man's Eternal Quest
The Divine Romance
Journey to Self-realization
The Science of Religion
Sayings of Paramahansa Yogananda (*The Master Said*)
Conversations With Yogananda (Crystal Clarity Publishers)
God Talks With Arjuna
The Second Coming of Christ

I put the last two at the end because they are so poorly edited–overedited, actually–that they can be a real labor to read. But their ideas are very important and I value them highly.

Advice Regarding Brahmacharya

Occasionally I receive letters from spiritual aspirants asking me for advice on the subject of brahmacharya. The following are pointers which are essential for the establishment of brahmacharya.

1. Daily meditation and constant japa throughout the day are essential foundations of brahmacharya. Japa and meditation cause the subtle forces known as prana to rise upward. Those who become adept in these spiritual practices will become urdhvareta yogis–those in whom the sexual energies flow upward and become transmuted into spiritual energies. I recommend that you read the book *Soham Yoga*.

2. Satsanga, the company of holy people–or at least those who are aspiring to holiness–is extremely helpful in the maintenance of brahmacharya. If you know like-minded people, then meet with them

regularly for spiritual study and conversation. It is not uncommon among both Hindus and Buddhists for spiritual aspirants to meet daily for meditation.

If you do not know any other spiritual aspirants—and this is not uncommon here in the West—then keep satsanga with saints and masters by reading their lives and teachings and keeping their pictures in your home. Holy images of divine forms are also beneficial.

Every day listen to spiritual music. Such music should be soothing and reflective—not the raucous banging and clanging that many shallow and worldly Christians and Hindus like. It is good to listen to devotional music, but shun merely emotional music, for it is linked to lower desires, no matter how religious the words may be.

3. Avoid asatsanga—the company of the unholy and the worldly—in the form of people who have no interest in spiritual life, as well as books, magazines, television, radio, and motion pictures that are centered on material consciousness. Absolutely avoid those which deal with the subject of sex or depict sexually suggestive (or outright) matters or images.

4. Avoid casual association with members of the opposite sex. Never be socially alone with a member of the opposite sex. This is an absolute. Make no exceptions based on seemingly spiritual character, age, or intention. When an older woman tells you that she is your "mother" run away! The same thing applies when a man tells a woman that he is her "father." This goes on in both India and America, including close—and private—association of men with female gurus and of women with male gurus. No one knows what impulses carried over from previous lives—many even from centuries past—are lying not far beneath the surface of the conscious mind, waiting to manifest.

"Spiritual" friendships with members of the opposite sex are doors to disaster. I have seen it over and over. Even in my early teen years I watched "spiritual" associations inevitably turn into sexual associations. And that had usually been the intention from the first moment, even if only subconsciously.

5. If you happen to be homosexual, then what I say above applies to both sexes. (The number of "gays" that end up fathers is remarkable. It may be cute or poignant on the movie screen, but it is tragic in real life.) In your spiritual associations try to be sure that there are always several people involved. This is a trial, but many saints and masters have coped with much worse.

6. Avoid absolutely any person or thing that argues against your aspiration to brahmacharya or tries to persuade or force you into sexuality in any form. The "just try it once/for a bit" people are worse than tigers. Run for your life–literally.

7. I have warned you about external factors that harm the life of a brahmachari, but the biggest threat or danger comes from your own mind and impulses. Ruthlessly cut off all overt or oblique thoughts of sex when they rise in your mind. Note what "innocent" subjects of thought "somehow" end up in ideas of sex and banish them the moment they appear in the future.

8. What about supposed physical "needs" and bodily "urges"? Never let them be an excuse for wavering in your ideal. But you must keep the body clean and pure to help you in maintaining brahmacharya.

9. Continuing the previous subject: Diet is an essential factor for the brahmachari and the yogi. Diet is a form of spiritual culture as well as physical culture. There should be total avoidance of animal protein in any form and to any degree whatsoever, and this includes dairy products. Gandhi said over and over that animal flesh, animal fats, and dairy products were detrimental to brahmacharya, that movements of lust could be attributed to the physical effects of their use. (This also happens to be the opinion of the Eastern Orthodox Church, especially the monks who watch their minds.) Become not just a vegetarian but a vegan: Also avoid sugar, and caffeine. Abstain totally from nicotine and alcohol.

To learn the scientific and practical basis of what I have advised, see the books of Dr. Neal Barnard (http://www.nealbarnard.org) and the information put out by the Physicians Committe For Responsible

Medicine (http://www.pcrm.org), Dr. Michael Klaper (http://drklaper.com), and Dr. McDougall (http://www.drmcdougall.com).

10. Food for the mind in the form of spiritual reading is also a tremendous help to the yogi. Two books are especially important for the aspiring brahmachari: *Meditation and Spiritual Life* by Swami Yatiswarananda (order from amazon.com) and *Practice of Brahmacharya* by Swami Sivananda. This latter book can be downloaded free from the Divine Life Society website (divinelifesociety.org/graphics/ebooks/swami_sivanandaji/introduction.html). It is #31 on the list.

Read the books of many traditions and teachers on spiritual life, taking what is useful and leaving aside what is not. Follow your intuition and don't get what Yogananda called "spiritual indigestion."

11. What if you fail in some area or to some degree—or completely? Just keep on trying and be more vigilant. Do not let the ego or foolish associates or "authorities" convince you that it is hopeless, you should not even try, you will not be able, blah, blah, blah…. Multitudes of holy people have struggled, some have failed at times, but all have succeeded if they kept trying. So will you.

12. Finally, know that God is on your side. And remember these words of the Bhagavad Gita:

"Though a man be soiled with the sins of a lifetime, let him but love me, rightly resolved, in utter devotion: I see no sinner, that man is holy.

"Holiness soon shall refashion his nature to peace eternal; O son of Kunti, of this be certain: the man that loves me, he shall not perish.

"You find yourself in this transient, joyless world. Turn from it, and take your delight in me.

"Fill your heart and mind with me, adore me, make all your acts an offering to me, bow down to me in self-surrender. If you set your heart upon me thus, and take me for your ideal above all others, you will come into my Being." (Bhagavad Gita 9:30, 31, 33, 34)

Some time ago I had an experience I consider enlightenment, but after a while things went back to normal. Still I think something real happened to me. Would you comment on this? What is the sign of liberation?

Just as an explorer will climb a mountain to see the surrounding country and then plan his route, in the same way our higher self sometimes lifts our awareness into a high level so we can realize that such a state of consciousness is possible. Then it is withdrawn, and we become motivated to seek to become established in that state. Once Sri Ramakrishna by a touch gave the future Swami Vivekananda an experience of the supreme state of awareness. When it was over–for that state was not really "his own"–Sri Ramakrishna smiled and said: "Now you have to work for it!" And he did. In the same way we receive "sample" experiences to encourage us to seek to make those heights our own.

As far as liberation is concerned, Yogananda used to say: "He who knows…he knows, none else knows." But this we do know: Buddha meditated and followed discipline like any other monk until the day of his mahasamadhi, even spending months in intensive meditation retreats.

Please study the Gita daily, as that gives a perfectly balanced and complete picture of spiritual life. I would also like to recommend *Meditation and Spiritual Life* by Swami Yatiswarananda, available from amazon.com.

I have dreams at night with sages from the past. I am wondering if these are just dreams or if the dead can make communication through dreams.

First, please see the previous questions on visions, because what applies to visions mostly applies to dreams. Ramana Maharshi's cautions about getting involved with visions and dreams is most important and trustworthy.

It is extremely difficult to figure out whether a dream is real or not. Yogananda said that if we dream of a saint and they look exactly like their photographs, then the dream is real, for the subconscious mind cannot reproduce the form of a realized Master. I have found that this is an extremely valuable principle, for a lot of the time our mind is just fooling around or even trying to trick us.

But even if the dream proves to be real, is it completely trustworthy? For often a dream has both superconscious and subconscious elements mixed together. It is not uncommon for the mind to splice in subconscious footage even if the basic part of the dream is real. I have known dreams to start out real and end up fantasy. How can the difference be detected?

It is best to just take note of what is dreamed but to go no further than that. In time life itself will reveal the truth or unreality of the dream, as well as its value or worthlessness.

Masters never die, but live forever, and they can communicate with us. It has been my experience that such communication is always backed up with more objective elements, that the communications are more a pointing out than a stand-alone kind of teaching.

There is no substitute for the intuition developed by meditation—not even visitations from saints and angels.

On your website you discuss some benefits of astrology for spiritual life. Do you recommend Vedic astrology over Western astrology? Can you recommend an astrologer to consult?

It is my experience that although Indian astrology is more complex and the most fully developed, still Western astrology can be as beneficial in most instances. The crux of the matter is finding a good astrologer. A good astrologer is invaluable, whichever type of astrologer is employed. I hesitate to recommend astrologers because for some reason different people can have differing experiences with the same astrologer.

What I do recommend is that when you find an astrologer you do not entrust them with many questions or extremely important ones, either. First you should do a "test" consultation on a matter of moderate importance and see how they perform. Only when they prove themselves should you have them do more complex (and therefore more expensive) work.

Be cautious and realize that you may not easily find a skilled astrologer right away. But the search will be worth it when you do.

What is the afterlife like for ordinary people or for those that are liberated? What does the liberated soul do in the afterlife? If one is liberated are they kept separate from those who are not? What decides where a person goes after death?

Because of their unique karma, no two people have the same experiences after birth in this world. It is just the same with birth into the astral worlds. Each person's experiences will continue to be distinctively theirs.

One thing and one thing only determines where we go after death: our level of consciousness—our evolutionary status. What happens after we get there is determined by our karma.

A liberated person will have control over where he goes and what takes place there. But no world is inaccessible to him—including the earth plane.

You might find Sivananda's book *What Becomes of the Soul After Death?* useful. It can be downloaded from: http://www.sivanandaonline. org/graphics/ebooks/swami_sivanandaji/introduction.html. It is #44 in the list.

Also good is *Through the Gates of Death* by Dion Fortune.

In reply to someone who wrote that they are trying to keep in mind that we are ever perfect:

It is true: we are eternally perfect in our true being—even when entangled (seemingly) in ignorance. We need only recover that perfection in our consciousness and know that we and God are one. And that is all that is needed—ever.

There is a foolish theism and a wise theism. The Gita and Upanishads present the wise theism. The rest we can forget about. As Krishna says to Arjuna: "Be a yogi."

Will God mitigate karma sometimes?

We must understand the nature of karma. Karma is not a force, some kind of stored up energy, or power of destiny. Karma is the effect on the mind (which *is* energy) of an action. It is purely internal—a conditioning. If the conditioning persists, the reaction to it comes about in the external life. If the conditioning is modified or lessened, so is the result. But such is possible only to the creator of the karma. God has nothing to do with it. Only relative beings have karma. You cannot eat junk food and ask God to give you the effect of good food. In the same way you cannot expect God to alter the reaction to your action. It is silly to the maximum degree. That is why saying we are sorry and whining or crying accomplishes nothing but more ego entanglement and self-pity.

But we can change our karma, so there is hope, and more than hope. Karma is changed or eliminated by the changing of consciousness. We alone can do that. And yoga is the best and surest way to do it.

What sort of help does God provide? Or, more to the point, what sort of help won't He provide, if any?

God has already provided all we need. What we do not need simply does not exist. Now it is up to us to start using what has been provided. First we have to wake up to the realities and the possibilities. Meditation is the process of awakening most accessible to us.

Do you believe that all religions lead to the same Goal?

They certainly do! They all lead right back to more rebirth. Only Dharma leads to liberation in God.

I thought the whole idea was to merge with God.

It is, but uniting or merging with God is not getting lost in God, to melt away or get absorbed so that we no longer remain. It is just the opposite–this is the teaching of the Sankhya philosophy on which yoga is based. Some Vedantists hold the idea that we cease to be individuals and only the Absolute remains. "One" is not just a number: it is a quality, a state of existence. Even when we are one with God a duality within unity remains. For there is an eternal distinction between us and God, as there is between a wave and the ocean.

Why is Yoga considered a science rather than a religion?

Because it is a precise methodology that has nothing to do with faith or the action of another being–including God. If you practice it, it works, if you do not, it will not. It is just like a machine. Doubtless there is such a thing as aptitude for yoga, as with any other practice, but the machine does not determine the success of the operator.

Facts are facts. And yoga is based on the highest facts. Also, even though a general philosophy has developed as a result of the unanimous experience of yogis through the centuries, the philosophy is a side effect and of absolutely no influence in success in yoga. We have lived so long at the whim of "authorities" that we just cannot imagine not needing someone interfering with us.

But yoga is a completely personal matter. You need not believe in it, and you can even laugh at it and deny its value. But if at the same time you are practicing you will get the same result as a person who has faith and values it. Oh, how wonderful it was to escape "If It Be Thy

Holy Will, O Lord" religion and find yoga that worked no matter how worthy or sincere I might not be.

When I was little I reached for a metal ring that was lying on top of a heater. "Don't touch it!" I was warned, "You will get burnt." I have no idea why, but I did not believe I could not manage, so I picked it up and got the most painful burn of my life, and hurt for a couple of weeks. My lack of faith did not affect the effectiveness of the ring to burn me.

No one need accept or believe in yoga. Just do it. As Yogananda pointed out, the critics and deniers of yoga are the ones that have no experience of it because they do not practice it.

When I was first learning yoga I often laughed at how funny the processes were, and how odd that they would produce the desired result. But they did. Always.

Now, can you equate that with religion? Hardly.

But yoga is the highest dharma. That is sure.

Please explain how the world goes–what is the starting point and the end point?

This is best explained in *Autobiography of a Yogi* (first edition facsimile published by Crystal Clarity Publishers). Some of the major Upanishads also give detailed descriptions of how the universe emanates from the Absolute–and also why. The Bhagavad Gita also deals with these matters. I recommend you get information directly from these authoritative sources rather than a synthesis from me.

If we consider this world as cyclic when will Satya Yuga arrive?

This is also discussed quite completely in *Autobiography of a Yogi* as well as in *The Holy Science* by Swami Sri Yukteswar Giri.

Please be aware, that Kali, Dwapara, Treta, and Satya are matters of prevailing consciousness at some point in time. But they are also indications of individual development. Therefore, we can inwardly be in Satya Yuga even when Kali Yuga prevails outside. And we can be in Kali Yuga inside even when the world in general is in Satya Yuga.

The answer to all this is meditation.

How long must I meditate to see God by my outer or inner eyes?

How long did it take you to become an adult? How long to get a university degree? Seeking Infinity takes a lot longer, so we have no time to waste. Seeing God is a matter of evolution.

Have you seen God?

I have seen forms of God ("gods") and the formless Light. Yet I am still here, so I keep on meditating.

In the twelfth chapter of *Autobiography of a Yogi*, Sri Yukteswar remarked: "Those who are too good for this world are adorning some other."

There are many more people on earth now than there were when Hinduism began and when Jesus lived and so forth. Where do these new souls come from?

They are not new. Some people are reborn on earth in a matter of decades and others not for centuries or even thousands of years. Depending on the general mental climate of the earth, fewer or more people are born at a particular time. Also, in the past so many died in infancy, and plagues would wipe out entire populations. If they had not died there would have been a great many more people on earth after awhile. So it has nothing to do with how many souls are stocked in God's pantry.

Does God continue to create new souls?

All are eternal, without beginning. They do not come from God, but exist forever in God. God does not predate us. We are as eternal as he–co-eternal with him. See Chapter One of *Soham Yoga*. Only those are in relativity who have decided to take the plunge and come down. Virtually infinite are those that are still thinking it over and have not entered into relative creation. There are no doubt many that never will. It is their choice.

If we plan everything before we are born, is that where we have free will or does it continue here?

You are not two people–one before birth and one after. There never is anything but free will.

If we do have free will here then can we choose to change something we planned before we were born?

If before birth we chose to be in a situation which we would then change or abandon–yes.

Do accidents happen?

There are no accidents.

If there are accidents and one senses help from a higher source, does that higher source help because It knows the accident wasn't part of our plan and would, therefore, interfere with the life plan we made before birth?

Why make a simple thing complex? Sometimes we choose to create a situation in which we are miraculously helped so we will wake up and realize there is more than we presently think. Don't forget, your true Self and God are one–even if not the same.

**Just how much is really planned? If we plan everything and noth-
ing is left to chance, wouldn't we advance sooner? We wouldn't
want to suffer if by just doing what we are supposed to do, we
could mitigate a lot of karma at once. You have said we can do this.**

Do not assume that before birth you are omniscient. Being out of the
body does not make us any smarter. So some people plan for themselves
lives that are idiotic. But even those lives push them toward learning.

**Someone once asked you if Jesus was an avatar. You said he
probably was but it did not do much for you. Since I've read the
Aquarian Gospel commentary and the obvious care you took
with it, I'm not quite sure I believe your professed indifference.**

The commentary is on the wisdom, not the person speaking it. The
status of Jesus is irrelevant. Look at the people who claim he is God, but
who have not been touched by him in the least. "Not every one that
saith unto me, Lord, Lord, shall enter into the kingdom of heaven; but
he that doeth the will of my Father which is in heaven. Many will say to
me in that day, Lord, Lord, have we not prophesied in thy name? and in
thy name have cast out devils? and in thy name done many wonderful
works? And then will I profess unto them, I never knew you: depart
from me, ye that work iniquity." (Matthew 7:21-23) Their "faith" in
Jesus is iniquity in his eyes! So why bother with what someone thinks
about him? What we *do* about him is what counts.

Can a Swami be released from his vows?

We do not take vows! Instead certain rituals are (usually) done, and then we make intense declarations of renunciation. We renounce the earth plane, the astral plane, and the causal plane. And that is that. It cannot be gone back on, any more than we can decide to not have been born. Of course we can commit suicide, and some monks do so spiritually.

Is Yoga also helpful for mentally ill people (people living with paranoid schizophrenia, etc.)?

A very adept Indian yogi once told me that crazy people should not be taught to meditate, for they will meditate in a crazy manner and make themselves crazier—and usually claim crazy experiences and revelations. He did, however, recommend that mentally ill people learn deep relaxation, and had cured a number of them in that way.

When did karma begin?

Karma means both action and reaction. Since action precedes reaction we can say that karma "began" as soon as we were able to act intentionally in any manner. Since intention implies conscious will, that would be as soon as we have evolved to that capacity—sometime during our manifestation on the animal level. ("Animal" is meant in a very broad sense that would include even micro-organisms.)

Would you describe your philosophy as pantheism, or panentheism?

"Truly has this universe come forth from Brahman. In Brahman it lives and has its being. Assuredly, all is Brahman. Let a man, freed from the taint of passion, worship Brahman alone" (Chandogya Upanishad 3:14:1). Once this is understood, such Western distinctions as pantheism, or panentheism are meaningless.

Can you help me find or choose a spiritual name, one that will express my understanding?

Since you are interested in a name that indicates your inner spiritual life, you can go about it in two ways.

1. You can choose a proper name, such as that of a great holy person, a figure in religious lore (such as the Mahabharata, Ramayana, etc.) or scriptures, or even the name or title of an aspect of God. (There are thousands in Indian religion.) Of course to do so you need to be well acquainted with such things.

2. You adopt a spiritual quality or state as a name. For example, you can take a Sanskrit dictionary and look through it for words that correspond to your inner feeling. I recommend that you start with *A Brief Sanskrit Glossary*, and if that does not yield what you need, then look into larger dictionaries. In India many people have names that indicate spiritual qualities, such as Abhaya (without fear; steadfast), Jnana (wisdom), Viveka (one endowed with discrimination), or Brahmavadin (one who follows the path to Brahman).

But this is very important: the name should be your choice, not one recommended by another. Since you want it to express your inner feeling (bhava), it must be determined from within, through your own intuition. Otherwise in time you may not feel completely satisfied with it.

In the Yoga Sutras of Patanjali, the section on Yama and Niyama does not talk about helping others, being compassionate and loving to others. Why is this?

If a yogi cultivates the qualities of non-violence and non-injury (ahimsa), truthfulness and honesty (satya), non-stealing and non-misappropriativeness (asteya), unselfishness (aparigraha), peacefulness (santosha), and spiritual orientation (Ishwarapranidhana), which are listed by Patanjali, he will have a truly positive attitude toward others and be very considerate of them.

Patanjali focuses only on yoga in a very specialized sense. A continual, in-depth study of the Bhagavad Gita will give a full picture of authentic spiritual life. For the Gita embodies the wisdom of the Upanishads and the discipline of the Yoga Sutras in a totally practical manner. It is the guide to higher consciousness in all aspects of life.

I am wondering what the Hindu view of mental illness is. Plato said that it is a gift from the Divine but in my case it has been a curse. Please let me know what your view is. Also, I try to stay focused in my karma yoga and be detached in my actions but I am constantly afraid that I have not done enough to enjoy Krishnaloka and will be reborn. Please let me know if this is a proper attitude to have.

It is the Hindu view that all persons bound in samsara, whirling around in the constant cycle of birth and death, are to some extent mentally ill—deluded and confused. The important thing is that we can be cured, can come to know who we really are and be what we really are. The Bhagavad Gita is a manual of self-healing. There are many who are not at present able to take up that therapy, but in time they will be. Until then we love and bless them, and have hope for their future. To be aware of our problem and our need is a sign of fundamental sanity. The seriously mentally troubled are those that think everyone else is the problem and that they are fine.

As far as your other question goes, in the sixth chapter of the Gita we find that Arjuna asked: "One who has faith but is uncontrolled, whose mind has fallen away from yoga without reaching perfection in yoga—which way does he go? Is he not lost like a dissolving cloud, fallen from both [worlds—here and hereafter], having no solid ground, deluded (confused) on the path of Brahman? You are able to completely remove this my doubt. Other than you there is no one who can dispel this doubt" (6:37-39).

To this Sri Krishna replied: "Truly there is no loss for him either here on earth or in heaven. No one who does good goes to misfortune. Attaining the worlds of the meritorious, having dwelt there for countless years, he who has fallen from yoga is reborn in a happy and illustrious family. Or else he may be born into a family of wise yogis. Truly, a birth such as that is more difficult to obtain in this world. There he regains the knowledge he acquired in his former incarnation, and strives from thence once more toward perfection. Truly, without his willing it his previous practice impels him on the yogic path. He who just desires to know about yoga goes beyond the Vedas. By persevering effort and mastery, the totally purified yogi, perfected through many births, reaches the Supreme Goal. The yogi is superior to ascetics (tapaswins), and considered superior to jnanis and superior to those engaged in Vedic rituals (karmakanda). Therefore be a yogi. Of all the yogis, he who has merged his inner Self in me and honors me, full of faith, I consider him the most devoted to me." (6: 40-47).

This is the way to understand the matter. Yogananda said that if he summed up his entire life, the one thing he had learned was this: God never forsakes the devotee.

Could you tell me something about the Antichrist?

Saint John the Evangelist wrote: "Ye have heard that antichrist shall come; even now are there many antichrists" (I John 2:19). Then he defines antichrist as anyone that denies that Jesus is the Messiah. There is also a spiritual meaning: Antichrist is anyone or any thing that opposes our inner Christ, or usurps the place of our inner Christ. In both the Roman Catholic and Eastern Orthodox churches there is a great deal of speculation and prophecy about a single person to appear in the future as Antichrist, but there is no basis for this in the Bible. The subject need not interest us. We need to know Christ. The rest will take care of itself.

How can I know if I am progressing in meditation?

By your habitual state of mind outside of meditation. Read the Gita carefully and consider if what Krishna describes there is being attained—at least in some degree—by you.

In *Journey to Self-Realization,* a collection of talks by Paramhansa Yogananda, at the end of the talk entitled "The True Signs of Progress in Meditation," he gives the following list of seven indications of progress in meditation practice:

1. An increasing peacefulness during meditation.
2. A conscious inner experience of calmness in meditation metamorphosing into increasing bliss.

3. A deepening of one's understanding, and finding answers to one's questions through the calm intuitive state of inner perception.
4. An increasing mental and physical efficiency in one's daily life.
5. Love for meditation and the desire to hold on to the peace and joy of the meditative state in preference to attraction to anything in the world.
6. An expanding consciousness of loving all with the unconditional love that one feels toward his own dearest loved ones.
7. Actual contact with God, and worshipping him as ever-new Bliss felt in meditation and in his omnipresent manifestations within and beyond all creation.

Certainly the yogi should be experiencing the effects of a yogic practice. They can take many forms, but Yoganandaji's list pretty well covers it all.

What is your perspective on the Virgin Mary? Should she be worshipped? And what about honoring images of the Virgin?

One of the most wonderful truths about spiritual life is its completely individual nature. The more evolved a species is, the more distinctive each of its members is. Those lower in evolution all look alike. It is the same with religion: those of lower evolution and spiritual insight try to make everyone the same. Religion of higher development encourages and enables each person to become more and more unique, and encourages them to follow their inner nature as much as possible. In India this is known as Swadharma, the mode of life that best evolves the person. So although I will tell you how I see things, it is your personal perspective that is really important and which you should value and follow. Also, be prepared for your ideas and insights to change as you change inwardly—as you evolve.

All that exists is a reflection of the Divine Source; and the fundamental trait of existence is duality, which also exists within the divine unity. All awakened (evolved) religion is aware of this, and acknowledges that the Absolute contains within itself both positive and negative, masculine and feminine. Those religions that do not hold this insight are almost always the coercive, hateful, "everyone but us is wrong" type that claim God harbors displeasure, anger, hatred, and vengefulness. Their God-concept is that of the quintessential abusive, bi-polar parent (usually male). They all originated in the Middle East.

When divinity manifests on earth, it is usually in a dual form to demonstrate the divine fatherhood and motherhood of God. This is well understood in Hinduism, Taoism, Buddhism, and original Christianity. Jesus embodies the fatherhood and the Virgin Mary the motherhood of God. Jesus said: "He that hath seen me hath seen the Father" (John 14:9). And those that saw Mary had seen the Mother.

This is proved by her appearances at Lourdes, Fatima, Mexico (Guadalupe) and other places throughout the world, as well as her miracle-working icons and statues. Her great healing and awakening power has been evident throughout the history of the Christian Church. As Jesus said to his beloved disciple: "Behold thy Mother!" (John 19:27).

Through Jesus we approach the Divine Father and through Mary we approach the Divine Mother. We need both, for we are all included in the biblical statement: "God created man in his own image, in the image of God created he him; male and female created he them" (Genesis 1:27).

When the Wise Men "were come into the house, they saw the young child with Mary his mother" (Matthew 2:11). Where there is Jesus there is Mary; where there is Mary there is Jesus. They cannot be separated. As a Syriac hymn says:

> Let us always remember
>> on Whose lap our Lord is seen.

> With the Lord of creation
>   will be found creation's Queen.

It is God Who is worshipped through both Jesus and Mary—as well as through many other forms. To honor a holy image is to honor the holy one it represents, and through them to honor God.

Those who do not grasp this are simply not evolved enough. Let them do what they want about it, and we should do the same. The ignorant should be ignored. As Jesus said to those like them: "Ye do err, not knowing the scriptures, nor the power of God" (Matthew 22:29). Never let yourself be bullied by such persons. They are antichrists, which is why their kind is so obsessed with the subject of a coming Antichrist. They are hoping for it. Look away from them to Jesus and his Mother—and therefore to God.

You made this statement in the Christian Vegetarian Diet post:

"When we realize that any physical object has all the levels which we do, namely, the physical, biomagnetic, sensory, intellectual and will bodies, we can understand the importance of the kind and quality of food we eat. For not only does the physical substance of the food become assimilated into our physical body, so also do the subtler energies become united to our inner levels."

How do you know ALL physical objects have an intellectual and a will body? How do you know a vegetable has an intellectual body for instance?

The Sankhya philosophy (and all the other darshanas—orthodox systems of Indian philosophy), which includes the oldest form of physics, postulates that all material objects possess five levels or koshas (sheaths/bodies).

The universe is considered to have five layers that correspond to the five Cosmic Elements (Mahabhutas or Panchabhutas). The Primal Element, of course, is Pure Consciousness Itself–God, Brahman, or Paramatman. On this ocean of Consciousness everything is based or "floating." Akasha, the Etheric Element, floats upon Consciousness; Vayu, the Air Element, floats upon Akasha; Agni, the Fire Element, floats upon Vayu; Apa, the Water, Element, floats upon Agni; and Prithvi, the Earth Element, floats upon Apa. Nothing can exist in the material world that is not supported by the other five levels or elements. Thus all things possess five layers or "bodies." These elements or bodies are really bands or bundles of energies.

In most objects, the levels are purely potential, or at best dimly awakened. But in sentient beings, they are all active, though in varying degrees according to the level of evolution. The bodies correspond to atomic, biomagnetic, sensory-mind, intellectual, and will energies or levels (faculties). In the human being these five are alive–but the degree of life also depends on individual evolution.

Vegetables possess all levels, mostly in the form of "raw" or unconditioned life energies (prana). Thus they are absorbed readily into our bodies and the subtle levels of our being, and become conditioned by our thoughts and the present vibratory character of our bodies.

This is not true of animals. Rather, all their levels are conditioned and locked into the vibratory patterns proper to their species. Thus, when we eat them we graft the animal bodies into our human bodies and create conflict and havoc, darkening and distorting our minds to an incalculable extent. Eating meat is one of the worst things we can do to ourselves, and it renders the practice of yoga and the awakening of higher consciousness virtually impossible. (I know you did not ask about animals, but it seemed good to complete the picture.)

Being "masters of our destiny" is mentioned in the article on the purpose of reincarnation. Does that include the two year old child in Haiti who is born into extreme poverty and contracts typhoid, malaria and yaws and dies a horrible death? That child is the "master of his destiny" due to free will? I simply do not grasp this.

It is quite simple, once you shake off the blindness of Western religion and come to understand the truth about the divine status of the Self, its absolute control over everything that happens to it in each lifetime, and the reality of karma—not only as an absolute law, but as a tool wielded by the evolving soul.

The sole purpose of the universe is the evolution of the individual spirit-consciousness. But the cosmos is not some kind of machine into which the spirit is dumped against its will, and subjected to a "sink or swim" situation. Rather, it is governed by very precise laws, all of which are being operated by the Self.

Our particular section of the universe is populated by people who, having made wrong choices (sankalpas), have come into conflict with the cosmos and its purpose. Just as it is not the fault of a wall if we bang our head into it, or the fault of a window if we fall or jump out of it, so it is with the world around us. When we touch fire it burns us—that is the law—but we are not being punished. We are experiencing the ultimately beneficial mercy of the universe which is using pain to warn us away from mistaken action.

I have said that our life is fully under our control, and that is so. However, we have made a great deal of wrong turnings and fallen into the quicksand of ignorance and confusion. The resulting suffering is great, but the only remedy is for us to quit making foolish decisions and actions and rectify what we have already done to our detriment.

As with every other aspect of life, the Bhagavad Gita deals with this matter clearly and very concisely. Arjuna asked Krishna: "Impelled by what does a man commit evil, even unwillingly, as if urged [commanded] by force?"

To this Krishna replied: "This force is desire, this force is anger; its source is the rajas guna. Voracious and greatly injurious, know this to be the enemy. As fire is covered by smoke, and a mirror by dust, as the embryo is enveloped by the membrane, so the intellect is obscured [enveloped] by this [i.e., rajas and its two forms of kama and krodha]. The knowledge even of the wise ones is obscured by this eternal enemy, having the form of desire, which is insatiable fire. The senses, the mind and the intellect are said to be its abode; with these it confuses [deludes] the embodied one, obscuring [or covering] his knowledge. Therefore, restraining the senses first, kill this evil thing which destroys knowledge and discrimination [intelligent understanding]. They say that the senses are superior. The mind is superior to the senses; moreover, the intellect is superior to the mind; that which is superior to the intellect is the Self. Thus having known that which is higher than the intellect, sustaining the self by the Self, kill the enemy which has the form of desire and is difficult to conquer." (Bhagavad Gita 3:36-43)

Most human beings have developed a form of schizophrenia in which the true Self and the body, emotions, mind, and intellect have become estranged by the arising of the negative ego which usurps the natural kingdom of the Self. Just as a person with multiple personality disorder is unaware of the other personalities, so it is with us.

Although the Self and the lesser self have become disconnected to a great degree, the Self is still fundamentally in command, and so it does all it can to awaken its alienated levels so reintegration can be accomplished in the manner indicated by the Gita. Because of our present status, pain and suffering are usually the only things that get our attention. So yes, the baby is born in terrible conditions and suffers accordingly. Even though it may not understand on the conscious level what is going on, a subliminal conditioning is taking place that will eventually surface in a future incarnation. In the meantime, between lives the individual becomes aware of what is going on during material incarnation, analyzes it, and arranges its next birth(s) accordingly. Consequently only benefit results, however long it takes for that to become obvious to us.

There can be no end to this karmic dilemma without an intentional, conscious, and thorough restructuring of consciousness. And this is accomplished only through yoga, as it is the only way to follow Krishna's instructions to Arjuna: "Become a yogi" (Bhagavad Gita 6:46). This does not mean that the individual cannot bring about a marked degree of relief by other means, but until the knowledge of yoga is gained the process cannot be completed and the freedom from pain made permanent. As the great Master Paramhansa Yogananda used to say: "Yoga is the beginning of the end."

Please explain how we can save ourselves from Satan.

First we must understand that Satan is not a person, but a negative cosmic force that is continually being fed by the negative thoughts and deeds of sentient beings (not just humans). It is like a vat of acid—if we do not touch it or breathe it, no harm comes to us.

By negative thoughts, words, and deeds we come into alignment with Satan and are influenced by it, just as a powerful river or its undertow will carry us away if we jump into it. If we are continually in alignment with Satan, in time we will become controlled by it and become its tool. This is the state of a large portion of humanity today.

We save ourselves from Satan by not going near it or touching it, just as we cannot get wet or drowned if we stay away from the river. What if we are already in the river? We get out by deliberately changing our words, deeds, and thoughts. After all, Satan is just a "thing" and we are intelligent beings with the power of will.

Do not worry and wonder if you are helplessly controlled by Satan, for if you were it would never occur to you that you might be. The fact you ask the question is proof that, even though you may be influenced to some degree, you are not its prisoner and can remove yourself from its influence.

Prayer and meditation are the surest ways to escape and distance yourself from Satan. Regular meditation and constant japa ensure your escape and freedom. Nevertheless, you must change your life, eliminating all that is negative and bringing into it all that is positive.

In conclusion, never forget the assurance of the Apostle John: "Ye are of God, little children: because greater is he that is in you, than he that is in the world." (I John 4:4)

What makes a holy scripture either holy or a scripture?

An excellent question, and one that more people should ask. Just because someone claims to have gotten a revelation from God, angel or whatever, does not mean the written record is holy scripture. Often it is fraudulent, stupid, or insane.

God is holy, and any writing that tells us how to communicate with God and our own innate spiritual, divine nature is a holy scripture. It does not make any difference if it was written thousands of years ago or only a few days ago. It is the content that matters. Holy scriptures contain demonstrable truths that can be proven by each person who applies their principles. They are not speculations of philosophy or metaphysics, but practical statements that can be assimilated into our lives and produce perceptible results—eternal facts.

Books that claim to tell us God's will and give us God's commands should be approached very cautiously. And do not forget that throughout centuries they may have been interpolated or edited by liars and lunatics (often both). Books filled with dire threats and "precious promises" are usually nonsense and often destructive.

A holy scripture tells us how to know God and awaken into our oneness with God. Any descriptions or expositions about the divine nature are not made for us to just accept and believe intellectually, but are intended to help us draw near to and awaken in God–and know when it is really happening.

Only God-realized Masters can write a holy scripture telling us what to do to know Eternal Verity for ourselves. After we have come to know That, then we can be assured that is a holy scripture.

A true holy scripture points us to God and makes it very clear that words are not truth: God alone is Truth. And they tell us that once we know God we have no need for them. "When the whole country is flooded, the reservoir becomes superfluous. So, to the illumined seer, the Vedas are all superfluous" (Bhagavad Gita 2:46). This is an essential trait of a holy scripture, along with the fact that a holy scripture never claims to be the one and only truth, threatening punishment or offering reward for our rejection or acceptance. That is sociopathy, not sanctity.

For all the foregoing reasons we unhesitatingly recommend that you investigate for yourself the various scriptures, and put them to the Reality Test.

When an animal that you have lived with for years and been as close to as another human being–maybe even more so–dies, what happens? Can they still stay with you, though unseen? Can they see you? Will you ever meet or reunite with them?

Death, like life, is solely determined by the individual, so there are no cut and dried answers or rules about it. However, in many cases the departed are aware–at least for a while–of those they leave behind, and this includes animals. Just as with humans, if the departed see their friends in grief and distress they are also grieved and distressed. So for their sake it is good to express our sorrow as little as possible.

There is no reason to think that you will not at some time in the future meet your friend. I have known two animals, a cat and a dog, that in a short time were reborn and reunited with their former human friends. There was abundant proof that they truly were the departed ones.

Animals are sentient beings; the only difference between them and us is the level of development of the organism through which they express. And that difference is only temporary, for they are evolving upward–as are we. This being so, you can pray for their welfare (which sends loving energy to them), and can even inwardly speak to them and express your love. Do your best to remember all the happiness of your time together, and express your gratitude for that, and hope for more in the future. Remember this: There are no dead. All are alive forever.

Someone recently wrote to me asking what mode of life he should live–and saying what it was he wanted to do. This was my reply:

Part of your evolution is learning how to live life, not having others tell you how to live.

Does hell exist? If so, why, and what is it like?

In Sanskrit the word for hell is *naraka*, which means "pertaining to human beings." That is telling us something, isn't it?

In the authentic (original) Christian tradition hell is simply the Anglo-Saxon equivalent of the New Testament Greek word *hades*, which means both "the unseen realm" and "the lower [under] world." There is no connotation whatsoever of a place of fire and torment, or indeed any quality whatsoever. It is just the invisible world of disembodied spirits. When many people converted to Christianity in the fourth century after the Emperor Constantine made it the state religion, they infused a great deal of their old pagan ideas into the subsequently modified Christian theology. Part of that importing was the concept of Tartarus, a place at the center of the earth ruled over by Pluto. This was a place of darkness and sorrow, and sometimes even of punishment by avenging spirits. Aristotle loved the idea and insisted that it was eternal. But Judaism never knew such ignorance, and neither did original Christianity.

That is what is not true. But what is the truth?

All that exists is brought into manifestation by God for only one purpose: the evolution of the individual souls to enable their perfection and union with God. There is no other purpose, and no other motive for any part of creation. To enable the souls to evolve, many worlds or levels have been created, this material world being the most objective. Beyond it are worlds of increasingly subtle energies. And all the existent worlds are rungs on the ladder of evolution, reaching ever upward unto divinity Itself.

The basis of evolution is knowledge–particularly self-knowledge. So the worlds are really mirrors in which we come to see our own face–however much we may dislike, deny or ignore it. Our whole life is a visual lecture on our own present state of development. Karma and rebirth are the two major factors in this lecture, as they determine what the lessons will be. Nothing that happens to us is ever intended to be reward or punishment. Instead, all that we experience is reaction–reaction to our past and present deeds and thoughts. And these reactions reveal to us the nature of those deeds and thoughts.

For example, if we heedlessly steal from someone, causing them pain and perhaps deprivation, we, then, shall be stolen from and caused to experience the identical degree of pain and deprivation. This is not to punish us, nor even is it meant to simply deter us from repeating the error of stealing. Rather, it is intended to show us the character of our act of stealing and reveal to us why stealing is wrong. It is not wrong because we get slapped for it, it is wrong because it causes another to suffer. Understanding that is a step upward in our development.

A person who abstains from wrong action out of fear of its attendant suffering is not evolving, but is simply being a conditioned animal. A truly evolving person refrains from stealing, even in time of need, because he does not want to wrong and hurt another person. This is the only right motive for honest action—or for right action of any kind. Part of the purpose of karma is to develop the divine traits of compassion and kindness in us. It is not rectitude but mercy that is the intent. Which is why Jesus more than once reminded his hearers of the divine principle: "I will have mercy, and not sacrifice" (Matthew 9:13).

Anyhow, as I have said, our life is a mirror that shows us our evolutionary face. This is not easy for our egos to accept, but it is nonetheless true. If people lie about us a lot, that shows us that we have lied about people in our past lives and that the root of that lying is still inside us on the subconscious level—even if in the present life we never lie. Therefore when people wrong us the first thing is to figure out how to correct ourselves of the trait that is being responded to. This is also why the wise have said that their critics and enemies were their best friends: they were showing them the aspects of their minds that needed correction. And that is what the world does for us.

Each time our physical body dies we pass into subtler worlds for some time. Those worlds more exactly mirror us, and in those worlds we are much more insightful than we are here. In the earth plane something can happen to us that seems inexplicable. But in those worlds as the thing is happening we see what is the force and purpose behind it. So we learn better there. Further, those worlds correspond to our subconscious mind, so they reveal what is usually only subliminal for the physically embodied.

Just as our dreams reflect the thoughts and experiences of the previous day, so the astral worlds reflect the inner character of our previous earth life. If our subconscious is harmonious and positive, we will automatically pass into a harmonious and positive realm at death. And that will be heaven. If, on the other hand, our inner mind is filled with negativity, especially such things as hatred, lust, greed, resentment, and suchlike, we will enter a world that vividly displays those forces to its denizens. And that will be hell.

Some people naturally associate with worthy and uplifting people. Others prefer to run with the rat-pack. Each will go to the worlds where that type of person is being instructed. And that is the key: *instruction*. Since that is necessary for our growth, we can see that it would be folly to want to deliver people from hell, for that would deter their growth. However miserable an academic examination may be, we would be doing no one a favor by kidnapping them from the examination place and taking them on a jaunt in the countryside. They need that exam! And we need both heaven and hell if we are to ultimately transcend the need for either of them.

So the only worthwhile prayer for the dead is a prayer for their increased understanding. That is why in the Byzantine Orthodox Church's service for the dead, they continually sing the refrain: "Blessed art Thou, O Lord, *teach me Thy statutes*." For that is the purpose of whatever world the departed might be in. This is why in the creation of a truly esoteric Mass, Bishops Wedgwood and Leadbeater formulated as the usual Gradual: "Teach me, O Lord, the way of Thy statutes, and I shall keep it unto the end. Give me understanding, and I shall keep Thy law: yea, I shall keep it with my whole heart."

I think I have somewhat indicated what hell is and what its purpose is. As far as what it is like, that is impossible to delineate, because there are many hells and many heavens, each portraying an infinite number of psychological states. In some worlds the pleasant or unpleasant qualities are more external, and in others they are mostly internal. The entire range of psychic possibility is covered by them.

The important aspect of all this is, that since it is our own inner state that determines where we go after death, we should get busy and clean our psychic house through right action, right thought, right worship, and right meditation. Then we need have no worry, but can say with Saint Paul: "I have fought a good fight, I have finished my course, I have kept the faith: Henceforth there is laid up for me a crown of righteousness, which the Lord, the righteous judge, shall give me at that day: and not to me only, but unto all them also that love his appearing" (II Timothy 4:7,8)

I understand that Vedanta is an accepted form of Indian philosophy. But what is it?

Vedanta means "end of the Vedas," and usually refers to the Upanishads which are appended to the Vedas, thus coming at their end. On the other hand, the philosophy of the Upanishads may be called Vedanta because it speaks of spiritual realization that results from—comes at the end of—Vedic study and practice.

Vedanta has three forms, and all three have been declared "orthodox"– that is, in conformity with the Vedas, the Upanishads and the Brahma Sutras (a philosophical exposition by Vyasa, the codifier of the Vedas). These three forms are Dvaita (Dualism), Vishishtadvaita (Qualified Non-Dualism), and Advaita (Non-Dualism).

Dvaita Vedanta says that God and the individual soul (as well as the creation) are absolutely separate and different from one another, although God pervades or encompasses all.

Vishishtadvaita Vedanta says that there is an eternal distinction between God, the souls, and creation, but at the same time there is a unity because God is the root, the ground, of everything. From the viewpoint of creation and the individual soul, there is duality or distinction. But from the viewpoint of God, which the soul can ascend to spiritually, there is oneness alone.

Advaita Vedanta says that duality or difference between God, souls, and creation absolutely does not exist at any time, and that any experience of difference is completely an illusion. Thus neither the individual souls nor the creation really exist in the ultimate sense, but are manifestations of the One. The Real is appearing as the unreal.

It is extremely important to understand that Advaita is not Monism. Monism means Oneness–that there is only One, and nothing else but the One. Advaita, however, only means "not two." It does not mean "one." So an Advaitist would say that there is no duality, but would not say there is only unity. He would simply say nothing except that there are not two. This is because the Real transcends both "two" and "one" and is ineffable and inexpressible. Therefore, as in Christian apophatic theology we can only say what is not, but cannot say what Is.

As already said, all three are true–are orthodox.

The three forms of Vedanta correspond to the Trinity: Advaita corresponds to the transcendent Father, Vashistadvaita corresponds to the immanent Son, and Dvaita corresponds to the Holy Spirit, Mahashakti, the very basis of duality. They are three ways of seeing reality according to which aspect of the Trinity in the individual is dominant.

The three Vedantas also correspond to the three Gunas: Sattwa, Rajas, and Tamas. If Sattwa Guna predominates, the individual experiences the Advaitic, non-dual state. When Rajas predominates, then both duality and unity are preceived–the Vashishtadvaitic view. And when Tamas predominates, then duality is the only perception.

The Vedantic views also correspond to the three states of consciousness delineated in Indian thought: the waking (jagrat), dreaming (swapna), and dreamless (sushupti) states. In the waking state only the duality of the world and spirit is perceived; in dreaming, their unity-diversity is experienced; and in dreamless sleep only unity is experienced. Jagrat=Dvaita. Swapna=Vishishtadvaita. Sushupti=Advaita.

But the Vedic sages tell us that there is a fourth state which transcends these three states of consciousness and is at the same time the substratum of the three. That state is called Turiya–Pure Consciousness. Those who attain that ultimate state perceive neither duality, semi-duality, or unity. What do they perceive? It is beyond words, and only those who have attained It know. So all three forms of Vedanta are eventually gone beyond as we enter that which is beyond all distinctions of views or states. Is not that state a state of unity–of Oneness? No, it is not, for it is no state at all. It is the true Nirvana in which these distinctions or labels simply cannot arise. That we must seek.

I would like to know what you mean by esoteric and exoteric religion or philosophy.

Esoteric religion and philosophy are completely oriented to the inner mystical and contemplative view of things–it would not be amiss to call it a psychic view of matters. Naturally, the emphasis is on the inner state of consciousness.

One of the major things that distinguishes esoteric from exoteric religion is the concept of spiritual evolution–a concept held by the mystics of all religions. Another trait of the esoteric view is its acceptance of many religions as valid, for the inner traditions of many are the same, the difference between them being in the mechanics of spiritual methodology or practice. But even there we find great similarity and much that is identical.

Adherents of exoteric religion views things in a very external way, being primarily interested in external observance, in external behavior, and externally expressed beliefs. This is because they are very interested in an external eternal destiny–that is, whether they will end up in heaven or in hell in a state of physical (certainly exoteric!) immortality. Their preoccupation is with where they will be forever after this life (only one to a customer in the exoteric view). Their state of mind or their inner disposition is of minimal concern to them. Of course the concept of spiritual evolution is utterly alien for them. Their focus is on just which bin–Damned or Saved–God will sort them into when they get judged after death.

In the esoteric perspective religion is not a stable or corral to hold people who are to be merely housed, fed, and broken into harness. That is the making of slaves, not gods or sons of God. The primary purpose of esoteric religion is to enable people to expand their life-sphere, to evolve without limit. It can offer nothing else–and nothing less. Those who want less than that can be well accommodated in the exoteric religions.

Inquirers should understand that religion can point the way and give aids on the journey, but they will have to do it all on their own, for that is part of their evolution. Each person is responsible for his personal application of what he is taught, without being wheedled, cajoled, or threatened. Esoteric religion gives him the tools and the knowledge and says: "Go to it." There is nothing more that can realistically be done. Moreover they understand that each one will progress according to both the effort he puts forth and according to his own karmic background produced by innumerable lives he has lived before.

How much does the afterlife concern a yogi?

To a yogi, where we go after physical incarnation–which happens many times–is only symptomatic. Where we end up after death (or within this life, since we believe in the law of karma) is just an indication of our interior condition, an indication of our inner status–the development of the consciousness of the individual.

Not only is the material universe evolving, the conscious entities within the universe are evolving as well. To the yogi, salvation is the attainment of perfection through evolution. It is not having our sins forgiven, or being classified by God as one of his chosen. Rather it is making the grade and graduating from this earth-plane school, having learned the necessary lessons—not intellectually, but through our own evolution beyond humanity, our ultimate goal being divinity.

Having used the expressions "school" and "graduate" I should explain that karma and reincarnation are fundamental realities for the yogi, providing the context in which he lives and acts. They are absolutes. Karma is the absolute law that everything we do must have a reaction—not as a reward or punishment, but for learning. Since we are so slow to learn, and life is so short, it is therefore necessary for us to keep returning to the school of earthly birth for many terms, many lifetimes, until we do learn. This kind of learning is not merely intellectual—in fact hardly so at all—but is a matter of evolving the consciousness to its full potential in the human status. Then we can pass on to the higher worlds and start evolving through and beyond those as well, until our innate divinity is totally revealed.

How important is belief in karma and reincarnation?

Comprehending the two principles of karma and rebirth is not needful just because they are facts of universal life, but because they give us a right perspective on all facets of life itself. Without knowledge of these two fundamental laws, a working concept of ourselves and our present lives is impossible. Seeing ourselves as fundamentally evolving consciousnesses confined in bodies and an environment whose only real purpose is evolution, we will naturally shape our lives accordingly and deal with our life experiences within that greater context.

We will also realize that salvation is not a matter of being stamped "approved" or "passed" as though we were nothing more than USDA-inspected carcasses. Most important we will comprehend that there is actually no such thing as approval or disapproval on God's part. It all lies in our hands. We alone must determine our future by the way we deal with the present. We can learn and graduate, or refuse to learn and be sent back again and again until we do. God is patient. He has eternity—and so do we.

What about belief in heaven and hell?

First, we must not equate the Eastern view of heaven and hell with the Western view. The Eastern view is that heaven and hell—as well as our situation during earthly incarnation—are valuable teaching instruments. They are mirrors revealing to us the state and qualities of our inner minds (but not of our spirits, for they are ever perfect).

In Western religion the view is that these are rewards and punishments, indications of whether God is pleased or angry with us according to whether we have been good or bad. This belief views the soul as a veritably inert thing that merely pleases or displeases God, rather than a living entity that grows. It only follows then that those who hold it consider salvation as no more than getting to heaven and avoiding hell. Seeing the soul as intrinsically static, exoteric religions treat people accordingly. They put their adherents through certain rites and rules of behavior whose only purpose is a guarantee of a place in heaven. But this approach is simply not viable because the soul is a growing and developing thing. Consequently salvation (liberation, moksha) is a process that can take millions, if not billions, of years.

How important is theology or formal philosophy?

Even the way Sanatana Dharma presents its ideas—its philosophy—is affected by the evolutionary view that is fundamental to it. We realize that no one can be coerced to believe something he does not believe, and that to force him to pretend to believe is a spiritual crime. True dharma cannot say to anyone: "This is the truth: believe it or else." What really matters is the person's present state of evolution and his interest in and capacity for consciously working toward higher states of evolution.

Intellectual theology or philosophy becomes insignificant unless it can help us in the practical application of evolutionary spiritual life and understanding. It is basically useless to believe that God exists unless we comprehend that we, too, are eternally part of the divine life. It means nothing to believe in Deity if we do not believe and act upon the fact of our own divinity. Nor is it of any value to consider anyone our absolute savior, for each one of us must realize and exercise our innate capacity to save ourselves from ignorance, from birth and death.

Every belief or principle should be looked at from the perspective: What does it do in my efforts for evolving myself? If it has no application (and we must be sure that we do not judge hastily about this) then why bother with it? The approach to beliefs should be thoroughly pragmatic. We should see Sanatana Dharma itself in the same light. If someone sees no meaning or value in what it has to offer, then they should pass on and keep looking for a religion that does. If they adopt Dharma without really seeing its value they will be thwarting their necessary freedom and growth. Any religion is a hindrance if it is not what the individual needs for his spiritual progress. There is no such thing as *the* religion or *the* philosophy for everybody at a single time.

How exactly do you consider other religions as valid?

The various religions of the world do great good for those who are on their wavelength. They all are necessary to those for whom they are intended. True exponents of Sanatana Dharma always ask seekers to be sure they understand other religious traditions–especially if they were born into one–before adopting the Eternal Dharma. It is good for them to experience other religions. Otherwise, how can they make an intelligent decision if they do not know the alternatives?

Here, too, the simile of a school helps us out. No teacher walks into a classroom with the idea that everyone in the school is supposed to be there. He knows that some are not ready for the class, some have already taken the class, and some are studying a totally different subject and they are never going to take that class. This is as it should be. And no responsible teacher would insist that every member of the class go out and get others to enroll because otherwise they would remain uneducated. Such a teacher would be considered a fool or insane. It is amazing to see how we tolerate and even expect people to behave in religion in ways that we would instantly repudiate in any other area of life.

This has perhaps come about because exoteric religion has no real practical application or demonstration of its worth. It is all emotion, theory and "pie in the sky when you die" for them. If we believe that this is the nature of all religion, we then become inured to utterly senseless behavior on the part of "believers." And God!

What is the purpose or mission of your religion?

Let us consider the basics of growth as it takes place on this earth. The sun shines and warms the earth and the seeds in the earth. This stimulates the life principle in the seeds and they grow upward into the light. It is a very natural thing. Here, too, we would think someone crazy who would sit out in a field and yell at the plants to grow, promising rewards if they do and threatening punishments if they do not.

When we are dealing with human beings we are dealing with potentially infinite consciousnesses, with gods in embryo. We consider that we are dealing with a spark of God's own life, because we do not believe God created the spirit. We believe instead that each individual spirit has existed eternally within God. So we consider that we are dealing with a potential god, and act accordingly. Gods should not be poked, pinched, and pulled.

Maria Montessori came to see that children should not be coerced to learn any subject. She proved that a subject need only be presented to them and when they are ready for it they will respond–until then they will not, and should not. Our present system of education fails because it assumes that chronological age determines readiness for learning. Maria Montessori, being a believer in reincarnation and a member of the Theosophical Society (though a Roman Catholic), understood that this was a matter of evolution, and that everything would come to pass in its own good and right time. This is why no child goes through the Montessori system and comes out having not learned. It is successful because it is based on the evolutionary nature of things.

We follow the same procedure. We present. The response is up to the individual. And any response, Yes, No, or Maybe, is fine. Certainly there are those who at their present stage of evolution need what we offer, but they have to recognize that themselves. It is not for us to tell them. It is definitely our duty to be there for those who need us, and we should let ourselves be visible. Beyond that it is their hands.

I learned something very early in my first visit to India. The fake teachers were more than volunteering their supposed wisdom, they were cornering people and forcing it on them. But the real teachers had to be asked for instruction. Otherwise they just conversed affably on unimportant matters. Their insight was that only when the question arises in the mind of the seeker is he ready for the answer. Until then the teacher can do nothing worthwhile

Consider the material on our website: it is a matter of simple presentation, of visibility. If someone reads the material and says that they believe what is in them because they convinced them, we are not satisfied. That means they are simply spinning in the realm of the intellect and not in touch with their real inner self—something that has to occur for conscious spiritual growth. Also, they should not be accepting *our* ideas. It should be a matter of their own conviction that arises from deep within. We cannot eat or digest for other people, and neither can we reveal wisdom to them. What we can do is present what we consider wisdom, and they may *recognize* it through their own inner response.

So what do we want people to say about the web material? We want them to say the truth. It they think it is nonsense, that is perfectly all right. For them it *is* nonsense. We do like someone to say: "I had never thought of it before, but when I read what you wrote I realized that it was the truth and that I had always believed it somewhere in the back of my mind." In other words, we did not convince them of the truth; they recognized it as already being part of their inner intuition that had not heretofore been verbalized.

The word "education" comes from the Latin, its literal meaning being "to lead out." That is, real education is the process of evoking the student's innate knowledge, of bringing it out so he can consciously work with it. It is a reminding of him of what he really already knows. Not many people are educated, then, nor are many people authentically religious or spiritual. And we cannot make them so. They have to grow into it. Then we can help further their growth by showing them how to pass from natural automatic evolution into intentional evolution through yoga.

From the lowest form of life up to and including a great deal of the human experience, evolution happens automatically with no intention or effort on our part. We just live and it happens. But a time must come—the real time of conversion or being born again—when the individual must take control of his own evolution and consciously direct and produce it. For at that point it will no longer come automatically. It is somewhat like a child who at a certain age must learn to dress himself and in time make his own living. He must finally do on his own, for himself, what others had heretofore done for him.

The earlier "child" evolution is natural or automatic. The "adult" evolution is completely in the purview of the individual. A religion that cannot show a person how to do this is not of much use to an awakening person. The wandering spirit has forgotten itself and its attendant realities. It does not need to be taught, it need only be reminded, profound as that experience is. That is the sole purpose of Sanatana Dharma.

Can the Infinite God—and all things besides—really be known?

All Eastern religions say adamantly that God is both knowable and unknowable. We must not forget that the Greek word for God is *Theos*: The Absolutely Other. God is the ultimate Alien.

In our view God is unknowable, inconceivable, unseeable. We hold that it is impossible to even make a statement about God—not even that he exists, because he is totally beyond our ideas of existence. We only know the relative, whereas God is the Absolute. Even to attribute any characteristics or qualities to God in his pure being is considered erroneous in Eastern religion. This is called apophatic theology—that is, we enumerate what we *cannot* say about God.

In Sanatana Dharma this approach is called *neti neti*, which means "not this, not that." The idea is that when we have negated anything we might say about God, then we are left with what God is. And it is beyond all words. So we both can and cannot know God. This sounds like some kind of Zen koan, but it is not.

Let me give an example from our external life. Can we, standing on the shore, see the Atlantic Ocean—in the sense of seeing the whole ocean? Of course not. We can only see a part since it is so vast. So we never see it. That is, we cannot encompass it within the scope of our sight. This helps us to understand what is meant by our incapacity for knowing God. It is a matter of the limited scope of our consciousness. We can know something of God, the hem of his garment so to speak, but in the sense of knowing God as he is in his totality, it is impossible. But we can enter into union with God—be drawn into his Being—and transcend all relative existence. This is the whole purpose for our being here. We are intended to evolve and expand our consciousness to the point where, by entering into union with God, we can indeed see the "all" of him. Or more precisely, we can evolve to the point where we can see God with his own eye of infinity. That is, he will share his vision with us. This is glorious.

Without doubt the instruments of knowledge we presently have—the sensory mind and the intellect—cannot embrace an infinite vision because of their inherent limitation. In the Upanishads God is defined as "That from which the mind and the senses turn back." Saint Thomas Aquinas used a very good expression about approaching God in our present condition: *sensum defectui*: the senses fail. There is also the implication in the Latin that the senses fall back or fall away in that endeavor.

But we have more to us than the mind and the senses. We have much higher faculties whose existence we have not even guessed. And they can be evolved to a condition in which they will not turn back or fail.

How can you know but not know, or see but not see?

God is not an object. Therefore no faculty of perception can see him. God is an eternal Subject–as are we. The higher faculties I have spoken of are not instruments of objective perception but capacities for spiritual union, the ability to link our consciousness with the consciousness of God and see with it. This seems incredible, I know, but it is even more wonderful and heartening. We are not worms before God or mere bugs or slaves. We are part of him. And this need not remain a beautiful principle of philosophy. It is a principle of possibility, the possibility of our own divine potential. Yoga is the way to realize it. And that realization is true Knowing–Gnosis or Jnana.

Yet, such knowledge is "unknowing" in the sense that it is beyond all our presently-active faculties of perception, a direct knowing beyond all objective knowing. It is, as I already mentioned, a subjective knowing which takes place through the evolution of our capacity for union with God without any intermediary "eye" whatsoever.

God-knowledge (Brahmajnana) is possible only in the state of direct, immediate union with God. When this occurs we know everything–not just God–but it is not *our* knowing, it is *God's* knowing in which we are able to participate. We can experience the state of being and consciousness that is unique to God. It is a sharing by God of his own knowing.

Rather than take up a long time explaining the implications, let me just say that the purpose of our unfolding evolution is the development of the capacity to eventually share fully in the Divine Life, to be "god within God."

Since you have Christian-oriented or Christian-based material on your website, will you explain to me what the Christians mean when they talk about a "spirit" and a "soul"? They seem to be two things.

Your question reminds me of the time when after twenty years of "Bible believing" I woke up and wanted to know what the Bible meant, not just what it said. And the only people who could tell me were yogis, especially Brother Premamoy of Self-Realization Fellowship. The actual teachings of Jesus are found in *The Second Coming of Christ* by Paramhansa Yogananda and his talks and articles.

Although in the West "spirit" and "soul" are used interchangeably, in the New Testament and the theology of Eastern Christianity they are different. The word translated "soul" is psyche (*psuche*), the psychic nature which includes the mind, intellect, astral and causal bodies. The word translated "spirit" is *pneuma*, which is the pure consciousness, that which gives life or makes alive–the spirit itself. So you can see that they are quite different.

It is very important to differentiate between them, as the psychic must never be mistaken for the spiritual. One of the reasons exoteric Christianity is so confused in its analysis of the human condition is the idea that a human being is only a physical and spiritual entity–the psychic is simply not in the picture. As a result it considers simple psychic phenomena and functions to be spiritual and has a totally erroneous conclusion and reaction to them.

Can you tell me what determines who is born as one's children?

A single thing: karma. Of course there are many types of karma, some personal and some general. For example, if it is your karma to have a child of a certain quality, a soul of that type will be born to you. On the other hand, a particular person you have lived with before and developed an intense bond with, either negative or positive, may be born as your child. In either instance, the karma must be dealt with, there is no avoiding it. The parents should keep in mind that the child is their karma, and they are the child's karma. The blame or the praise is on both sides. However, your duty is to learn from the part that is your karma. The child has to deal with its own, though you may be able to help in some instances.

Can the parent-child bond be broken? Since the bond is karmic, it can be dissolved through one or both learning the karmic lesson or reaping the karma to the full. (Spiritual practice is the way to do the first, and is the surest and the safest.) Otherwise the ties will not be loosened and there may even be a "repeat performance" in a future life.

Is the knowledge gained in a lifetime carried over to the next life?

The conditionings, the samskaras, of one life do continue into future lives if they are strong enough and relevant to those lives. Usually the samskaras manifest as instincts rather than intellectual knowledge, but if strong enough the past life knowledge can carry over into the intellect. It is not uncommon for people to know something they never learned in that life.

In the matter of spiritual-knowledge karma, if we build on it we will increase it from life to life. If, however, we neglect it, it will weaken and may be lost to us in the next life. Our evolution does not take place in a steady ascent, but in a series of back and forward steps until our spiritual consciousness has become strong enough to carry itself forward in each subsequent life. Then no spiritual effort is ever lost.

I was wondering about the Yugas. It is mentioned in your Sanskrit glossary that we are currently in ascending Dwapara Yuga but in descending Kali Yuga in the cosmic scale. I am quite familiar with The Holy Science and the 24,000 year cycle, but not so much with the cosmic cycle. Was wondering about your conclusions that we are in the cosmic Kali Yuga, and how that might tie into the 2012 predictions and Kali and Dwapara?

These are not my conclusions but the standard view in India. If you will look up references to the yugas in *Autobiography of a Yogi* you will find the relevant information. Here is the entire entry from *A Brief Sanskrit Glossary*:

"Hindus believe that there are four yugas: the Golden Age (Satya or Krita Yuga), the Silver age (Treta Yuga), The Bronze Age (Dwapara Yuga), and the Iron Age (Kali Yuga). Satya Yuga is four times as long as the Kali Yuga; Treta Yuga is three times as long; and Dwapara Yuga is twice as long. In the Satya Yuga the majority of humans use the total potential–four-fourths–of their minds; in the Treta Yuga, three-fourths; in the Dwapara Yuga, one half; and in the Kali Yuga, one fourth. (In each Yuga there are those who are using either more or less of their minds than the general populace.) The Yugas move in a perpetual circle: Ascending Kali Yuga, ascending Dwapara Yuga, ascending Treta Yuga, ascending Satya Yuga, descending Satya Yuga, descending Treta Yuga, descending Dwapara Yuga, and descending Kali Yuga–over and over. Furthermore, there are yuga cycles within yuga cycles. For example, there are yuga cycles that affect the entire cosmos, and smaller yuga cycles within those greater cycles that affect a solar system. The cosmic yuga cycle takes 8,640,000,000 years, whereas the solar yuga cycle only takes 24,000 years. At the present time our solar system is in the ascending Dwapara Yuga, but the cosmos is in the descending Kali Yuga. Consequently, the more the general mind of humanity develops, the more folly and evil it becomes able to accomplish."

Opportunists and alarmists (usually the same people) are continually creating "coming events" and "impeding crises" to worry about and obsess on and wonder how to prepare for. Then the indicated time comes and passes, and nothing has happened—all is the same as before. In the last fifty years we have had 1) the stellium in Aquarius, in which we were told California would fall in the ocean, and many people sold their homes and moved inland, 2) the Comet Kahoutek about which many books were written, 3) Haley's Comet (ditto), 4) the Harmonic Convergence (a lot of fakes got rich on that one and a lot of fools ended up in the desert, having sold everything back home), 5) the "end" of the traditional Buddhist calendars, which sparked off conferences of Buddhist leaders throughout the world, 6) Y2K, and 7) 2012!

May I make a prediction? Nothing will ever happen except the scrapping of books and revision of websites and a lot of thought being given as to what people will buy into next.

If all the interest and energy and dedication wasted on these bugaboos had been channeled into spiritual life, this world would now be a much better place.

In response to a Christian's letter listing differences between "orthodox" Christianity and the beliefs presented on our website, and asking our explanation of those differences:

It has been our experience that when Christians write to us with a list of Biblical "what abouts?" and we take the time to answer, the response is simply another list of "what abouts?" As you yourself say in your email: "There will always be questions of course." Therefore we hope you will permit us to answer in a straightforward manner, interpreting it as you will. (On previous occasions when we have been direct in our reply we have been accused of hostility, defensiveness, ignorance, or–horrors!–anger.)

Your questions should be asked of yourself, rather than your condescending comment that we have presented our views "with obvious good intentions." If the principles espoused on our website are true, then why does the Bible contradict–or seem to contradict–them? That should be your concern, not ours. If the principles we present are not true, then what does it matter to you? (Hopefully you are not concerned for our souls.)

The members of our ashram all have a Christian background, and are not unaware of Protestant, Catholic, and Eastern Orthodox beliefs. We consider that we cannot in good conscience be "Christians" that are actually Churchians and be able to follow Sanatana Dharma and Jesus. *The Christ of India* presents our view of Jesus as a Sanatana Dharma missionary–neither Jewish nor Christian. Further, our posting of *The Aquarian Gospel* text and extensive commentary on it underlines our beliefs on these matters.

As indicated on our website, we recommend the writings of Paramhansa Yogananda regarding the teachings of Jesus as a correct presentation of their meaning.

In response to a letter in which someone expressed discouragement over having made some mistakes in spiritual life.

Many mistakes–and even falls–can occur in spiritual life, but a person can always get up and keep journeying onward, for his essential divine Self (nature) is unchanged. As long as this is done there is always hope for eventual success. There is only one thing that can prevent this: discouragement. If the sadhaka becomes discouraged at his failures and begins to feel hopeless and gives up his efforts, then no improvement is possible. Because of this, discouragement is the worst thing that can happen to a sadhaka, for it will end all spiritual progress. Be sure that you never give into this most harmful thing, and you need never fear failure. If it comes, arise and keep on moving. Then nothing will be able to stop you in reaching the Goal.

Are you aware of the current scene in N.? Do you think that true spirituality still exists in N. and other holy places in India, or is it being replaced by a market-place spirituality? Can such holy men as Sivananda still be found there? I would appreciate your honest opinion.

The French have a most insightful proverb: "The more things change the more they stay the same," the idea being that changes in externals only point out the fact that human nature stays just what it always was. Only the childish and foolish think that they are different from preceding generations.

India is just what it always was. As in any other country there have been saints, sages, scoundrels, fools and hypocrites. It is all a matter of magnetism: we encounter those that are on our own wavelength. I knew some people that went to India to find a guru and ended up making connections with drug dealers instead.

Throughout my first trip to India I was always in walking distance of at least one saint. But at the very same time other Westerners were searching and searching—even for years—and met not one worthy spiritual teacher. Others met the saints and thought they were bores and fools, so the result was the same.

It is all a matter of karma, of mental vibration, whether or not we meet holy people and whether or not we benefit from the meeting. This I can tell you: the saints do not waste their time on non-yogis or those that do not have the potential to be yogis.

The key to whether you will meet great souls in India is in you alone. If you meditate—really meditate—and are leading a purified life, observing the moral precepts of yama and niyama (and not just for a few weeks), then you will find the saints and the saints will find you. And be careful who you have as a traveling companion. They can spoil everything.

Market-place teachers have always existed in India for market-place seekers. Unfit disciples get unfit gurus. The unclean and impure easily meet unclean and impure gurus who will eagerly help them ruin their mind and life. Water does find its own level.

Right in N. there is one of India's spiritual gems, living in total obscurity and even secrecy. A true jnani, this holy one does not play the guru game, dresses like any rural Indian—no gerua, big beads, or big tilak—does the housework, cooks and cleans, and only lets a few people come at designated times for satsang. Westerners who have pushed in and demanded teaching have been sent right back out the door. Others have been welcomed and conversed with freely and openly. But they had to be prepared for some straightforward and pungent truths! They left uplifted and inspired to work on themselves—not to "take refuge in Sri Guru" or any such nonsense. Please do not ask me the saint's name or location—it would do no good if the saint did not want the meeting. And if the saint wants the meeting it cannot be avoided.

Work on yourself. As Buddha said: You are your only refuge; all else is external and therefore ultimately delusional.

In response to a letter in which someone expressed concern over "drifting from my Christian background" through esoteric interests.

If your Christian background lacked esoteric knowledge and insight into Eastern religion, then you have drifted from ignorance and should thank God for it. Keep drifting!

If we don't remember our past lives, how can we make ourselves better people?

Actually it works the other way round. As we begin bettering ourselves by living according to the principles of dharma, and most especially by the steady practice of meditation, the purification of mind and heart enables us to spontaneously remember our past lives as they relate to the situations of our present life.

There is no value in just knowing about our past lives if it has no practical purpose. Just saying: "I did this" or "I was that" in a previous life means nothing. Those who apply themselves to yoga meditation will find that they will automatically remember a past life, if remembering it will help them understand their present situation in life and help them in finding the best direction for their life in the future. So the attempt to live a higher mode of life and spontaneous past life recall go hand in hand. But first take the advice of Krishna: *Tasmad yogi bhavarjuna*: "Therefore become a yogi, Arjuna" (Bhagavad Gita 6:46).

When we are reincarnated as lower beings of life, how can we get good karma to became a higher being? If you are a tree or snail or something, what can you do to get good karma?

For most subhuman species, simply living according to nature is sufficient. The presence of the atman in each one of them is the force that draws them upward into higher forms. However, selfishness, greed, hatred, and other passions can be seen in them, and this will determine the kind of animal bodies they will be taking on. For example, there are beneficial snakes and poisonous snakes. In many species we find this to be true—some are harmful and some are not. Both insects and animals suffer from disease and from "natural predators." Cunning is to be found in all animals, but the most intelligent are the vegetarians, for they are preparing to take on human form. Unfortunately humans fall back into the way of carnivorous animals that can lead to animal births, though rarely. Instead they are born among other "humanimals" that hate, fight, and kill one another and end up being far worse than any animal. Though in human form, they have become demons and take on demonic form after death and retain the demonic nature when they are reborn.

Human beings create human karma, so once we come to the level of human beings we rarely if ever return to animal form. Instead our karma, even if unfortunate, impels us into further human births. We have instances of humans taking animal form, such as Jada Bharata (see Glossary), but when that is done the person has full awareness as a human even in that body. In this way the intended lesson is learned. Their misery ensures that they will not make that mistake in future births.

In Jada Bharata's case the lesson was the unwisdom of over-attachment. Sadly, some people take animal form because they have made many animals suffer greatly in their previous life. Those who own or work in slaughterhouses run the risk of animal incarnation, as do those who experiment on animals. And what then about those who eat the flesh of animals? By the end of their lives they have incurred the karma of the slaughter of thousands–tens of thousands–of sentient beings.

I want to experience sweet fellowship with God. Also, how do I get to know God without giving my mind away while still being surrendered?

Intimate communion with God is not just a possibility–it is your actual nature. Even at this moment you are absolutely one with God, but the focus of your consciousness has slipped away from the divine center into a state of disunity in which the dream has hidden the divine dreamer. Nevertheless, nothing has really changed any more than dreaming you are someone other than your waking self makes you that someone. When you wake it is all over. In the same way, when you awake from this prolonged dream we call samsara and maya, you will not be attaining something or becoming something, you will be remembering the reality of yourself and the Reality that is God.

How to go about awakening is the crucial question. Even though awakening is a purely spiritual process, we cannot forget the body and mind that presently are blinding us to the Divine Vision. So here are some recommended steps:

1. For the body: Become a vegetarian if you are not already so, eliminating all meat, fish, and eggs totally from your diet. Further, abstain absolutely from alcohol, nicotine, and mind-altering drugs. Best of all: Go vegan.

2. For the mind: Obtain and read:

The Song of God: Bhagavad Gita, translated by Swami Prabhavananda of the Vedanta Society of Southern California.

The Upanishads, Breath of the Eternal, by Swami Prabhavananda.

Autobiography of a Yogi, by Paramhansa Yogananda—the first edition facsimile by Crystal Clarity Publishers (with the exception of this and editions also published by Philosophical Library, the original publishers, later printings are so altered and falsified they are misleading.)

Meditation and Spiritual Life, by Swami Yatiswarananda of the Ramakrishna Mission of India (in America: the Vedanta Society).

The Philosophy of Gorakhnath, Akshaya Kumar Banerjea, Motilal Banarsidass.

And the other books recommended in *A Yogi's Recommended Reading List* on our website.

3. For both body and mind: Adhere strictly to the principles of yama-niyama as outlined in the article *The Foundations of Yoga*.

4. For the spirit: Begin meditating seriously and regularly.

Now about your second sentence. First of all, the idea of "surrender" in spiritual life is a Western concept and a colossal aberration. God is not your enemy, so why would you surrender to him? Surrender is a tool of cult domination intended to bully people into giving up their intelligence and personal welfare. Guru cults traffic in this propaganda of surrender, but they are spiritual criminals, not true dharmic institutions. In Sanskrit the word they mistranslate is *sharanam*, which means refuge, protection, and shelter. Taking refuge in God is hardly surrender: it is safety and assurance, the end of doubt and fear. It is loving trust placed in the only worthy Protector.

As far as giving your mind away is concerned, it is the same situation. This is why the Bhagavad Gita should be studied. Krishna keeps speaking of the necessity for Buddhi Yoga, the cultivation of the intelligence and discrimination. There is no giving up of the mind in the path to

Self-realization. It is just the opposite, for the spiritual cultivation of yoga enables us to master our mind and use it as a tool for furthering our evolution. In the final chapter of the Gita, not far from the end, Krishna says to Arjuna: "Now I have taught you that wisdom which is the secret of secrets. Ponder it carefully. *Then act as you think best*" (Bhagavad Gita 18:63). There is no hint of "surrender" here!

What is needed is reclamation of what we have never really lost. That is one of those glorious contradictions in which Eastern wisdom abounds, but whose realities can be experienced by the yogi.

"Therefore become a yogi" (Bhagavad Gita 6:46).

According to the Aquarian Gospel, Jesus was born at the beginning of the Piscean Age. The question is, in which Age would Jesus come during his Second Coming? Would it be The Aquarian Age? and would The Aquarian Age begin in December 2012? I am just a seeker of Truth and hope and pray to the Almighty One to guide us all to complete truth and wisdom.

The Piscean Age began 2,000 years ago, and the Aquarian Age in the year 2000. This is calculated according to the vernal equinox and the astrological point on which it falls.

As to the next birth of Jesus we will just have to wait and see and make sure we are not deceived. I have met three people claiming to be Jesus and one claiming to be the Virgin Mary! They were the embodiments of foolishness and ignorance. (One of the Jesuses was in an adulterous relationship with the self-proclaimed Virgin Mary.)

God being present here and now to each one of us, we need not worry much over the future.

I have read a lot of information on Christian websites about meditation and its ability to attract "demons" to you. How would you counter the Christian point of view?

First, this is not a Christian viewpoint, it is the propaganda of ignorant bigots—including some sects in India, by the way. "The moment you sit for meditation you are opening yourself to evil entities," said one adherent of an Indian sect to me in my beginning days of meditation. East and West have people who will try to tell meditators that they are in danger of either going insane or coming under the power of (or possessed by) evil spirits. It is simply not true. I do not bother to counter it—I meditate and prove it false.

However I will give you some examples: Many times the intoning of Om or other mantras that are used in meditation have exorcised evil spirits from people. Yogananda recommended intoning Om in the right ear of a person for this purpose, and Swami (Papa) Ramdas in his autobiography *In the Vision of God* tells of a woman being freed from an evil spirit simply by hearing singing of the Ram Mantra.

The most haunted house I ever encountered was the home of a young man who was attending one of my meditation classes. The place was filled with spirits, and the entire building emanated negative energies. I said nothing to him about it, but waited. Two weeks later I went back and the house was free of all negative entities and energies—just because he was meditating thirty minutes twice a day. I then told him my impressions and he replied that for nearly his entire lifetime he and his sister had been plagued by spirits in that house. But now all was peaceful and positive.

I have been practicing meditation, specifically to get through some severe anxiety and panic I suffered after an accident (and to get closer to God). I believe I am plagued by some type of oppression and have been for a long time. I am experiencing a great amount of fear now when I meditate–despite the fact that it helps me immensely.

A situation such as yours is impossible to comment on, as it can be very complex. I would advise you to consult qualified medical practitioners as they have the means to determine if your problem is physically-based. I say this especially because you say your trouble began after an accident. A friend who was a healer told me that feelings of fear and oppression can arise from problems with the adrenal glands. If for some reason they leak small amounts of adrenalin, the person can experience unexplained anxiety, panic, or fear. He had helped many people who thought they had a psychological problem simply by correcting the condition of the adrenals.

Diet, which determines the chemistry of the blood and cells, can also play a part in these matters, especially through food additives. Meat is often saturated with chemicals and with the toxins (including adrenalin) released by the fear and suffering of the animal when being killed.

The relaxation produced by meditation can be of help, but it is only wise to seek a medical solution in case the problem is based on a physical condition.

Is there a difference between "unnecessary experience" and karma?

There is no such thing as unnecessary experience, nor is there anything that is not karma. That is why in Yoga Sutras 2:18, Patanjali says that the entire range of relative existence "has for its purpose (providing the purusha with) experience and liberation." (The words in parentheses are added by the translator I. K. Taimni in his commentary *The Science of Yoga*.)

To someone who wrote about conflicts between his Eastern Orthodox Christian tradition and the principles of Sanatana Dharma–which he was increasingly accepting as true:

The prime question each human being should be asking is not "What is the true religion?" but "How can I find God?" When you learn how to find God and start doing so–that will be the true religion.

Sanatana Dharma cultivates respect for all religions, but often those religions cover up the teachings of their founders, and even substitute themselves for the founder. Many are more interested in a church as "the Body of Christ" than in Jesus himself. "Outside the Church there is no salvation" should be seen as nonsense by any Christian. There is no salvation outside Christ–that is the truth. But unfortunately they have very little understanding of the nature of Christ, who should not be confused with Jesus.

This I will say: If the Holy Spirit is guaranteed to lead Christians "into all truth," why do they know so little truth? I think it is because they do not really possess the Holy Spirit. Although all Orthodox Christians are chrismated, Saint Seraphim of Sarov spoke of their need for "the acquisition of the Holy Spirit." He apparently saw things quite differently from the official Church. The Orthodox Church thunders that anyone who prays with heretics is to be excommunicated and suspended from clerical functions, but Saint John of Kronstadt prayed with Moslems who came to him asking assistance. Saint John Maximovitch cured a dying Jewish woman by calling out to her: "Christ is risen!" And he never tried to convert her. Christ and contemporary Christianity are just not the same

I believe that Jesus lived in India for most of his life before returning to Israel, and that after his resurrection he returned there. More to the point, I believe that he was a Sanatana Dharmi–not a Jew or a Christian.

We must ask of all religions: Do they reveal or do they veil?

I hope it is clear that our website presents Sanatana Dharma and not popular Hinduism.

The final word is this: It is not what you *believe* but what you *know* that matters. And all knowledge comes from God, Who is seated in each heart. Seek there for the truth.

To someone who wrote asking if eating fish would be a "blemish" on the character or personality of a sannyasi, or whether it was not necessary to be a vegetarian:

Yes, it is a terrible blemish of character that an Indian sadhu–or anyone claiming to be a yogi or sanatana dharmi–would ever eat meat, fish, or eggs. To eat meat is to break with thousands of years of sacred tradition–and to what purpose? No supposed sadhu or even "avatar" however famous and revered can make their own rules. Dharma is dharma, and exceptions cannot occur. *Satyam eva jayate.* Truth alone conquers (prevails).

What is the point in worshiping the Divine forms as God? Do they have any existence apart from the imagination? Since the reality and goal is pure consciousness, does it distract our attention from the truth? Is the saguna worship meant for developing concentration?

In the Gita we find these two very important verses: "Others worship me, knowing Brahman in all things: some see me as one with themselves, or separate: some bow to the countless gods that are only my million faces" (Bhagavad Gita 9:15). "Whatever wish men bring me in worship, that wish I grant them. Whatever path men travel is my path: no matter where they walk it leads to me" (Bhagavad Gita 4:11).

From these verses we see that God is merciful and takes into account our weakness and lack of understanding. However, it is certainly more correct to worship God in a formless manner. Here is something I recently wrote on the subject:

"This is very important: When we want to swim in the ocean, we do not dive into a particular wave, but into the ocean itself–though we may pass through a wave. Also, the wave, being only a manifestation on the surface of the ocean must be left behind if we are to sound the depths of the ocean. If we stay with the wave, we will remain as separated as the wave is from the ocean. If we 'ride' the wave like a surfer we will find ourselves being thrown onto the shore and out of the ocean. It is the same with meditation on names and forms–whether of 'gods' or liberated 'masters'–rather than diving down where name and form cannot go. We must meditate on the Self–not on external deities or symbolic forms of psychic states. As Sri Ma Sarada Devi said: 'After attaining wisdom one sees that gods and deities are all maya' (*Precepts For Perfection* 672)." The major Upanishads, Gita, and Yoga Sutras know nothing of meditating on 'gods' or 'ishta devatas'–only on the Self.

The usual excuse for saguna worship is that it enables the devotee to concentrate his mind and prepare him for meditation. But in fifty years I have never found this to be true for anyone. You must start out with what you want to end up with. Right meditation alone concentrates the mind in a meaningful manner. That is why Sri Gajanana Maharaj of Nasik said: "Some people say that meditating upon Nirakara [the Formless Reality] is difficult. But in my opinion it is very easy and in addition it is natural. A man easily gets into the state of samadhi by meditating upon Nirakara. The path of doing so is, however, concealed and secret. Once you get it you can be in that state although outwardly you may be talking, laughing, playing, or sleeping. This power is concealed like the river Saraswati. As some people have not understood this secret path, therefore, they say that it is difficult, and that it would require the passing of various lives to obtain success in it."

How are kundalini and pure consciousness related? Does a seeker have to bother about kundalini?

All Shakti is really Shiva. That is, there is nothing but Pure Consciousness, really, but in projecting the creation there is the appearance of movement or vibration. Kundalini is Primal Power and therefore Primal Consciousness in evolutionary activity. As a consequence, when your atmic consciousness is awakened, so is your kundalini–which is the same thing. So you need not give it a thought. Everything will happen as it should from your meditation. I recommend you read *Philosophy of Gorakhnath* by Akshaya Kumar Banerjea, for an excellent explanation of this.

Is the return of Christ–as spoken of in the Gospels of the Bible–a bodily return or is it the spiritual return of the Christ in man? We are entering a new age–the age of Aquarius, or the revealing age. I feel that the book of Revelation is a picture of the true reality of the struggle within man himself and what every man must face and overcome.

The Greek word translated "coming" in the New Testament is *parousia*, which literally means "presence," but it means both to be near ("at hand") and a returning. As is usual in spiritual writings, words that have more than one meaning give a latitude in interpretation. Yogananda said that all scriptures should be considered as having three levels: physical, mental, and spiritual, both literal and symbolic, both external and internal.

Each person should be seeking the advent of Christ in the sense of Divine Consciousness. Yet there is a tradition in Jewish mysticism that says the Messiah will come twice: first as Son of Joseph and be rejected, and later as Son of David and be accepted. Jesus was born at the beginning of the Piscean Age and we may assume that he will be reborn at the beginning of the Aquarian Age–and perhaps already has been.

Obviously Jesus can manage things for himself so we need not do anything about this, but should be intent on the birth, resurrection and ascension in us of the Christ Life (Consciousness). As he said: "My time is not yet come: but your time is alway ready" (John 7:6). So it is wisdom to stay focused on our own personal Advent. Nevertheless there is nothing wrong in praying to be aware of his second physical appearance and to meet with him. Nor is it amiss to pray for the hastening of his birth and revelation to the world.

Yogananda wrote a thousand-page commentary on Revelation as a yoga scripture rather than an earthly prophecy, but it has not been printed after nearly sixty years. So a person will have to meditate deeply and use his intuition in figuring it out. Of course, the four Gospels are the same: a symbolic presentation of the path to Christhood. The early church not only interpreted them as symbols, it denied that some parts of them were literal history. Chances are they are both literal and symbolic, with maybe a bit of alteration. (For example according to Anna Catharine Emmerich the stigmatist, Jesus was born in an Essene family that never worshipped at Jerusalem because of the animal sacrifice, but on Mount Carmel. So the stories of Jesus being presented in the Jerusalem temple after being born and questioning the elders at the age of twelve are not accurate, but took place on Mount Carmel.) Anyway, it all comes back to the need for us to learn truth for ourselves.

You have written: "All spiritual life is self-initiated from within; we are both guru and disciple as Krishna and Arjuna symbolize in the Bhagavad Gita." Do you believe Krishna to be a real person who came to earth, and spoke the Bhagavad Gita, or do you hold that the Gita is purely symbolical? I feel confused on the idea of what the avatars of Vishnu/Krishna really stand for.

Certainly Yadava Krishna was a historical person as was Arjuna, and they were involved in the Mahabharata war–also a historical reality. But it is stretching it to believe that Krishna and Arjuna spoke to each other in poetic meter and that the seven hundred verses of the Gita were a continuous conversation just before the battle.

We can be sure that Krishna spoke to Arjuna regarding the war and his obligations in relation to it, but it seems a bit silly to think that at that time he discoursed at length on such subjects as diet being a reflection of the predominant guna of a person, the constituents of Maya/Prakriti, and other technicalities of the Sankhya philosophy.

Someone once remarked to Paramhansa Nityananda of Ganeshpuri: "In the Gita Krishna said…," and Nityananda interrupted him, saying: "No. *Vyasa* said that Krishna said…." Although the Mahabharata war actually took place, Vyasa used it as a symbol of the battle that faces all serious sadhakas, and Krishna and Arjuna are symbols of the internal dialogue that takes place between the higher and lower selves of the individual.

The Bhagavad Gita is the supreme scripture; none are equal to it. Even the Upanishads that are extensively cited in the Gita are not its equal, because they are only philosophical and the Gita is the perfect synthesis of philosophy, practical dharmic life, and yoga.

The Gita should be the daily study of the aspirant to liberation, because it describes the attitude, the entire psychology, of the person who is going to attain liberation. Many of the deluded and fraudulent "yogis," "masters," and "avatars" that abound in India and throughout the yoga world would not succeed if people looked at them with the perspective of the Gita on what is the real nature of enlightenment.

The razor's edge path to the Supreme is extremely difficult to traverse because of the many ways in which our clouded and deluded mind can lead us astray or spoil our needed focus. The Gita alone keeps correcting us and holding us on the right path–provided that we do not approach it with preconceived, sectarian ideas.

As I have pointed out, the teachings in the Gita are those of the Sankhya philosophy, as were the teachings of Paramhansa Yogananda. According to Sankhya (and therefore Yogananda), an avatar is a totally liberated jiva who has attained such perfect union with Brahman that all differences (but not distinctions) have been erased between his consciousness and that of Brahman. When such a one is born–not by karmic compulsion but through his liberated will–practically speaking that jiva is an avatar, a manifestation of Divine Consciousness which acts and speaks through him.

Since the real question is "Who am I?" it is a waste of time to go round and round as to who Krishna or anyone else might be.

In Gaudiya and other Vaishnava traditions, the view seems to be that the devoted bhakta eventually goes to Vaikuntha to be eternally with the Lord, whereas they believe the lesser, advaita way of doing things will leave the advaitin to merge with "the void/Brahman" instead of enjoying Vaikuntha. On the other hand, Advaita Vedanta seems to advocate that all will essentially merge with Brahman, regardless of the path. Could you help explain your views on all this? I am feeling somewhat lost in the big city that Hinduism can be.

You are right, Hinduism is "the big city," but that is because it is all-embracing. Every possible truth and view of that truth was long ago set forth by the sages of India. However, in contemporary India we can find a lot of errant nonsense, for some parts of the big city have become slums and others are really outside the city limits even if they appear to be inside.

The truth as set forth in the Upanishads and the Bhagavad Gita is the same: the goal of the individual is to unite with Brahman the Absolute. Then, like Brahman they can do/be whatever they like. Just as Brahman is both with and without qualities and both with and without form, so they can be. To say that one is superior or more ultimate than the other is to miss the point: Brahman is beyond such distinctions, for Brahman is absolutely ONE. In fact, Brahman transcends anything that can be said about It. The wise seek the Goal and leave the talk to others. As they say in the American South: "The empty wagon rattles the most."

The Upanishads and Gita affirm the eternal, divine nature of the atman-self. It, too, is part of Brahman. This perspective is essential to right understanding of any philosophical point.

You mention both the personal and impersonal aspects of God in an article. You say that since Brahman can manifest as the transient universe, then obviously he can manifest as a deity (according to the particular devotee) as well. I certainly agree with you. My only thing is, the existence of the personal God in that way seems dependent upon an individual to perceive and need such a thing.

Brahman and the jiva are really one and inseparable and in a sense interdependent. Consequently as the jiva moves toward the Goal, whatever it needs will come to it or arise in its consciousness.

Are paths like bhakti and the impersonal advaitic path of yoga and meditation equal? Do they all lead to the same thing?

Certainly, because there is only the One to realize. The Bhagavad Gita affirms this unequivocally. Yoga is advaitic, but not Advaita. Yoga, like the Yoga Sutras, is based on Sankhya philosophy.

Are a personal God and the impersonal Brahman on the same level, or is one more ultimate than the other?

There is only The One. Our distinctions rise from our limited, unenlightened consciousness. As the verse says:

> This is the Complete; That is the Complete.
> The Complete has come out of the Complete.

If we take the Complete away from the Complete,
Only the Complete remains.

This can be applied to many things, including Saguna and Nirguna Brahman.

I experience "pressures" in my body–mostly in the third eye area. It gets quite intense sometimes, for example, when I read your web site–expanding the pressure through my forehead, etc. I have not found anyone to help me understand this and wondered if this may be something written about that I have not discovered yet. It seems to happen randomly, sometimes throughout the day. But I seem to have an effect on it when I open to spiritual matters. I cannot say that it is painful, especially if I "breathe" it or kind of "ride it." I sometimes experience vibration or radiation in my throat chakra–sometimes along with this. Would you address this? I am grateful for any reply.

I understand your situation. In my beginning years as a yogi I sometimes had such intense energy and pressure sensations in the third eye that I more than once lay down on my bed and waited to die, I was so sure that my brain would rupture. But I did not die, and the sensations stopped after a while.

The mind and the body are not just interrelated, they are fundamentally the same thing: cosmic energy in conditioned form. That is why when we see appealing food the digestive system immediately reacts and gets ready for digesting food.

Our mental (manas) and intellectual (buddhi) levels can be profoundly and dramatically affected by our thoughts according to the nature or primary vibration of those thoughts. Therefore when a person begins thinking more and more of spiritual matters, and especially meditation, reactions may be experienced on the physical level. Many people are perplexed or even worried about this, and sad to say most religious and even yoga teachers have no understanding of it.

Such sensations are evidence of a change in the vibratory structure of our body and mind. They are normal and natural–for the yogi. Sometimes the energy sensation can be very intense, but no harm results, and in time the process transmutes into a subtler form until it becomes purely intellectual, resulting in insights and intuition.

Strong creatures eat weaker ones day and night. How can one say God is great? The world is seen to be very painful. If God is the creator, why did He create like this?

What God permits is not the same as what God wills. God manifested the creation many creation-cycles ago as a perfect entity, but humans have spoiled it by their misdeeds and murderous ways and corrupted the lesser forms of life as well. The individual human life and the cosmic life are interrelated. Just as a human being carries his karma along with him, and that karma determines what his future lives will be, so it is with the world. Humans have progressively caused the creation to be increasingly flawed and painful. Until they change themselves and thereby change the state of the world, things will keep on as they are or get worse. The choice is ours, not God's. That is what free will is all about.

If I kill another person for money and feel good about it and believe I am right, does that mean I will have no bad karma? If

I cheat another person for money and believe it is justified and
that I am right, does that mean I will have no bad karma?

No, it just means that you are a murderer and cheat that has no
conscience. It also means that you are going to be cheated and killed in
the future by someone who does not think he has done wrong. And it
will not stop until you become a changed person.

Buddha said that karma is determined by the mind. That is, if we
do something accidentally we are not guilty; but if we intend to do a
wrong, then we are guilty, whether we succeed or fail in carrying out
our evil intention.

The day our Original Christianity and Original Yoga website was
launched we received an irate communication from one of those
Western "Hindus" that believe they are more truly Hindu if they
hate other religions–especially Christianity–and deny that Jesus
ever existed. Here is our answer:

If Jesus did not exist, how is it that great spiritual masters of India
have seen him in visions, researched and proved not only his existence
but his having lived in India, and expounded his teachings as being the
same as (not just consistent with) Sanatana Dharma?

Sri Ramakrishna, his great disciple Swami Brahmananda, Swami
Rama Tirtha, Swami (Papa) Ramdas, and Paramhansa Yogananda all
saw Jesus in visions–some more than once, and some actually spoke
with him. Sri Ramakrishna kept a picture of Jesus in his room at the
Dakshineswar Kali Temple. He also told several of his disciples that he
had seen in visions that they had been disciples of Jesus. Both Swami
Rama Tirtha and Swami Ramdas had visions of Jesus while staying at
Vashishtha Guha north of Rishikesh in the cave where Jesus had lived

for a while (though they did not know that fact at the time of their visions, but learned it later).

Swami Abhedananda and Swami Trigunatitananda, disciples of Sri Ramakrishna, at separate times journeyed to Ladakh and verified the existence of ancient Buddhist texts recording the life of Jesus. Swami Trigunatitananda was also shown two paintings of Jesus by the Buddhist monks, and had a copy of one made from his memory when he was living in America as a Vedanta missionary. Swami Abhedananda, also for a while a Vedanta Missionary to America, printed a translation of the part of the Buddhist text on Jesus and defied the British government's ban on Nicholas Notovitch's *Unknown Life of Jesus Christ* which contained the complete text. He not only brought copies of the book from America, he had an edition printed in India. He also wrote the pamphlet: *Why a Hindu Accepts Christ and Rejects Churchianity*. A friend of mine gave me a copy of a letter Sri Ramakrishna's disciple Swami Saradananda wrote to her aunt, Edith Grey, who had gone to India and become a disciple of Sri Ma Sarada Devi, the consort of Sri Ramakrishna. Miss Grey had written to the Swami about how she felt equal devotion to Sri Ramakrishna and Jesus. The Swami wrote back: "Our Master assured us that they were just the same." Later in the twentieth century the Shankaracharya of Puri, Jagadguru Bharati Krishna Tirtha, found what he called "proof positive" of Jesus actually having lived in the Govardhan Math, the present math of the Order of Shankara in Puri. He even wrote a book on the subject, which he found had been thrown away by an illiterate servant when he returned from his world tour, and which he did not live long enough to rewrite. Before that, Swami Sri Yukteswar Giri, the guru of Yogananda, wrote a study in which he proved that Jesus had lived in India and that his teachings were identical with the Sanatana Dharma which he adopted and preached in the West. That was borrowed by a Christian missionary who refused, in Sri Yukteswar's lifetime and even after his death, to return it.

Paramhansa Yogananda wrote and lectured extensively on the teachings of Jesus. In fact, at his first speech given in this country he announced that he would be holding classes in Boston which would consist of three half-hour periods each: one on the teachings of the Bhagavad Gita, one on the teachings of the Gospels, and one demonstrating that their teachings were the same. His two-volume commentary on the Gospels, *The Second Coming of Christ*, is perhaps the only complete and reliable presentation of Jesus' real teachings—which are mostly unknown to Churchianity. Swami Prabhavananda of the Hollywood Vedanta Society wrote *The Sermon on the Mount According to Vedanta* and often referred to Jesus in his lectures. Swami Akhilananda of the Boston Vedanta Society wrote a valuable study called *Hindu View of Christ* and also cited Jesus as a spiritual authority. (Both Vedanta Societies celebrated Christmas, too, as does Belur Math, the world headquarters of Ramakrishna Mission.)

As a final example which I witnessed myself, my beloved Swami Sivananda, founder of the Divine Life Society in Rishikesh and perfect example of Sanatana Dharma, not only wrote and published a life of Jesus for popular circulation and celebrated Christmas each year, in the daily evening satsang kirtan he led us all in singing: "O my Jesus, O my Jesus, Lord Jesus: Come, come to me! O my Mary, Mother Mary, Virgin Mary: Come, come to me!" And often at the end, along with other exclamations in praise of Dharma, would call out: "Jesus Bhagavan: ki jai!"

All these great yogis of India did not just believe Jesus existed, they honored him as a liberated son of God and considered him a Sanatana Dharmi just like themselves.

Our irate correspondent concluded with the statement: "Hinduism/Yoga is not Christianity."

We agree. But like so many Westerners he has it all backwards. Sanatana Dharma and Yoga are not Christianity, *but authentic Christianity is indeed Sanatana Dharma and Yoga* and not Churchianity at all.

In response to our recent blog posting about the reality of Jesus in the experience of India's great yogis, we received a most heartening letter from India. I want to share parts of it with you and my reflections on it for I feel it presents the most authentic perspective on these matters.

> "I agree with the contents of the blog that the truth of Christ's coming should not be doubted. In fact, if someone whom I can accept as a good Christian were merely to tell me Christ is for real, I would believe him. I would tell him that my mother, a practising Hindu, taught me that long ago, and had read out his parables to me in my childhood!! Christ is as real to me as my mother."

More than one person has told me that they never met anyone who really understood Jesus until they went to India. My doctor told me that the only meaningful discourse he ever heard about Jesus was given by a sadhu in South India one Christmas. One of my most valued acquaintances made in India was a French lady who told me: "You will be surprised to learn why I am in India. My local Catholic priest sent me. He told me: 'You will never understand the Gospel of Saint John if you do not go to India and study the religion there.'" She did so, became a disciple of Swami (Papa) Ramdas, and later permanently moved to India and became a resident of Sivanandashram in Rishikesh. It is my conviction that intelligent belief in and understanding of Jesus is impossible without the perspective of Sanatana Dharma. (In fact, I don't think any valid religion can be comprehended without that perspective.) Our friend continues:

> "I already believe. But I am not alone. It is a natural way for most of my fellow-Hindus. Sri Ramakrishna and Swami Sivananda were representative Hindus who gave all faiths their due. Though they were Hindu spiritual giants, it is not because of them that the ordinary Indian people are magnanimous in religious belief. The Sanatana Dharma (even in the form of Hinduism) is beginningless and endless. It is a way of life, a way of thinking for the

Hindus, of which the above-mentioned sages were spokespersons. Everyone has freedom of faith and worship in India, that is its ageless tradition of openness and religious egalitarianism.

"On the reality of Christ's advent, therefore, and his ascension, there can be no doubt."

This is the unique glory of India—only there have people's minds and hearts been fully opened to Reality. I often comment to people that it is all very well for people of various religious backgrounds to say that all religions are true and lead to the same goal, but only Indian religion teaches that as a real principle. Absolutely those great souls mentioned are representative of Sanatana Dharma, not unusual or unique. I know, because I received my faith in Jesus from India. In the university I had come to completely disbelieve in Christianity and therefore in Jesus. But when I read the Bhagavad Gita and Paramhansa Yogananda's *Autobiography of a Yogi* I gained real faith in Jesus, but not in the religion that betrays him in his name. The more I understood Dharma, the more I understood Jesus, and the less regard I had for Churchianity.

Our friend then asks:

"What would interest me is to know whether you and the followers/monks of ocoy.org would also keep pictures of Sri Ram/ Siva in their rooms like Sri Ramakrishna or sing the name of the Hindu god(s) like Sri Sivananda in their "Light of the Spirit" monastery, in line with the Hindu sages you have cited. And it is my fervent hope that they would."

I really had to smile when I read this, because I knew exactly what our friend was wanting to know. Quite some time back when I was in Delhi an Indian friend asked me to go with him to visit some "open-minded" and "ecumenical" Christian monks who were "friendly" to Hindu Dharma. I had my doubts, but I went—and got my doubts confirmed.

The abbot was very gracious and showed us around, commenting in the chapel that quite a few Hindus sometimes came to their church services and appreciated them. Then we went to the monastery's common room where all the monks were in conversations with one another, and the abbot and the senior officers of the monastery began talking with me. Again, the abbot remarked about how "open" Hindus were to their Christian worship. So I replied: "But tell me, Father, what would you do if one of those Hindus said to you: 'Father, I have worshipped your Christ; will you now come and worship my Krishna?' What would you do? Would you go worship Krishna?" His response? NONE. Literally he acted like I had never spoken those words. So I asked the same thing. No reply. A third time I asked, and he just turned to one of the monks and began a conversation as if I were not even there and had not spoken a word. My Indian friend was shocked at this revelation of the hypocrisy of the "good fathers."

There is indeed in our office a picture of Shiva (Umapati Shankar) and Sri Rama (Ayodhya Pati Ram). At first in writing this I listed every holy image in our office, but the list was much too long to impose on you, so I encapsulate it in this way: In our office there are twelve Christian images, nine Buddhist images, and eighteen Hindu images. Yet they are all images of the One Reality and we reverence them all. Such sacred depictions can be found throughout our monastery, and outside as well, among them many photographs of saints–Hindu, Buddhist, and Christian. Yet, as I say, to us it is all ONE.

I would like to mention here that we have daily satsang in the late afternoon at which we always have three readings from spiritual texts. Right now we are going through: *Man's Eternal Quest*, a book of talks by Paramhansa Yogananda, *The Christian Gnosis*, by Charles W. Leadbeater the renowned Theosophist and founder of the Liberal Catholic Church, and *Philosophy of Gorakhnath*, by Akshay Kumar Banerjea. I want you to understand from their nature that our approach is not a mere tinge of the East.

It has been our custom for years to attend and participate in (not just observe) Buddhist and Hindu temple worship. Of course we will sing the Names of God in kirtan. There is only one God, and he is all his "many faces." Any religion that makes people sectarian is a false and destructive religion.

There is more:

> "And further that the Light of the Spirit Church has unequivocally and publicly repudiated the principle and practice of proselytisation. In fact, an assertion/clarification prominently in the web-site to the above effect would go a long way to confirm the 'Sanatana Dharma' aspect of the monastery and the ethical integrity of the 'Original Christianity' that is professed, and set the Light of the Spirit Church apart from the 'Churchianity', besides drawing more and more readers to your excellent blogs."

This is most important. Each person's religion is a matter of his swadharma as expounded in the Gita. And swadharma is determined by samskara and karma. No one should ever try to persuade someone to adopt any religion. Each person must decide this for himself. Nor should anyone try to dissuade a person from following a path he feels drawn to. After all, see how many paths Sri Ramakrishna followed and discovered that each one led to Brahman.

There is really only one ultimate religion: Brahmajnana or atmajnana (knowledge of God or knowledge of the Self, however a person prefers to view it). Without jnana, religion becomes superstition and distraction. Yet if that is what a person likes he should be free to follow it. After all, he has eternity to learn for himself the way to God. This is part of the divine plan.

Do you want to know if we believe that Jesus is the only way or the best way? NEVER. God is the only and the best way. How we reach God is part of our personal evolution. Great world-teachers like Krishna,

Buddha and Jesus only show the way to God. As Buddha said, they are a finger pointing to the moon. It is good to learn and apply the wisdom of great Masters, but God must be the focus of our search, for Patanjali says: "He is Guru even of the ancients."

Why then are we followers of Jesus? (The word "Christian" has been so ruined, just as the Nazis spoiled people's impression of the Swastika, that I don't much like using it.) It is not my place to answer for others, so I will say this:

1. I follow Jesus because I believe he was a teacher of Sanatana Dharma alone and that his teachings cannot be understood apart from that Dharma.

2. What is distinct about Jesus is the fact that he presented spiritual life in terms that Occidentals could relate to and that were in accord with their psychology. He was bringing the eternal wisdom of India to the West that simply had no background to help them in relating to it. Therefore he translated those truths into forms they could comprehend. The Trinity is a prime example. Instead of Brahman, Ishwara and Shakti he used the terms Father, Son and Holy Spirit—not as perfect as the Sanskrit, but still conveying the concepts.

3. Knowing that the traditional Samskaras of Indian religion were very important as a foundation and fostering of spiritual consciousness, he created the Sacraments to accomplish the necessary openings and empowerments in forms the West could relate to and benefit from, even if their philosophical understanding was not perfect. This is the living heritage of Jesus still remaining in the world, however poorly it has been understood through the centuries. For those outside the spiritual environment of India these rites have an inestimable value in imparting spiritual stability and perseverance. I have written about this at length in *The Yoga of the Sacraments*. Again, no one thing is absolutely necessary in spiritual life except the aspiration to liberation (moksha). As Sri Ma Anandamayi often said: "The desire for God is the way to God," and: "There are many ways to the One Way." And in conclusion:

"I may kindly be pardoned if I have written in ignorance but I felt like telling you what I have and so I out-ed with it!"

And I hope you will forgive my long response! But I wanted to leave no doubts as to our position on these things. Christian bigots and Hindu bigots will both hate what I have written, but hate is their favorite pastime, and that is their choice. We, dear friend, can join hands and hearts and walk together along the path from the unreal to the Real, from darkness to the Light, and from death to Immortality.

Please explain the twenty-four elders standing around the throne of God.

It is most important to realize that the book of Revelation is purely spiritual symbolism and not prophecy at all. It is a book of mystical teaching, relating especially to the esoteric experiences of the evolving consciousness. Paramhansa Yogananda stated that it is a book of yogic wisdom, and he wrote a (yet unpublished) commentary of one thousand manuscript pages to expound that fact.

One of the symbolic pictures given in Revelation is that of a throne in heaven around which twenty-four venerable persons known as presbyters are seated. The Greek word *presbyter* literally means "elder," but in Christianity it referred exclusively to a priest. The elders are mentioned in chapters four, five, eleven and nineteen of Revelation.

Before I begin to tell what I consider their meaning to be, I want to point out that spiritual symbolism can usually be interpreted in many ways that are accurate and were intended to be applied. So what I am going to say is not the only way to understand this subject.

"Heaven" is the sahasrara chakra, the thousand-petalled lotus of the astral and causal brain. This is the highest center of consciousness in the human being and is the point where Cosmic Consciousness is first experienced. The sahasrara is a reflection of creation, a miniature universe containing many levels of consciousness (existence). Consciousness Itself–Spirit–is the core of existence and is "he that sits upon the throne." The twenty-four presbyters are the twenty-four cosmic principles of creation that are expounded in the original philosophy of India: the Sankhya philosophy on which yoga is based. They are also the twenty-four basic forms which consciousness can take in relative existence, and no doubt correspond to twenty-four intelligences that are the creators, supervisors and maintainers of all that is. They are given several names, none of which is sufficient to indicate their nature. This is because they are as ineffable as God whom they "sit around." In our present level of evolution it is impossible for us to comprehend anything about them any more than we can comprehend God. But the ancient yogis of India, particularly Guru Gorakhnath, insisted that eventually every yogi will attain perfect comprehension of them as well as all else in creation. (See *Philosophy of Gorakhnath* by Akshaya Kumar Bannerjea.)

The twenty-four elders exist in each one of us as twenty-four centers of consciousness-power, or chakras, in the sahasrara chakra. In their midst is our spirit-self, the atman, the divinity in each one of us, the jiva (individual spirit) that is essentially Shiva (infinite, cosmic Spirit).

Therefore meditation and japa done with the awareness centered in the sahasrara, is the way to enlightenment. That will bring about our own personal Revelation, the realization of the Self. (See *Soham Yoga* for more on this.)

Revelation 4:6 speaks of "a Lamb...having seven horns and seven eyes, which are the seven Spirits of God sent forth into all the earth." What are the "eyes" and what are "the seven Spirits of God"?

In Ezekiel and Revelation various supernatural beings are described as being "full of eyes" to indicate that they are fully conscious, "eyes" symbolizing their awakened faculties of perception. In some esoteric writings "eyes" also symbolize the points of spiritual power and consciousness that the yogis call "chakras." Although yogis mainly focus on seven chakras, we really have hundreds of chakras throughout our bodies, which is why the Bible speaks of "eyes" within and without, before and behind. But all of them are dependent on the seven major chakras.

Regarding the Seven Spirits of God, there is this from *Robe of Light*:

"These are the seven great creators who project and direct the universe. We read about them in the book of Revelation: 'Grace be unto you, and peace, from him which is, and which was, and which is to come; and from the seven Spirits which are before his throne' (Revelation 1:4). 'These things saith he that hath the seven Spirits of God' (Revelation 3:1). 'And there were seven lamps of fire burning before the throne, which are the seven Spirits of God' (Revelation 4:5). 'In the midst of the elders, stood a Lamb as it had been slain, having seven horns and seven eyes, which are the seven Spirits of God sent forth into all the earth' (Revelation 5:6).

"These are the seven greatest and most highly evolved beings in existence, so near to Divinity that they might even be called the seven fingers of God since their consciousnesses are to so great a degree merged with God. Only the slightest tinge of separate consciousness remains in them so they may carry out the divine creative plan. Yet so nearly total is their oneness with God's Consciousness that their wills are flawless reflections of the divine will and their actions are truly acts of God. With God as their inmost Guide, they project the entire universe from the most subtle to the grossest realms and enclose all conscious entities in those body vehicles which correspond to their individual levels of evolutional development. The principal thing to realize in all this is that in the final summation of things there is really only one source of the entire creation: God."

I have practiced meditation for many years. But, I feel I only achieved a very little progress. I have tried several methods of meditation, but when one would seem to produce no progress, I soon got dissatisfied and changed from one method to another. Is it a must to have a personal guru who can provide me initiation? Can one do meditation without a guru but just practice through the guidance of books?

Certainly a person can learn and practice meditation without a guru in the present-day sense, though it is good to have the advice of a person with experience in meditation. Nevertheless, the way can be learned even from the written word. It is practice that matters.

It is first necessary to understand what indicates progress in meditation. Because yoga is being peddled like a kind of drugless drug, its salesmen want people to think that visions, revelations, and "kundalini experiences" are the purpose of yoga practice. But as Paramhansa Yogananda said: "The path to the Divine is not a circus." Progress in meditation manifests as both the deepening and expansion of consciousness, as well as the purification and correction of the mind. Real meditation is basically the cultivation of spirit-consciousness, the knowledge of our true Self.

Without devoting a great deal of time to meditation very little benefit can be obtained. Nor can anything be attained if the practice is not correct. Furthermore, unless a person observes purity in thought, action, and diet, nothing can be attained in any practice. The Yoga Life is absolutely necessary for success in yoga. If you have not already done so, I urge you to carefully read *How To Be A Yogi*, paying special attention to chapter three: The Foundations of Yoga.

Since there is a Law of cause and effect or the Law of Karma is it still necessary to pray and ask God for something like world peace, elimination of our financial problems, good health, etc.? If God fulfills or answers one's prayer does it not mean that God is breaking the Law He himself has created?

It is absolutely true that God, being all-knowing and all-caring, need not be constantly pestered with prayers. Sadhana is the supreme prayer in action. However, prayer itself is an action, and therefore a producer of karma. So prayer can result in various benefits since praying in a positive manner generates positive karma. It is still a matter of the law of cause and effect. Also, prayer is often a sending of positive thoughts and vibrations to those who need help. All my life I have seen blessings and even miracles result from prayer. Ultimately, though, it is up to the spontaneous feeling of the individual and not to be dictated by anyone else.

Can I follow the right path without a spiritual leader to initiate me and guide me?

It is certainly necessary to have a guru, but everyone already has one: God himself. Patanjali very clearly says about God (Ishwara): "He is guru even of the ancients" (Yoga Sutras 1:16). This indicates that at no time in creation has there been any other guru than God.

But how can we get in touch with this guru? Through meditation. And for that we certainly need teaching either from a personal teacher or from studying the teachings of a good instructor in meditation. It is beneficial to have someone experienced and qualified to answer questions about practice and experiences in meditation, but Vyasa and Shankara both say that yoga itself becomes the teacher when our practice is correct and prolonged. I know this to be true. My first meditation teachers in America were extremely limited, though sincere, and often could not answer my questions. But in time my meditation experience gave me the needed answers. Later in India I met highly qualified teachers, all of whom answered my questions and gave me practical instruction—never with the demand that I make them my guru. They were rare for India, that is true, but they were there and I found them by the grace of the One Guru. Twice I fell into the guru-trap, but both times I escaped through the mercy of that One Guru, and learned my lesson permanently.

I read your article "Rainproofing Our Mind" about desire and spiritual liberation. It raises this question: How can someone live without desire in the world today?

"Desire" is the usual translation of the Sanskrit word *kama*, which means egocentric desire, passion or lust. Desire arises from the ego and is always "I want" with little regard for the principles of spiritual life or the ultimate consequences of fulfilling such desire. That is why the Gita says: "Renounce all your desires, for ever. They spring from willfulness" (Bhagavad Gita 6:24). And: "He knows peace who has forgotten desire. He lives without craving: free from ego, free from pride" (Bhagavad Gita 2:71).

On the other hand, the wise person is to live by *sankalpa*–resolve and act of will and intention based on enlightened intelligence (*buddhi*). This is a manifestation of *icchcha shakti*, the power of will (*ichcha*).

For example, someone can desire to become wealthy so they can have whatever they want and impress others and perhaps even have power over them. This is *kama*, and egotistic evil. Someone else may decide to do their best to become wealthy so they can repay personal debts and help others. I know of an entire family in India that is of this second type. The family members have united in forming the largest charitable trust in India. The individual members engage in many personal charities, as well. One whom I met, Sri Jagannath Roy, always traveled third class on the train, had only two changes of simple cotton clothes, and lived extremely frugally. When a friend of mine asked him: "Mr. Roy, why don't you spend any of your money on yourself and your comforts?" he replied: "Then how would I be able to give that money to help others?"

"Getting ahead" in the usual sense is not a worthy intention, but success in doing good and benefitting others and enabling one to follow dharma more easily and effectively is laudable.

Desirelessness is attained only by the yogi. Therefore the Gita says: "When a man can act without desire, *through practice of yoga*;...when his heart is poised in the being of the atman no bonds can bind him" (Bhagavad Gita 4:41). And: "He puts aside desire, offering the act to Brahman. The lotus leaf rests unwetted on water: he rests on action, untouched by action" (Bhagavad Gita 5:10). And most importantly: "The abstinent run away from what they desire but carry their desires with them: when a man enters Reality, he leaves his desires behind him" (Bhagavad Gita 2:59).

This is why we must heed the exhortation of Krishna to Arjuna: "Therefore, Arjuna, become a yogi" (Bhagavad Gita 6:46).

It is important for you to also consider the principle set forth by Jesus: "Seek ye first the kingdom of God, and his righteousness; and all these things shall be added unto you" (Matthew 6:33). This is not a promise—it is a law.

If everyone presently on this planet did not take birth again because they had attained liberation, does that mean the planet would be empty of human beings but only be occupied by flora and fauna? Is this condition possible?

Individual spirits (jivas) are coming into manifestation all the time in the most basic form and evolving upward in ever more complex forms throughout the cycles (kalpas) of creation until as human beings they attain liberation from earthly rebirth. And then, since this world is only the first of many levels (lokas) that comprise relative existence (samsara), they have many more creation cycles to keep evolving until they eventually attain total union with God (Brahman). So some are entering at one end and others are leaving at the other. It never stops. There has never been a beginning to this process and there never will be an end. It is as eternal as God, because it is all the manifestation of God.

Is the faith and destiny of us human beings completely due to God's will without anything to do with our karma? In other words, is it predetermined because we have no control? Is it just like a drama, a human being only an actor, but God being the author of the scenario?

In the universe, karma is the law of God. But we alone determine our karma by our thoughts, words, and actions. That is under our control completely.

God has built the theater, the cosmos, and equipped it. We have come into the theater by the actors' entrance and come onto the stage by our own will. The drama is written by us by our own actions and karmic reactions. How it comes out is determined by us, no one else. Life is like a musical instrument that has been made by someone else, but how we play it and what kind of music comes out is up to us.

Even though we pray every day, it seems to me that without God's will our prayer shall never be fulfilled. So what is the use of praying? Why shouldn't we just surrender our fate to the will of God?

It is God's will that we live in such a way that we fulfill our own prayers. But we can refuse to do that, and end up with a tangle of confusion instead of a worthwhile and worthy life.

We can ask the help of God in living rightly, and if our prayer is sincere we will receive divine assistance. God has not left us on our own, but we can be if we so choose. As Krishna explains in the Gita (3:5), no one can remain without action, as that is the nature of relative existence, but we can live according to divine, spiritual principles or ignorant, human whims. It is all up to us.

There are devotees who never ask God for anything, trusting him to guide and protect them. When they are sincere and devoted, not just trying to avoid using initiative or taking responsibility, it works. But if we consider the matter, we will see that this, too, is a form of action and taking charge—just in a different direction.

In the next life will we reincarnate in the same family or nationality as in this present life? Or will we be born in some other family, nationality or even a different religion?

I think by now you know my answer: It is all according to your karma, which includes your desire.

For nearly my whole life I have heard and read that the religion of India is what turned it from one of the wealthiest countries in the world into one of the poorest in the world. What do you say to this?

A single word: Nonsense.

Vivekananda, upon his return to India from the prosperous West, said that after having been outside India every square inch of India's soil was now a sacred place (tirtha) to him. He of course deplored India's poverty, but he said: "The problem is not the religion of India, but the fact that it has not been followed."

This is true, but there is a far more obvious reason for India's economic plight at Vivekananda's time and even past the midpoint of the twentieth century: one thousand years of rapacious foreign domination and oppression, including in the last three hundred years, deliberate sabotage of India's economy. I will not start on that subject because it is too horrible and infuriating. But it is a matter of history and many of my friends in India have told me of their own experiences in this matter.

Why cannot people notice that after India gained Independence the economy began to rise–slowly, yes, but surely? And consider India now. It is emerging as one of the leaders in global economy! Why? Have the people of India abandoned Sanatana Dharma? Not at all. They practice it more openly and freely than ever before. Therefore India is rapidly progressing beyond a "third world" status. I have myself seen amazing changes since my first pilgrimage to India at the end of 1962. Others I know marvel at the tremendous strides they see in India every time they visit.

This is only to be expected, since: "In the beginning the Lord of beings created all men, to each his duty. 'Do this,' He said, 'And you shall prosper. Duty well done fulfills desire like Kamadhenu the wish-ful-filler'" (Bhagavad Gita 3:10). Now that India is free both politically and spiritually, this is being demonstrated.

Do you believe that the Virgin Mary is an incarnation of the Holy Spirit?

It is our belief that the Virgin Mary is a perfect reflection or image of the Holy Spirit. Only in that sense is she an incarnation of the Holy Spirit. The same is true of Jesus: he is a perfect reflection-image of the Son, the Second Aspect of the Trinity.

Both Mary and Jesus are divine, gods as are all spirits, but God alone is God.

Why are animals sacrificed at Kali temples in India? What is the purpose? Isn't it against the principle of vegetarianism?

The killing of animals is always an offense against Life Itself. But in perverted religion throughout the world animal sacrifice is found. Only a misunderstanding of Kali could seem to justify such a terrible practice.

Holy Mother Sarada Devi absolutely forbade animal sacrifice at the time of Kali Puja at Belur Math. Sri Sri Ma Anandamayi also banned such barbarism.

Animal sacrifice is not just a violation of vegetarianism, it is murder.

If I am not mistaken, the Bhagavad Gita says that to attain spiritual awakening it is mandatory to have a guru or spiritual master....

No; that is the usual interpretation, but it is incorrect. Krishna (Vyasa) tell us to seek out worthy *teachers*–acharyas. This is not same as the mythological guru figures of degenerate Hinduism. That is why the great master Swami Sivananda often said: "I abhor gurudom," and Neem Karoli Baba: "I make devotees of God, not disciples."

Is initiation necessary in the search for spiritual awakening?

Definitely not. Spiritual awakening arises from within the individual when a certain level of evolution is reached. This is why Buddha is referred to as Self-Awakened. The same is true of all of us.

There are a number of religious scriptures in the world. But some of them are in contradiction to one another. If these are all really divine revelations from God why then do different religions war with one another?

Scriptures are not divine revelations directly from God. Those that claim to be so are false and should be ignored. Rather, scriptures record the insights of those who have gained some experience of spiritual realities. The limitations of those authors naturally limit what they write. Their own understanding of their experiences may also be limited or even mistaken. That is why the Bhagavad Gita urges us to seek direct spiritual experience for ourselves. This is why the Gita tells us to become yogis. Without yoga there is no hope of full spiritual understanding, much less enlightenment.

Within Hindu religion ritual animal sacrifice is still being practiced in some parts of India, Nepal and Bali which quite contradict the teaching of ahimsa. How can we explain this?

Contemporary religion in India is often a mishmash of the most sublime truths and the most profound ignorance and superstition. Like the ant we must take the sugar and leave aside the sand. Many spiritual associations and ashrams follow the pure traditions of India's enlightened sages, and these should be sought out. It is not philosophy we need, but our own inner experience through personal yoga practice.

What is meant by "messiah" versus "avatar"? How are Jesus and Krishna similar and how are they different? Are they both Messiahs? Are they Avatars?

"Messiah" is a Hebrew word meaning "anointed one" as does the Greek word *Christos* from which "Christ" is derived. Almost always "messiah" refers to that single person whose coming was predicted by the Jewish prophets. He was expected to be both a spiritual and a political figure, both teaching and leading Israel. Many people have appeared over the centuries and been considered the Messiah by differing numbers of people. Also, in Jewish mysticism "Messiah" refers to a supreme level of enlightenment and is also the name of the high spiritual realm in which those who have attained such enlightenment usually dwell and from which they may descend into lower worlds for the welfare of others. (This is the basis of the concept of Christ found in the Aquarian Gospel.)

An avatar according to Sankhya philosophy is someone who has attained total enlightenment and perfect union/identity with God and then returns to lower worlds for the upliftment of those living there.

Only God, Jesus and Krishna know their spiritual status, whatever their devotees may believe about them. Certainly Jesus taught some of the same things that Krishna did, but Jesus lived most of his life in India and would have known the Bhagavad Gita, as he also knew the teachings of Buddha. One thing both Krishna and Jesus have in common is the exaggeration and misunderstanding regarding them on the part of those who claim to be their followers.

This we can know: both Krishna and Jesus pointed people to God. As Buddha said, a true teaching or teacher is like a finger pointing to the moon. The moon is the message–not the finger. Both indicated that Self-knowledge and God-knowledge are interdependent and fundamentally the same. Again: yoga is the path.

When the Self leaves the body at the time of death, who carries the memory of the karma, which is going to be the foundation for the next reincarnation?

Karma exists as energy impulses, waves or whorls in the astral and causal levels of the subtle mind body. They depart the present body, remain for a while in the subtle worlds, then create the next body, enter into it and manifest through it.

What do you say to some pious individual who uses his or her "religion" like a weapon? If I am a believer in Sanatana Dharma, how do I defend myself against wing-nuts who have convinced themselves that I am going straight to hell? The relentlessness of the judgment is quite unbelievable, pretty psychotic and irrational, in my opinion. It actually has nothing to do with me! The next time I get called a godless heathen and a great disappointment to humanity, what do you think I should say?

First: Congratulations. If you weren't on the right track those on the wrong track would not be so hysterically fearful of you and your spiritual path. Whenever emotion enters into a matter, the emoter is in the wrong. This is a principle I have found to be true for over fifty years when encountering the self-righteous and the willfully ignorant. The Sanskrit proverb, *Satyam Eva Jayate*: Truth Alone Conquers (or Is Victorious) is true. Evil and ignorance (basically the same thing) are terrified of simple truth. The evil and the ignorant therefore hate and fear spiritual reality in any form. So their reaction to you is a trustworthy assurance that you are in the light they detest. You are right: it has nothing to do with you. It is all on their shoulders and in their hearts.

All right: what should you do?

1. Remember that you were just like them in some previous life and reacted just like they are doing now. Otherwise this would not be happening to you. It is part of your karmic purification and will benefit you if you respond wisely.

2. Realize that they are suffering. Their religion is a hell in which they are trapped. Oh yes, they hold to it and exalt it, but that just shows what a terrible trap they are in.

3. Be aware that their reaction to you may be a sign of their own awakening–an awakening they do not like, but which you can assist if you always respond to them calmly, reasonably and even with humor, unless that sets them off even more–you will have to be cautious with this. I have seen the most argumentative and obnoxious people turn completely around in a short time and change permanently in their thinking.

4. Yogananda said foolish people argue and wise people discuss. Never argue or let them draw you into their emotionality. Be very firm about this. Just speak quietly and to the point. Say what you have to say and then be silent.

5. Consider if the situation requires silence from the very first. Sometimes you have to refuse to even speak with such people.

6. On occasion you have to just leave and make it clear that you will not be around in the future if the unpleasantness persists.

7. Do your best to love them throughout. If you can't love them, try to respect them. If you can't do either of these, then fake it.

These seven points are not easy, but by following them, I have lived to see people (including my parents and some relatives) who declared me crazy and a devil-worshipping heathen come to believe in reincarnation and karma themselves and even consider their former beliefs foolish and false. Others have kept to their ideas but decided that God must somehow accept mine. And the incurables have not bothered me because I have not given them a chance. There is no place in my life for them.

Again: Congratulations. You are going to manage just fine, because truth does prevail and conquer.

What is the best time to meditate?

Whenever you can and do meditate–that is the best. However, it is my experience that the Brahmamuhurta, around 4:00 a.m., is the best because the mind is calmest then. Here in the monastery we meditate from 4 to 7 each morning and prefer that. Some people find they meditate best in the evening, so it is really an individual matter.

I would like to advise you to meditate for at least three hours in a single session whenever you can manage. Once you can sit for three hours you can sit for much longer.

Will you please be so kind as to tell me: what is the practice of contemplation of the Divine Name and how may I begin to practice it?

It is surprisingly simple. I will tell you what I personally learned from Sri Anandamayi Ma and from reading the printed diaries of Sri Gurupriya Devi (Didi), Ma's oldest and most faithful devotee.

Ma said you can choose any Name of God that appeals to you. When asked if it should be a formal mantra, she emphatically said No; it should be a simple Name of God–a form of God (deity) or incarnation of God (avatar), for such a being is also God. The Name you choose must be your choice. She was very insistent on this.

When asked if it should be prefaced by the mantric syllable Om, Ma said No: just a simple Name. When asked if it needed to be given by a guru or through diksha, Ma also emphatically said No; all the power of enlightenment is already present in every Name of God. (And, I might add: in you, the spiritual aspirant, as your eternal, divine Self.) She further said that as time went by if you found you preferred to take up the japa of another Name instead of your earlier choice, that was perfectly all right because all Divine Names embody and invoke the One.

Occasionally Ma would announce that anyone who wanted to take up the sadhana of the Divine Name could come on a certain day between certain times and formally adopt the practice in her presence. This was done on one of the days of her birthday celebration in the Agarpara Anandamayi Ashram, north of Calcutta, in 1963. Unfortunately I was not able to be there that morning because I had become ill. But two devotees of Ma described it to me later that day. Each person came individually before Ma, who asked them what Name they wished to choose. When they told her, she took a japa mala of the type used for sadhana of that Name (usually rudraksha or tulsi) and handed it to them with the instruction to keep repeating it. Usually, they told me, she simply said: *Thakur Nam karo*—"Say the Name of the Lord"—as they took the mala. Then the next person came before her and did the same. Most of the people who did this brought fruit and/or flowers as an offering of respect. And that was all. This was not initiation. Ma often said: "I do not give the initiation a guru gives."

When one of the residents of our ashram was with Ma one time in the '70s, much the same thing took place in the Ranchi ashram, as he told me in detail.

I last saw Ma in 1981 in Kankhal. On the next to the last day I was standing outside the enclosed veranda of Ma's house next to the main ashram building. Twenty or so young women had come by a private bus from Hoshiarpur where they attended a school named in Ma's honor. I could see everything very clearly and hear all that was said. At one point Ma urged them to take up japa of the Lord's Name. One of the girls asked what Name they should repeat and Ma asked each of them individually what Holy Name they wanted to use in japa and meditation. Each one replied to Ma with a Name (not a formal mantra). And each time Ma responded: "Good [sometimes "Very Good"], say That always!" That was all. I sincerely hope they still do remember the Name they chose that day.

Now I would like to relay to you what Ma told me about japa of the Holy Name. I am adding nothing of my own to this.

Japa. Ma told me that the highest form of japa is to intone the Holy Name once as you inhale and once as you exhale, fitting the length of intonation to the length of the breath: if short, then short; if moderate, the moderate; and if long, then long. Do no kind of visualization during this, but just listen to the sound of your inner repetition-intonations. "Singing" the mantra mentally on a single note (whatever pitch is natural) makes it easier to remember and become absorbed in the Name.

Meditation. Meditation is just the same as japa, but you sit upright in a comfortable posture, turn your eyes gently downward at a slight angle and close them. Sit there intoning the Name in time with your breath as just described.

If you wish to keep an image or picture of the deity whose Name you are repeating where you meditate, look at it carefully and reverently, make a salutation and then sit upright, close your eyes and do japa of the Name without visualization, just intent on the inner sound of the Name. At the end of meditation, open your eyes, look at the deity's form and bow, offering the meditation to God.

Alternately, Ma said that if a person wanted, at the beginning of meditation they could sit, close their eyes and visualize the Divine Form that corresponded to the Divine Name. They should calmly visualize the

Divine Form in this manner: Start at the feet and move upward ending with the face of the Deity. Then dismiss the visualization and begin the japa as I have described. As I say, Ma emphasized that absorption in the sound of the Divine Name alone was the highest form of japa. At the end of meditation, do the same visualization and bow, offering the meditation to God.

After meditation return to japa of the Name and keep it up until you fall asleep. Begin the japa as soon as you awaken in the morning, or happen to awaken during the night.

In my second visit to Ma, she spoke at length on the value of lying in the Corpse Pose (Savasan) and continuing to mentally intone the Divine Name in time with the breath. She said this greatly accelerated healing when the sadhaka was ill.

How can I succeed in maintaining brahmacharya? It is not easy.

Whenever we begin any positive endeavor it is only natural that opposition to it will arise, both from without and within. However, "greater is he that is in you, than he that is in the world" (I John 4:4). That is, your pure spirit is greater than any force out in the world, and also greater than those aspects of your own makeup that are also "in the world." Perseverance is needed as well as careful vigilance to see that no subtle elements are entertained in the mind that will lead to endangering brahmacharya. Often delusion wears a mask so the nature of its presence is not recognized.

This I can assure you positively, three factors are crucial in the matter of brahmacharya: environment, diet and meditation. Without purity of all three there is simply no hope.

The environment must be free of all elements that are incompatible with perfect brahmacharya both physically and mentally. This includes anything that coarsens our mind and senses, even if not specifically related to sex. It also includes people who are coarse and sexually oriented. As Yogananda often said: "Company is stronger than will power."

The diet must be very pure and truly healthful. Merely being vegetarian or vegan means very little as there is a lot of junk food that has no animal elements. Nevertheless, all animal protein should be avoided in any degree, both animal flesh and animal glandular secretions–i.e. dairy. Gandhi had a tremendous struggle to achieve and maintain brahmacharya. He found that milk of any kind was very detrimental to brahmacharya. Sugar, caffeine and chemical additives are enemies to health as are mind-altering drugs, including nicotine.

Most important is meditation–not just twenty minutes in the morning and night. Even an hour morning and night is not sufficient. You may have heard a lot about living a life "with a balance of meditation and activity" from people who live no such thing. Take the time these people meditate and put it up against the hours in the day they do not. A balanced life requires some hours a day of meditation. A truly balanced life would be eight hours of meditation, eight hours of activity and eight hours of sleep. Understandably, that cannot be managed by most people, but it puts the lie to the pop yogis who do not come near that. Do not pay attention or follow them.

Also, to keep the mind where it should be, continuous mantra japa is absolutely essential. Without it nothing can be done with the mind. Go to the website: http://www.dlshq.org/download/download.htm. Book 33 in the list is *Practice of Brahmacharya*. Download it or read it on line. From Sivananda's own sacred lips I heard the teaching that of all methods to preserve brahmacharya, japa is supreme.

Be a 24/7 yogi. If you succeed in this, then your life will be directed by divine grace and your spiritual future will be assured.

I want to convert to Christianity–can you help? I am a Hindu.

If you want to convert to the religion popularly called "Christianity" then you need only find a church and join it.

IF, however, you want to be a follower of Jesus Christ, then like him you must become a dedicated student and practicer of Sanatana Dharma. According to the *Bhavishya Maha Purana*, a book of Kashmiri history, when a king of Kashmir met Jesus in the Himalayas and asked him about himself, Jesus told him: "I hail from a land far away, *where there is no truth*…the land of mleccha darkness." This proves that Jesus did not believe in Judaism. Nor, as can been seen from the whole account of this conversation (see *The Christ of India*), did Jesus teach Churchianity. Rather, he learned and taught the pure principles of Sanatana Dharma. His disciple Thomas did the same, as you will see by reading *The Apostle of India* section in *The Christ of India*.

Please study the following:

1. The eleven principal Upanishads: Isha, Kena, Katha, Prashna, Mundaka, Mandukya, Taittiriya, Aitareya, Chandogya, Brihadaranyaka, and Shvetashvatara, as well as the commentaries written on them by Shankara and Ramanuja.
2. The Bhagavad Gita and the commentaries by Shankara and Ramanuja.
3. The Yoga Sutras (Yoga Darshana) of Patanjali. If you do so, then you will know what Jesus really taught, because they were studied by Jesus himself.

The books by Swami Sivananda of the Divine Life Society are also invaluable, especially the ones about sadhana. Many of them are posted online and can be downloaded for free. (Go to http://www.dlshq.org/download/download.htm.)

It may seem strange to you that I have answered your question as I have, but it was my interest in the real teachings of Jesus that led me to India and its eternal wisdom. Only there did I come to understand what Jesus really was and what he really taught.

I hope you will do the same.

Jesus lived around 2 BC to 33 AD. Adi Shankaracharya (who founded the Govardhan Math) lived between 788 AD and 820 AD. In your website it is mentioned that Jesus lived in Govardhan Math. How can it be?

Quite simple. Shankaracharya lived sometime between 500 and 300 BC.–so I was taught as a young monk by more than one sadhu of Joshi Math, the "home base" for all members of the Giri branch of the Dasanami Order, and I have never had cause to doubt them.

A later dating for Shankara is simply without basis and is from the influence of Western "scholars" and those in India who are influenced by them. Like the fabricated "Aryan Invasion of India," such a dating is intended to both deny the ancient character of Sanatana Dharma and to imply that the wisdom of India is post-Christian and perhaps even influenced by Christianity.

During his world tour in 1958, Jagadguru Shankaracharya Bharati Krishna Tirtha stated to various people, including some of my acquaintances, that he possessed "historical proof positive" that Jesus had lived in the Govardhan Math. He told them that he had found evidence of this fact in the archives of the math, and had written a book on the subject which he intended to publish on his return to India.

Unhappily, when he returned to the math he was told that a servant had thrown away the manuscript thinking it was waste paper. That may or may not have been the situation, considering that in the nineteen thirties a Christian missionary had borrowed and destroyed the manuscript of a book by Swami Sri Yuketswar Giri, the guru of Paramhansa

Yogananda, in which he proved the same thing: that Jesus had lived in Govardhan Math and had been a student and teacher of Sanatana Dharma, a spiritual son of India.

A useful online source on this subject is: http://www.hindu-blog.com/2008/02/year-of-birth-of-adi-shankaracharya-509.html

What are the indications of purification of memory in the context of the Nerve of Memory?

In the *Sri Sri Ramakrishna Kathamrita* (English version: *The Gospel of Sri Ramakrishna*) we find the most authoritative teaching about both the nerve (nadi) and its indications. On March 9, 1884, a devotee named Mahimacharan asked Sri Ramakrishna: "Sir, why does a man become deluded by worldly objects?"

Sri Ramakrishna replied: "It is because he lives in their midst without having realized God. Man never succumbs to delusion after he has realized God. The moth no longer enjoys darkness if it has once seen the light.

"To be able to realize God, one must practice absolute continence. Sages like Sukadeva are examples of an *urdhvareta*. (A man of unbroken and complete continence. [A yogi in whom the sexual energy flows upwards.]) Their chastity was absolutely unbroken. There is another class, who previously have had discharges of semen but who later on have controlled them. A man controlling the seminal fluid for twelve years develops a special power. He grows a new inner nerve called the nerve of memory. Through that nerve he remembers all, he understands all."

I am aware that some people are interested in this subject to improve their ordinary memory, but that is like seeking a king's ransom in order to buy chewing gum.

Is an exoteric religious tradition necessary?

An exoteric religion tradition is certainly not necessary for everyone, but everything in this world is necessary and has a purpose.

There are two classes of human beings: 1) those that are mostly aware of external existence and therefore think and act with an almost total degree of outer awareness, motivation and response, and 2) those that are also aware of internal existence to such a degree that it affects their thinking and behavior to a marked degree. These people are mostly affected by psychological and even psychic awareness. Though living side by side, they live in two different—even contradictory—worlds. Origen called the first type Somas–Bodies, and the second kind Pneumas–Spirits.

For the externally-oriented people, exoteric religion is a necessity, for by continually bringing God and spiritual principles to bear on their outer material life they very slowly begin to spiritualize their thinking and living. This can take a lot of lives, but it does inevitably happen.

For the internally and psychically aware people, esoteric religion is a necessity for it furthers their growth into progressively higher awareness until they transcend this purely material life and and become capable of passing into higher, subtler worlds where their evolution will be greatly accelerated. Until then, yoga can be the major factor for their development, not mere religiosity even if extremely "spiritual."

So for some people exoteric religion is necessary and for others esoteric religion is necessary and some need both together. It is all a matter of karma, samskara and intuition, and must be determined by the individual, not some external person, factor or authority.

The prime necessity is that each person figure this out for himself while respecting the needs of others, however different they may be.

Can you please guide me as to how to increase the predominance of sattwa guna so as to move steadily in the path of devotion while continence is being practiced?

Three things are necessary to help the sadhaka increase in sattwa, and all are very simple and easy.

1. Follow a strict vegetarian diet, for only that diet is sattwic, and since as the Chandogya Upanishad tells us that our mind substance is formed of the food we eat, we must have a sattwic diet always.
2. Carefully study and apply all the passages in the Gita which outline sattwa guna as it manifests in various aspects of the spiritual life, including diet.
3. Meditate regularly and for an adequate amount of time each day. Success will be assured.

I am wondering if the Soham mantra requires initiation.

The Soham mantra does not require initiation because it is innate in each sentient being. Please see our publication *Soham Yoga*.

Can you please tell me about signs of awaking of Kundalini? How is a sadhaka supposed to detect it?

Here are the words of Sri Ramakrishna on the subject:

"The mind of a worldly man generally moves among the three lower centers: those at the navel, at the sexual organ, and at the organ of evacuation. After great effort and spiritual practice the Kundalini is awakened. According to the yogis there are three nerves in the spinal column: Ida, Pingala, and Sushumna. Along the Sushumna are six lotuses, or centers, the lowest being known as the Muladhara. Then come successively Swadhishthana, Manipura, Anahata, Vishuddha, and Ajna. These are the six centers. The Kundalini, when awakened, passes through the lower centers and comes to the Anahata, which is at the heart. It stays there. At that time the mind of the aspirant is withdrawn from the three lower centers. He feels the awakening of Divine Consciousness and sees Light. In mute wonder he sees that radiance and cries out: 'What is this? What is this?'

"After passing through the six centers, the Kundalini reaches the thousand petalled lotus known as the Sahasrara, and the aspirant goes into samadhi.

"According to the Vedas these centers are called 'bhumi', 'planes'. There are seven such planes. The center at the heart corresponds to the fourth plane of the Vedas. According to the Tantra there is in this center a lotus called Anahata, with twelve petals.

"The center known as Vishuddha is the fifth plane. This center is at the throat and has a lotus with sixteen petals. When the Kundalini reaches this plane, the devotee longs to talk and hear only about God. Conversation on worldly subjects, on 'woman and gold', causes him great pain. He leaves a place where people talk of these matters.

"Then comes the sixth plane, corresponding to the center known as Ajna. This center is located between the eyebrows and it has a lotus with two petals. When the Kundalini reaches it, the aspirant sees the form of God. But still there remains a slight barrier between the devotee and God. It is like a light inside a lantern. You may think you have touched the light, but in reality you cannot because of the barrier of glass.

"And last of all is the seventh plane, which, according to Tantra, is the center of the thousand-petalled lotus. When the Kundalini arrives there, the aspirant goes into samadhi. In that lotus dwells Satchidananda Siva, the Absolute. There Kundalini, the awakened Power, unites with Siva. This is known as the union of Siva and Shakti."

And also:

"Can one attain knowledge of God by merely repeating the word 'God'? There are two indications of such knowledge. First, longing, that is to say, love for God. You may indulge in reasoning or discussion, but if you feel no longing or love, it is all futile. Second, the awakening of the Kundalini. As long as the Kundalini remains asleep, you have not attained knowledge of God. You may be spending hours poring over books or discussing philosophy, but if you have no inner restlessness for God, you have no knowledge of him.

"When the Kundalini is awakened, one attains bhava, bhakti, prema, and so on. This is the path of devotion."

Are you Saint Thomas Christians or Hindus?

To us they are the same thing. Jesus lived in India from the age of fourteen until he returned to Israel when he was thirty. There he taught the dharma he had learned in India and incurred the wrath of the religious authorities who eventually brought about his death by the Romans who were occupying Israel. His guru, Chetan Nath, a leading figure of the Nath Yogi Sampradaya, revived Jesus by his yoga powers and they returned to India where Jesus lived the rest of his life mostly in the Himalayas in Kashmir.

A short time after Jesus returned to India Thomas, one of his twelve apostles, also went to live in India, first in Kashmir and then in what is the present-day state of Kerala. He had many disciples who were called Ishannis ("of Isha"–Isha Nath being the Sanskrit name of Jesus as a Nath Yogi). The Ishanni Sampradaya was fully a part of Sanatana Dharma as were the sampradayas of other acharyas such as Shankara, Ramanuja, etc. All of the Ishannis were Brahmins who adhered strictly to Sanatana Dharma. Only after the coming of the Portuguese and other Europeans did the Ishannis become known as Saint Thomas Christians.

It is important to understand several distinctive characteristics of the Saint Thomas Christians who adhere to the original principles of Jesus and Saint Thomas:

1. They consider Jesus of Nazareth to be a perfected yoga siddha, a jivanmukta like the great acharyas such as Shankara. They honor him greatly as all sampradayas honor their founders, but they do not believe him to be God the creator or somehow the only savior of the world in whom people must believe to be "saved."

2. Their beliefs are completely those of Sanatana Dharma, the religion of the ancient rishis of India as found in the eleven major Upanishads, the Bhagavad Gita and other scriptures.

3. Just as each sampradaya in India has distinctive features, mostly ritualistic, in the same way the Saint Thomas Christians are distinguished by the rituals instituted by Jesus and known as sacraments. However these rituals reflect and express the principles of Sanatana Dharma such as karma, rebirth and the divine nature of the Self in all human beings.

To understand the Saint Thomas Christians fully we recommend that you read *The Christ of India* which you can find on our website, ocoy.org. It is now available in a print edition as well.

Where is the atman (soul) located in our body?

The atman is everywhere in the body and beyond as the basis of the aura.

Should we focus on the atman when we do meditation since the atman is a part of God?

The object of meditation should be identical with the atman itself. Otherwise the meditation will not lead to atmic experience (atmadarshana) or knowledge (atmajnana). This is extremely important for the yogi to realize. Otherwise a great deal of time and even an entire incarnation can be wasted. Please read *Soham Yoga*, which discusses this.

When we meditate should we close or open our eyes? Which one is better?

Closing the eyes is best because it removes visual distractions and reduces brain-wave activity by about seventy-five percent, thus helping greatly to calm the mind. A person who cannot meditate with closed eyes is in a pathological condition and needs the attention of an adept yogi he knows personally (not someone at a distance like myself) or even a neurologist.

Tell me, please, where is the Mother God in Saint Thomas Christian Dharma?

Where She was originally, we have no idea because all the books from the time of Saint Thomas were burned by the Portuguese. (See *The Christ of India*.) Jesus and the Virgin Mary certainly represent the divine masculine and divine feminine in God. It is sufficient for us that the basic scriptures of India present the concept of the Mother God. But to make up for what was destroyed we use *The Aquarian Gospel of Jesus the Christ*. There we find:

"And Spirit breathed, and that which was not manifest became the Fire and Thought of Heaven, the Father-God, the Mother-God." (Aquarian Gospel 9:16)

"And Jesus went into an ancient plaza and taught; he spoke of Father-Mother-God; he told about the brotherhood of life." (Aquarian Gospel 34:3)

"And in the tomb I will remain three days in sweet communion with the Christ, and with my Father-God and Mother-God." (Aquarian Gospel 127:28)

I am full of doubts about my ability to realize the Self. What is the right course for me to follow?

First: Understand that since you ARE the Self, you cannot help but realize it. So relax and fear not.

Second: Become a yogi, for it is the nature and purpose of yoga to reveal the Self.

Third: Persevere.

It is said that reincarnation is due to our own karma and we alone are responsible for the past, present, and future life. But what part within every individual living entity actually can create words, thoughts, and deeds either good or evil? Is it the atman (soul), mind, or a particular organ of the body?

Someone said that life is suffering. This means that every birth is accompanied by suffering. But what or who really suffers, the soul or atman by getting rebirth (taking a new body after death), or what?

Presently we are functioning in and as a duality. Our atman (self) is encased in various bodies or koshas that are formed of vibrating energies of various frequencies. The atman never acts, but only experiences. All action is done by the bodies; they alone create good and evil karma. But the atman experiences the effects of the actions. That is why the Mundaka Upanishad says:

"Like two birds of golden plumage, inseparable companions, the individual self and the immortal Self are perched on the branches of the selfsame tree. The former tastes of the sweet and bitter fruits of the tree; the latter, tasting of neither, calmly observes. The individual self, deluded by forgetfulness of his identity with the divine Self, bewildered by his ego, grieves and is sad. But when he recognizes the worshipful Lord as his own true Self, and beholds his glory, he grieves no more. When the seer beholds the Effulgent One, the Lord, the Supreme Being, then, transcending both good and evil, and freed from impurities, he unites himself with him. This Effulgent Self is to be realized within the lotus of the heart by continence, by steadfastness in truth, by meditation, and by superconscious vision. Their impurities washed away, the seers realize him" (Mundaka Upanishad 3.1.1-3, 5).

I have come across the word "prana." What is the relation between atman and prana?

"Prana" means "life," and is the vital energy, life-breath and life-force. One of the bodies in which the atman is encased is the pranamaya kosha, the pranic body. It consists of vital forces and the subtle energy system that is the power behind the physical nervous system. It is a covering of the atman, not the atman, which is independent of the bodies (koshas).

What is "chitta"? What is the meaning of "when the mind and Self are one"?

A Brief Sanskrit Glossary defines chitta in this way: "The subtle energy that is the substance of the mind, and therefore the mind itself; mind in all its aspects; the field of the mind; the field of consciousness; consciousness itself; the mind-stuff." This covers a lot of territory, but that is because in Sanskrit all the aspects of a thing are considered and included.

The meaning of the mind and Self being or becoming one is impossible to determine unless we know the word used for "mind." For example, it could be chitta, manas or buddhi. Certainly whatever word is used, it is based on the conviction that vibrating energy (shakti) is really one with consciousness (chaitanya), with spirit (atman), that it is an emanation from the atman even if only in the sense of a temporary illusion—not a reality but an idea or concept. In that case, when the Self is revealed the sadhaka realizes that everything is the Self and in that sense everything, not just the mind, "becomes" the Self. Another view is that the mind is truly an emanation of the Self, and that the Self withdraws the mind-thought into itself.

There is certainly a difference in saying that the mind and the Self *are* one or that the mind *becomes* the Self. I have read both, but they were English translations of Indian languages. So we must be very careful before we attribute a particular meaning to a teacher, even if we are quoting a translation of his words. Naturally, translations are done according to the level of the translator's understanding and experience (which is often nil).

So what is the solution? To find out for ourselves by practicing meditation and experiencing the results. And even then, we may find that there are no words to accurately express our experience, and we will remain silent.

Will meditation alone improve one's moral sensibility? Will one naturally move toward the good as one meditates?

If meditation alone would improve one's moral sense or automatically move us toward the good, Patanjali would not have outlined the ten principles of yama and niyama for us:

1. Ahimsa: non-violence, non-injury, harmlessness
2. Satya: truthfulness, honesty
3. Asteya: non-stealing, honesty, non-misappropriativeness
4. Brahmacharya: sexual continence in thought, word and deed as well as control of all the senses
5. Aparigraha: non-possessiveness, non-greed, non-selfishness, non-acquisitiveness
6. Shaucha: purity, cleanliness
7. Santosha: contentment, peacefulness

8. Tapas: austerity, practical (i.e., result-producing) spiritual discipline

9. Swadhyaya: introspective self-study, spiritual study

10. Ishwarapranidhana: offering of one's life to God

Although these are presented as prerequisites for meditation practice by Patanjali, it has always been considered that meditation can be practiced at the same time the aspirant is striving to embody these observances and non-observances. However, if these are not developed early on to a goodly degree, the yogi will fail to attain any significant realization.

What is the difference between atman and jiva? Also do you believe that we are all one soul, or many living entities?

The atman and the jiva are the same thing, though since atman is derived from the root *at*, which means "I breathe," you could say that atman is the jiva in relative existence and experience, and the jiva is the pure spirit-Self. Still, they are the same.

There is only One Reality: Satchidananda Brahman, the Paramatman. Yet in a way beyond our comprehension there are a virtually infinite number of individual spirits or jivatmans existing within Brahman, absolutely one with Brahman. They are not separate from Brahman, but there is a very real distinction between them and Brahman–distinction, but not difference. Only those yogis who have attained Brahmajnana (atmajnana) can comprehend this.

When will Jesus be born on earth again?

As far as I know that has never been exactly revealed. But considering that he was born at the very beginning of the Piscean Age it is likely the same with the Aquarian Age. If so, then he is in his teens at this time. Considering the prophecy it is definite that he has been born in a Jewish family, but whether in Israel or not is not sure. The major unknown factor is when he will reveal himself. Until then it is wise to begin spiritually preparing ourselves now in hope that we will have the opportunity to meet him then.

The Ribhu Gita seems to say that the mind and its concepts are all unreal, that all is Brahman. Does this mean that they have no reality or that they are within Brahman?

It is important to realize that in the East a statement can mean many things simultaneously. Also the East believes that all verbal statements are only hints or approximations of the way things really are; that human beings are not at all capable of seeing or grasping the full truth of anything. Consequently words are always far from the full reality of anything. Please keep this in mind always when considering anything relating to the Eternal Dharma.

Brahman alone is real; everything is Brahman. This is the fundamental position of the enlightened. But they also tell us that all things are held in the consciousness of Brahman and their essential nature is consciousness alone. So there is a sense in which they are unreal, but remember that a dream or a hallucination is real as an experience.

I prefer the way Yogananda explained it. God is the Cosmic Dreamer, dreaming (holding in his consciousness) all things, and we are co-dreamers with him, living and moving in his dream as we dream the dreams of our individual lives. The reality or unreality of it depends entirely on what we consider to be the nature of reality. If we hold a materialistic view of existence, then in actuality all that we see or seem is unreal however much we "believe" it. But if we hold a spiritual (spirit-based) view, then everything is real, since God is real and God is All.

Do advaita and Buddhism teach non-existence upon liberation or nirvana?

This is another of those Eastern riddles!

Advaita teaches that all is One: Brahman. Since Brahman is existence itself, non-existence is impossible. In the Gita Krishna says to Arjuna: "That which is non-existent can never come into being, and that which is can never cease to be. Those who have known the inmost Reality know also the nature of *is* and *is not*" (Bhagavad Gita 2:16). Just before that he said: "There was never a time when I did not exist, nor you.... Nor is there any future in which we shall cease to be" (Bhagavad Gita 2:12).

Mahayana Buddhism teaches the existence of the Buddha Nature within each sentient being. Therefore they exist forever. As far as the Theravadins are concerned, I do know that the monks of the Thai Forest tradition believe there there is an eternal part of each one of us that exists forever.

Within your system of yoga, is time considered as linear or cyclic?

The yogis of India have for centuries been assuring us that time, along with space, is an illusion, a mere appearance of a misperceived reality. They also say that time is both linear and cyclic according to how we look at it. They do not take it very seriously, because in the terminology of *The Maltese Falcon* time and space are really "the stuff of which dreams are made."

To someone who wrote asking how to cure the habit of negative thoughts.

The solution to negative thinking is immersion of the mind in positive thought–specifically in meditation and japa. Regarding negative thought patterns, Shankara says: "They are dissolved along with the receptacle, the chitta.... Because they have no effect, they are not given attention, for when a thing is falling of itself there is no point in searching for something to make it fall." I. K. Taimni says: "As the object of meditation continues to fill the mind completely there can be no question of emptying the mind." It is simple. Not easy, but worth the effort.

Someone wrote the brief message: I AM A SINNER AND I DO NOT DESERVE FORGIVENESS.

All human beings have sinned and may sin, but they are not sinners by nature. Rather, they are divine, eternal spirits ever one with God. But many births in the material world have darkened their consciousness and they have forgotten their real nature.

No one needs forgiveness because God cannot be "offended" or "angered." A religion which teaches he can be is demonic falsehood and should be abandoned. What is needed is awakening to actual spiritual realities. Buried within each one is the divine light, covered over so only darkness is presently perceived. Yoga is the means by which the holy light is uncovered and we know ourselves as we really are. Meditation and continual japa is The Way.

To someone who wrote juggling all kinds of statements about how much better it would be to not believe in reincarnation and the problems such a belief caused.

In the West the question about a belief is its utility, its plausibility, its acceptability (appeal) and its practicality. In the East it is a simple question of: Is it true? No other question really matters. That each person settles for himself.

Those who purify and refine their consciousness through yoga meditation have no problem, because their intuition and their own memories of past lives settle the question, as well as the testimonies and the research of many, many others.

Reading the words [about God as guru] in *Soham Yoga* a bell went off: the realization that the teacher we need to "introduce" us to God is him who already is within us and he comes into our lives when we "see" this. Am I right?

You certainly are. Along the way we often do need teachers–but not enslavers such as those who would have us believe that without them or their meditation methods we cannot know God–or even worse, those that would addict us to their "love" and "blessing" and insist on "loyalty" to them. God leaves us free at all times, and so does a true spiritual teacher such as Swami Sivananda and Paramhansa Nityananda. All true masters, including Patanjali, teach that God is the ultimate guru.

I eat meat, however I have decided to adopt a strict vegetarian diet for sixty days. If it does enable me to go deeper into meditation, I will never eat meat again. My question is, is sixty days long enough for me to experience a difference? Or how long (approximately) should it take for me to see results?

In yoga everything is individual, and that includes yogic diet. The present condition of your bodies, gross and subtle, determines your usual state and function of mind. Therefore I could not at all say when a perceptible change will come about from a vegetarian diet.

Many years ago I taught a two-week seminar on yoga at a university in northern California. A friend had been slated to teach, but asked me to take his place. I agreed to do so free of charge, on one condition: that everyone in the seminar would have to be purely vegetarian for the two weeks. This was worked out with the university and accepted by the nearly twenty students in the seminar. To my surprise, after only one week they had noticed such a difference in their minds—which included better functioning in their other classes and even one examination—that they declared they would be vegetarians for life. Three years later I met some of them in India, and they were still vegetarians.

For a really dramatic change I find that six months and three years are somehow magic numbers. By that I mean that after six months of being a vegetarian a very marked difference is noticed, and after a total of three years as a vegetarian the change is seen to be astounding. The bacteria in the digestive tract of meat-eaters is anaerobic. Since oxygen is inseparable from evolving life, such bacteria are literal death-bearers, and one of the reasons that vegetarians have been proven to have at least three hundred percent stronger immune systems than non-vegetarians. Anyhow, if a person becomes a strict vegetarian (no lapses and no cheating), after three years the bacteria in the digestive tract will have completely changed over to aerobic bacteria: oxygen-based and life-giving. This is, I expect, the reason for the three-year period.

So enter upon the Great Experiment and see what happens. This I can tell you: if you eat junk food, even if vegetarian, do not expect much improvement. And if you use nicotine or alcohol, both of which are much more harmful than meat, then who knows what will result?

This person wrote back and said that in a few days the benefit of a vegetarian diet became so evident that he did not need sixty days to decide that a vegetarian diet was the best for a yogi.

To someone who wrote describing many kinds of psychic experiences including astral travel and kundalini manifestations.

So many kinds of experiences are possible that even the yogis of India have not listed and classified them as to their character and value. For the yogi there is a single question: What is or was the lasting effect of an experience, if any? Did it impart knowledge and wisdom or did it leave me asking, "What happened to me?"

An experience may be real, but our response to it may be mistaken. For example, I knew a man who believed he was the present King of India because someone told him so in a dream. He would also dream someone was dead and would spend hours praying for their soul only to find out they were alive. Yet he never questioned the accuracy of his experiences. I knew a very intelligent woman who supposedly had a revelation that she was a part of the Divine Mother that had broken off (???) and incarnated as her, and her husband was the Archangel Michael who was born on earth to protect her.

Another question to ask is: Have I learned anything from this experience, or do I just have more questions? It is extremely important to approach these matters with great caution because it is so easy to misunderstand and come to a wrong conclusion about them.

Astral travel is certainly real, but whether or not it is beneficial is the question. I have known several people who astral traveled from childhood because in a previous life they had been forced to develop psychic powers including astral projection. In this life it caused them great confusion.

I grew up with people who were visionaries and spiritual clairvoyants, but they were very stable and understood everything. One of them was a great healer and miracle worker. On the other hand I have known others that were confused and ultimately harmed by taking their experiences seriously. Quite a few people have reported to me receiving "initiations" when out of the body, but they neither understood their experience nor learned anything from it.

I am telling you these examples to urge you to carefully analyze everything and determine for yourself the character of various experiences.

Do you have some kind of test to apply during these various kinds of experience? It is very important to do so. I recommend that you intone a mantra such as Om over and over and see what occurs.

I advise you to forget experiences that do not come with understanding, and put your attention on those that give you insight and practical knowledge. It is very common for psychic life to consist of both worthless and worthwhile events. Sand and white sugar look alike, but an ant knows which is which. So the yogis say to be like the wise ant and take the sugar and leave the sand.

To someone who asked about Saint Bartholomew the Apostle in India.

In ancient documents Ethiopia is often called "India," as in the case of Saints Barlaam and Ioasaph. Saint John of Karpathos wrote a book of spiritual instruction entitled "For the Monks of India," but he meant Ethiopia. It is much like Columbus thinking he had reached India, and the way Native Americans are still called "Indians" today.

To someone who wrote about vegetarianism.

This I can tell you, the longer you are a vegetarian the more crazy meat-eating appears. But a real vegetarian never pesters non-vegetarians, and those that carry on about how disgusted they are when they see meat are often wishing they could have some. People who are the real thing in any area of life are always content and keep quiet, never pestering others.

Peggy Dietz, one of Yogananda's secretaries, told me that a woman who fancied herself a spiritual light in the Los Angeles area sometimes came with some of her followers to visit Yogananda on Sundays when people gathered with him in what had been the lobby of the hotel that then was the ashram. She would monopolize the event by carrying on and on about vegetarianism, finally declaring: "I have no meat in my body: I have never eaten meat in this life. I have no meat in my astral bodies: I have never eaten meat in any of my past lives, either!" She would go through this monologue every time, ending only with her departure. One time Yogananda went with her to the door and said goodbye. Then as she walked away from the building he turned to everyone there and said: "My God, I wish somebody would slip that woman a ham sandwich. It wouldn't hurt her a bit and she would never know the difference!"

Do you believe that there are individual atmans? Also I wonder if you feel that jivas retain their individuality or merge in Brahman as Shankara believes?

Absolutely there are individual atmans, though they are all in eternal union with Brahman. There is no difference between them and Brahman, yet a distinction is also eternal. This we cannot figure out intellectually but have to experience for ourselves through yoga sadhana.

The idea that everyone melts back into a cosmic lump is a misunderstanding. This is not the position of Shankara, although it is mistakenly attributed to him. In the Gita Krishna tells Arjuna: "There was never a time when *I* did not exist, nor *you*, nor any of *these kings*. Nor is there any future in which *we* shall cease to be" (Bhagavad Gita 2:12). So the distinction is eternal. The jivas retain their individuality forever, but their consciousness is merged completely in Brahman.

This is why the Yoga Darshana is based on Sankhya Philosophy and not on Advaita Vedanta. And why the Bhagavad Gita should be the daily study of the yogi to retain the correct perspective.

Is consciousness an attribute of the Self, or is it the Self?

Spirit is consciousness itself, and the Self is spirit. Consciousness is not an attribute, it is essential being, the nature of God himself. Consciousness does not depend on anything else for its existence, but is itself the basis of all things.

Also is the "I" the ego as Shankara believes or is the "I" the self as Ramanuja believes?

Both are correct. The ahankara, the ego, is the false Self–a mirage. The true Self is the eternally existent "I." That is why Sri Ramana Maharshi said that it was good to say "I" a few times at the beginning of meditation to attune to the true Self.

Considering the occult anatomy of a human being, how do you feel about the principle: Brain=seat of mind, and mind=tool of Awareness?

The astral/causal brain, the Sahasrara chakra, is both the seat of the mind and the instrument of the mind. Mind itself has two levels in Sanskrit terminology: manas and buddhi. The manas is the sensory mind, the receiver of impressions relayed by the senses. The buddhi is the higher mind, both intelligence and intuition. The buddhi in its higher levels is so subtle that it is indistinguishable from spirit whose nature is pure consciousness. But of course in the philosophy of India everything ultimately is spirit, so we must not exaggerate the distinction between material, psychic and spiritual.

Can we underestimate the (physical, even subtle) healthy/sick condition of brain as the seat of mind?

We certainly can underestimate the condition of the brain in yoga. Frankly a lot of psychotic people in India, many of them sociopaths, claim enlightenment experiences and are believed. Actually, there is more gullibility shown in India regarding these false yogis than anywhere else. You would think that centuries (millennia) of yogic knowledge would make the people of India more cautious than anywhere else in the world, but that is not the case at all. Of course in both East and West the disciples have an incredible ability to rationalize outrageous words and behavior on the part of their so-called gurus.

"Living in the abyss of ignorance, yet wise in their own conceit, the deluded go round and round, like the blind led by the blind" (Mundaka Upanishad 1:2:8). "They be blind leaders of the blind. And if the blind lead the blind, both shall fall into the ditch" (Matthew 15:14) said Jesus, who had surely read (or heard) the Mundaka Upanishad in India.

Some say anyone can practice meditation and some say only initiated persons should meditate as it could be dangerous for some. What is true?

Over half a century of yoga practice and observation of other yogis has demonstrated to me that anyone can practice authentic, traditional yoga safely and with benefit. By "authentic" I mean what is taught in the eleven principal Upanishads (Isha, Kena, Katha, Prashna, Mundaka, Mandukya, Taittiriya, Aitareya, Chandogya, Brihadaranyaka, and Shvetashvatara), the Bhagavad Gita and the Yoga Sutras.

Initiation is not needed to practice such meditation. Other forms such as Tantra are dangerous even for those who receive an initiation into them. That, too, I have seen for half a century.

To someone who wrote asking about involvement in an avocation for the enjoyment of it.

Our lives are an unimaginably complex system composed of innumerable influences. Any simplistic view or opinion must by its very nature be irrelevant and often (usually) wrong. Karma is an irrevocable and all-encompassing law. Nothing can be done that is not in our karmic store, and nothing can be avoided that is. Certainly karma can be mitigated or altered, but it rarely is because the question does not arise until it is too late, anyway.

So we can all say: My Karma Made Me Do It. Especially when we realize that karma is purely psychological, not an outside force except in the sense that all things are external to our true Self, the spirit.

My advice is to enjoy your abilities and interests. Being creative and constructive is manifesting our divine image.

I am looking for a type of meditation that focuses on the heart in order to attain pure love: a loving path, a way to be purified in heart as Jesus said. Can you help me in this?

It is important to realize that the heart is not a place in the body, but rather is all-pervading spirit-consciousness which certainly includes the heart region and even the physical organ, but is actually infinite in its potential.

All authentic yoga leads to the heart, for the heart is everything. Love is the very Consciousness of God. This is why Paramhansa Yogananda said that yoga must be practiced with devotion, the practice itself being a gift of loving aspiration toward God.

Please help me: In some religions if one commits a sin and then sincerely asks for forgiveness the same is granted. On the other hand in the Hindu philosophical thought, one has to keep on being reincarnated until all the Karmas have borne their fruits. How do we reconcile this?

Karma is a law: whatever we sow we reap—for every action there is an equal and opposite reaction. That is the way the universe is set up. However, we need to understand the nature of karma. Karma is not some blind force set loose in the universe. Rather, karma is totally psychological.

The acts we do condition the mind, which is really a field of vibrating energy. Negative actions create negative conditions in the mind, and positive actions create positive conditions in the mind. As a result, negative karmas can be mitigated or wiped out completely by positive actions, especially in the spiritual realm: meditation, prayer, worship, almsgiving and good deeds of many sorts. Of course they must be done with the right disposition and intention—not as a bribe to placate God or the gods. The heart must be pure in its intent. Only then can the defiled mind become pure through such tapasya.

In the Gita Lord Krishna tells us: "If even an evildoer worships Me single-heartedly, he should be considered righteous, for truly he has rightly resolved. Quickly he becomes a virtuous soul and goes to everlasting peace. Understand: no devotee of Me is ever lost. Truly, those who take refuge in Me even though they be from wicked origins, they also attain the Supreme Goal. Having come to this impermanent and unhappy world, devote yourself to Me. With mind fixed on Me, devoted, worshipping, bow down to Me. Thus steadfast, with Me as your supreme aim, you shall come to Me" (Bhagavad Gita 9:30-34).

Please study the Gita daily. There you will find the highest truth set forth in a totally practical manner.

Do you think people somehow ever meet again after passing?

Yes, we do meet again in various ways. Sometimes we see the departed, sometimes we may hear their voice, sometimes ideas or memories pop into our minds that are definitely from them, and sometimes we feel their presence.

Even more significant, often our lives are influenced by them, by events that take place which are life-changing. My life was totally changed by my grandmother on the anniversary day of her passing. Later she came and told me where she was going to be reborn and who her parents would be. When I went near her expectant mother, her presence was remarkably strong.

Our monastery's "life" was greatly changed throughout some years after the passing of one of our monks, and I fully believe that it was all his doing "from the other side."

And of course we often meet again in subsequent lives.

Life itself is much more interesting than most people realize!

We seek the intervention of the gods and goddesses to alleviate our sufferings or to seek boons. Isn't this in violation of the law of karma?

No. Seeking the intervention of the gods and goddesses to alleviate our sufferings or to seek boons is a legitimate application of the law of karma. All actions are karma and have results. Praying, worshipping and making offerings to God, gods, goddesses and holy people are holy actions that create merit (punya–positive karma) which can invoke blessings in the form of various beneficial responses.

What is your opinion on ghosts? Are they departed spirits or something else?

The word "ghost" comes from the German *geist* which simply means "spirit." Certainly spirits can be seen and sometimes communicated with. (The wisdom of that is debatable.) There are many kinds of spirits, some of which are departed human beings, and they are "ghosts." However, other kinds of spirits can be seen. There are animal spirits, nature spirits and spirits that wander in from other worlds or dimensions and get trapped here.

Some spirits are positive, some negative and some neutral. Sri Ramakrishna said to a young man who was a spiritualist medium: "My boy, if you think of ghosts you will become a ghost; if you think of God you will become God. Which do you prefer?"

It is good to not get too involved with spirits, especially those that are earthbound and seek help. There is some kind of "spook network" that passes around the word if you help a spirit, and others start showing up and asking for help. One time I helped some spirits in a local cemetery, and the next time I went to a church in a distant city, the president of the church committee who had just left his body came right up to me and said: "Do for me what you did for those people in the cemetery." If you are not careful you will be drawn into unwise or too much contact with spirits. I had to learn when to say No. Pray for troubled or wandering spirits and then let the matter rest. You must always be very cautious regarding contact with spirits lest you become distracted and over-involved with them. Sometimes you have to be very firm about not doing so. I speak from experience.

I am a Hindu but am confused about our gods and goddesses. Who are they?

The words god (deva) or goddess (devi) can mean different things:
1. Those highly evolved beings who rule or direct natural forces on the material plane, such as Indra, Surya, Vayu, Varuna, etc.
2. Highly evolved beings who rule or direct the worlds beyond this earth.
3. Those divine forms through which the Absolute (Parabrahman) has appeared and communicated with human beings, such as Brahma, Vishnu, Shiva, Lakshmi, Saraswati, Durga, Kali and others who are recorded in the Puranas and other scriptures.
4. Avatars of the foregoing deities, such as Rama, Krishna, Sita, Radha and others whose lilas are also found in the Puranas and other scriptures.

The main question to ask ourselves is: Who Am I? When that is known, everything is known.

In response to someone who wrote about spontaneous knowledge of yoga and various experiences resulting from yoga sadhana or spontaneously, "out of the blue."

As you have seen for yourself, yoga practice itself becomes the yogi's teacher, as both Vyasa and Shankara wrote in their commentaries on the Yoga Sutras.

The yogi must pay attention to his experiences, and at the same time must question them. The basic thing to ask is: "Did this experience strengthen my spiritual life?" If Yes, then it was real and of value. If not, and it was just a curiosity, then even though it may have been an indication of general development, it was of no great value.

An authentic and meaningful experience imparts understanding of itself. When the yogi does not understand what has happened to him, he need not reject the experience, but should just file it away in his memory in case it becomes clear in the future. But until then it can safely be forgotten.

It is extremely chancey to tell one's experiences to others, since they are profoundly individual and it is not likely that others will understand them or have anything significant to say. They may even misunderstand and misdirect the yogi.

As to how/why you spontaneously came to know about Yoga, God is the prime factor, and past life practice and knowledge are involved, too.

It is pure ignorance to insist that things can only happen in one pre-approved way. Everything in the universe is individual, thank heaven (who made it that way). My beloved friend, the yoga-siddha Sri Dattabal, who worked miracles in his infancy, asked many yogis about his experiences and none of them could tell him anything. Finally he met Anandamayi Ma and she understood everything and explained everything. But he could have managed very well if he had not met someone who understood and explained. Yet it is nice to know.

You and God seem to have been doing pretty well together so far.

To someone who wrote about recent prophecies regarding the world and the destinies of nations.

Personally, I never pay much attention to prophecy because I have seen that even very special people can get it wrong.

Paramhansa Yogananda made prophecies that never came true. One example was his prophecy made to Sister Meera who was in charge of the Hollywood Cafe. He told her in detail of a time when she would have to contend with people picketing the restaurant because only monastics worked there and they did not hire "real" people who thereby earned money. She is no longer in the body and the café is long closed. Nothing like his prediction ever happened. Yet during World War II he made a prophecy to her about huge buildings one day being built on the three corners next to the Hollywood Center. It happened just as he said. In fact, in 1961 I was living across the alley from the church when the prophecy was fulfilled by the Kaiser Foundation.

William Branham the great healer whom I personally saw work astounding miracles, made many predictions based on his visions, and not a one came true.

Swami Swarupananda, when he was in charge of the Delhi Anandamayi Ashram told of ancient prophecies of world cataclysm that he had read in manuscripts written by renowned sages that even gave the approximate dates. Nothing whatsoever came true.

The Bhrigu Samhita, an ancient, gigantic "library" of prophecies in India, makes absolutely accurate predictions and absolutely inaccurate predictions. It is really hit or miss.

Anandamayi Ma made predictions that never came true. Yet she made a couple of predictions to me about my personal life and they happened exactly as she said.

Edgar Cayce's world prophecies were worthless but his diagnoses were one hundred percent right.

Why is this? I really do not know. Totally correct prophecies are very rare indeed.

This I do know: karma and reincarnation are absolutes and the wise seek through yoga to neutralize them and attain liberation. So I try to act on that and keep that perspective always.

How would you describe what it was/is that Christ truly taught the people of the Middle East, Kashmir and India about how to lead a truly authentic spiritual life? Is it still valid in modern times?

The main purpose of our website is to show that Jesus lived in India for many years, then returned to Israel as a missionary of the religion he became part of in India: that eternal truth known as Sanatana Dharma. After his resurrection he returned to India and lived there many years.

Saint Thomas, his "twin," also lived in India, first in the Himalayas and then in the southern tip of India, the modern state of Kerala. He, too, professed and taught Sanatana Dharma, which is just as viable today as it was the first time the sages of India received it in direct revelation from Parabrahman, the Absolute. That is why it is called the Eternal Dharma/Religion. It is pure spiritual mathematics applicable to all who aspire to total consciousness in union with that Absolute. It alone is Universal Religion.

Sri Ramakrishna said: "All the religions of the world have come into existence through the will of God, and all will cease to exist through

His will. But the religion of India will never cease to exist, for it alone is the Sanatana [Eternal] Dharma."

If pure consciousness is all and everything, how do the "I" and "mine" arise?

This is the effect of Maya. But how can Maya affect that which is pure consciousness? It cannot, but it can affect that which is energy. Our body, feelings, emotions, sensory mind and intellect are all formed of vibrating energy, and as a result can be affected and even modified. The mind, as we can observe, can be totally deluded.

So the question arises: How does pure consciousness come into contact with and seemingly touch and experience energy-maya? That is the subject of the Shiva Sutras, a major treatise of Kasmir Shaivism which is carved in stone in two places in Kashmir. I recommend that you obtain the commentary on the Shiva Sutras by I. K. Taimni which is entitled: *The Ultimate Reality and Realization*. Then if you want to go deeper, *Shiva Sutras, the Yoga of Supreme Identity*, by Jaideva Singh, is quite valuable.

But in the final analysis, only the accomplished yogi will ever really know the answer to these questions through his own experience.

To someone who asked about the astral plane and the hells it contains.

The earth plane and the astral plane are mirror images of one another. Just as there are places on this earth that are hells, heavens and in-be-tweens (mixed), in the same way in the countless levels of the astral plane there are hells, heavens and mixed levels, including worlds that are virtually identical to this world in many aspects. Just as life in this world is determined by karma, so is life in the astral world. Whichever world we enter at death is a matter of our level of consciousness and also our karma, because our actions are a manifestation of our level of consciousness. It is all interdependent.

The way to not go to hell is to not have a hellish mind and heart, but a heavenly mind and heart. This is totally determined by us. Those who meditate, study spiritual wisdom and follow only positive ways of life will become literally "too good for hell" and go to heaven–which is only a way station on the path to realization of our divine Self.

Who or What is Ishwara?

Ishwara means "God" or "Lord" in the sense of the Supreme Power, Ruler, Master, or Controller of the cosmos. "Ishwara" implies the powers of omnipotence, omnipresence, and omniscience.

Ishwara is the aspect of God whom the Gospels call "the Only-be-gotten of the Father." Many holy ones may bear the title Christ, but each is *a* Christ, not *the* Christ. Ishwara is The Christ. Unfortunately Christians get Christ and Jesus confused.

Jesus, Buddha and Krishna were one with the Christ, with Ishwara, and we are all made in the "image" of Ishwara.

Jesus' Aramaic name was Yeshua, and his Hebrew name was Yahoshua. Both are from Yah, which means God the Lord–which is the meaning of Ishwara.

Jesus became a Nath Yogi in India and his spiritual name was Isha Nath. Isha and Nath both mean "Lord."

When joined with other words, Isha often becomes "esh" or "esha." For example: Yogeshwara (Lord of Yogis), Parameshwara (Supreme Lord),

Ganesha (Lord of the Ganas, a kind of spirit), Romeshwar (Lord of Roma, the Divine Mother), etc.

To someone who wrote about what seemed a conflict between yoga philosophy and Advaita Vedanta:

It is important to keep in mind that Advaita Vedanta is not the basis of yoga. In fact they are not really compatible. Rather, Sankhya, the original philosophy of India, is the basis of the Yoga Darshan (Yoga Sutras) of Patanjali, and serious yogis need to be very aware of this. That is why Vyasa speaks of it five times in the Bhagavad Gita and entitled the second chapter "Sankhya Yoga." Yogananda's teaching was always consistent with Sankhya, not Vedanta.

Are angels and archangels real individual consciousnesses, or are they some kind of energy constructs?

In Oriental cosmological view (including that of Christianity, which is an Eastern religion) the individual consciousness evolves from the simplest form of manifested existence, the atom of hydrogen, to the most complex. And that includes angels and archangels, which in India are known as various kinds of devas: gods, gandharvas, apsaras, etc. They are all stages along the way to infinity. Human beings evolve into angels, and angels evolve into archangels, and onward to divine perfection.

There are no human, angelic, archangelic, etc., beings as entities in themselves. Rather, there are spirits (atmas) who are presently evolving through those forms. More simply: there are no beings known as hats, coats, shoes, dresses, and trousers—those are just the clothing assumed

by us humans. In the same way there are only individualized consciousnesses that are clothing themselves in various states of embodiment for
the purpose of evolution. The angelic/archangelic condition is just that:
a condition or state of being which is experienced by the evolving spirit
in its upward passage to divinity.

**It has been my understanding for years that angels are in a
completely different evolutionary stream from that of human
beings–that they have not passed through the evolutionary forms
that lead up to the human form. I have been taught that angels
are of a completely different mode of being than us, and that
their evolutionary paths are irrevocably separate. Could you
comment on this?**

There are throughout the universe–and including our own planet–
numberless types of psychic entities that are evolving along lines of their
very own–beings that shall indeed never be in the human evolutionary
stream. I use the term "psychic entities" to designate beings that have
bodies formed of astral (psychic) energies, rather than material energies.
The term "spirit" is properly applied only to the divine spark within all
beings, rather than to their relative conditions. These range from the
type of entities we call "elementals" to the guides and guardians of plant
and animal life, even up to great entities who look after the welfare of
solar systems. Each of these entities may be given a proper name of their
own, such as sylphs, undines, pixies, kelpies, devas, gandharvas, kinnaras,
etc. Christians tend to lump them all together under the term "angels."
This certainly does no harm, but is not very accurate.

Although there are indeed many "species" of non-physical entities
which dwell within, upon, and above the earth, mostly affecting its
mineral, plant, and non-human life, they are not properly called angels.

Perhaps to use the Sanskrit term *devas* is more appropriate even if not exact. Further, it is true that these residents, though evolving, will never enter into that particular evolutionary current which produces humans and angels. They are nevertheless the moral and spiritual equals of the beings within that current—as are those within all the various evolutionary streams within creation.

Who or what is "Satan"? And "Lucifer?"

Satan is the force of cosmic delusion. But since it is to a great extent the collective energies projected by deluded intelligences (souls), it is also a kind of energy being that has a form of independent (though reflected) consciousness. Those who talk about how "if God did not exist, man would invent him" have intuited a fact. Humans can create thoughtform entities that become energy robots with a dim life and consciousness of their own. Many of the "gods" that have been worshipped through-out history were such creations of human will and consciousness. It is fashionable to sneer at the declaration by Judaism and Christianity that many of the "old" gods were demons, but they were.

Satan is much more powerful than the thoughtform gods, being drawn from countless beings over a vast span of time. Satan can be thought of as an immense blind shark that swims around and intuits who can be engulfed or eaten and perhaps even assimilated in time. In this way it perpetually increases in power and effect. As Frankenstein's monster was composed of parts taken from many bodies, so Satan is also a composite of energies or intelligent beings that are yet somewhat individual though submerged in a collective darkness of consciousness. So Satan is not an individual but a collection of both negative forces and negative trapped souls. This is far more hideous than anything most of us can imagine. This awful conglomerate moves through the universe, both material and psychic, indeed seeking whom it may devour (see I Peter 5:8) or debase. It both knows what it is doing and does not know, since much of its function is subliminal.

Lucifer is an altogether different matter, being a highly evolved creative being—an archangel or prajapati—that has turned negative while maintaining his definition as an individual entity. Since he is in total harmony with the cosmic Satanic force and has for ages added to its power as its agent, he can also be called Satan—just as Jesus "turned, and said unto Peter, Get thee behind me, Satan: thou art an offence unto me: for thou savourest not the things that be of God, but those that be of men" (Matthew 16:23).

What are "demons"?

In ancient Greek, *daimon* simply meant a discarnate intelligence and could be either positive or negative. What we presently call demons, or evil spirits, are fallen (i.e., negative-turned) angels and earthbound human souls—many of whom are under the thrall of other evil entities. There are swarms of these distorted souls that also move here and there seeking whom *they* may devour—that is, dominate and eventually assimilate. They are like gangs of murderers that will to be what they are and yet are at the same time slaves of their commanding masters. We can think of them as divisions of a demonic army.

Just as moths and other insects are drawn to light, so Satan, Lucifer, and the evil spirits are drawn to those whose auras shine forth. And just as the moths smother the flames of lamps and candles, so these beings wish to extinguish the light of souls and seize them in the resulting darkness. Each commander of a demonic platoon wishes to be as God. And the first step is the collecting of souls to rule. Such beings often reveal themselves as gods to those susceptible to contact with them. They can even give benefits and answer the prayers of their devotees, but in time they devour them and possess them through long ages. This is absolutely the situation with the "gods" of Voodoo and its variations. Though in time their slaves escape–for none are "damned" forever–the experience is nonetheless monstrous and traumatic. Those who enter into the path of communication with them shall find it leading into a darkness and agony that is hardly escaped–and for most cannot be escaped at all until the end of the creation cycle. Why does God allow it? Because it is the consequence of free will. We might as well complain about God allowing people who put their hands into fire to be burned. There is no learning otherwise.

So we must learn that defence against such horrible wanderers is necessary for both inner and outer survival. The pretty-think people may not like the truth about these beings, and even deny it. But that only guarantees that they will not have any immunity to their onslaughts. I well remember assisting in the exorcism of a wholistic health center run by a positive-thinking metaphysical church. The entire place was infested with earthbound entities, including a particularly dangerous being that had gotten trapped there. Since the church denied the existence of such beings, how could they deal with them? Consequently this beautiful expensive facility was completely unusable. Within a short time of entering there anyone would leave in fear. As a result they had to call those of us who were too ignorant to know such things did not exist to come and get rid of the non-existent beings. As the little boy says in the folk story: "I was afraid of the ghosts that did not exist!"

Such things do exist, and we who strive for higher life must not naively think that we are thereby automatically protected. We must not make the mistake of the deer in *Bambi* (I am referring to the book, not the movie) who believes that humans are kind and friendly and is shot trying to get near them. Sincerity and good motivation have never shielded anyone from the consequences of folly. Even Jesus would not agree to risk psychic danger when Lucifer urged him to jump off the pinnacle of the Temple (Matthew 4:5-7). The principle not to tempt God by foolhardy confidence is wisdom.

On a cosmic level these entities and forces need to be pushed into "the outer darkness" of chaos where they can harm no one and can in time be healed.

Being miniature universes, we, too, have inner Satan, inner Lucifer, and inner demons–all created by our own negative deeds and thoughts in this and previous lives. They, too, must be "thrust down"–back into the subconscious from which they arise–and be recycled into good forces. Just as in time Satan, Lucifer, and all demons shall be healed and restored to their original state of perfection, so we should be working even now to restore their inner counterparts within ourselves.

Just how and why did Lucifer fall?

As far as the how and why of Lucifer's dilemma: I have no idea about my own "fall," so any speculation on my part about another's fall would be worthless. It happened. I cannot say any more, except that being an Archangel is no big thing on the evolutionary ladder, and Lucifer's situation only proves the statement of one great Master: "Until you are There, you are *not* There." That is, the possibility of reversing the process of evolution is as open to us as is the path of progression. Evolution is really a two-way street. In the ultimate analysis, it is a matter of *will*, which, whether it is exclusively ours or is really God's, is always free. Therefore the option of falling is essential to our freedom to rise.

Then what about Lucifer—is he evolving, too?

Lucifer is still playing the fool, directing other similarly deluded beings in their mutual self-destruction, but in time he will truly come to himself and take the path of return—so the saints and masters have told us. But I do not plan to wait around for the event.

Do animals have souls?

Indeed they do. What is more, so does every living thing upon the earth, including plants and stones. Actually, every single atom that exists bears within itself a spark of the divine consciousness that we call "a soul." Thus, every atom is a "person" in its own right—or, more correctly, every atom is the vehicle of a soul that is beginning its evolution. It will pass through gas, mineral, plant, animal, and human forms in a series of countless rebirths until the soul is evolved beyond the earth plane and ascends to continue its evolution in higher and higher realms of existence until it attains the capacity for infinite consciousness. Thus everything around us is alive and evolving and must be respected and treated accordingly.

Where do animals go after death?

They usually fall asleep for a very short period of astral rest and then reawaken in another incarnation. When they draw near to human form, however, they spend longer times in certain astral regions where they experiment with being human. That is, they take on temporary human forms and learn to function in them. This is of course done under the guidance of those angelic guardians who foster the evolution of lower forms to higher. On occasion animals remain "earthbound" for a while, usually because of attachment to their "owners." Thus they may be heard barking, meowing, or whatever for some time after their death. Incidents have been recorded of disembodied animals defending or warning their former owners in time of danger.

Do animals reincarnate?

Absolutely–according to the principles I have already outlined. There are many instances of such reincarnations, and I have myself met rein-carnated animals whom I had known in their previous lives. And we *both* knew it was a reunion.

Does God love animals as much as humans?

Yes, for they are His immortal children, dreaming that they are animals until after passing through many forms they shall awaken and be with Him, "gods with God." In truth, there is not an atom that God does not love with an infinite love, a love that is itself the force of evolution, the call to come back to their Origin for a perfect union of Love which is God Himself.

Therefore we should indeed love animals and not eat them. They are our brothers and sisters, evolving just as are we. To destroy their innocent bodies for the sake of food (Romans 14:20) is a crime against our and their nature.

If we are all evolving, including animals, how do they fit into this statement? Will they be humans at some time in their evolution?

When the individual consciousness comes forth from the Absolute it begins as a single atom of hydrogen, moves upward in evolution through mineral, plant, animal, human, angelic, archangelic forms, and beyond. We have all lived in each animal form upon the earth in turn as we worked up to human life. And now we are hopefully growing beyond even that.

Yes, those divine sparks that are now manifesting in animal form are destined to become human beings one day. Morally and spiritually they are even now our equals, our brothers and sisters. Therefore to exploit and injure them is a crime against Life itself.

How well I remember my first lessons in these truths when I was in India nearly forty years ago. I was staying at the school founded in Ranchi by Paramhansa Yogananda. One morning I went with a young man to gather flowers for the early morning worship. There was a particularly fine marigold on a tall plant. "Here, pick this one," I told him. "No!" he replied. "It is the only bloom on the plant, and if I pluck it the plant will cry." I am glad to say that I did not think he was silly, but realized that what he said was true. Some weeks later I was helping in the cleaning and decorating of the Guru Mandir for the celebration of Christmas. I lifted a picture off its nail, and out ran a lizard (gecko). I jumped back and expressed disgust. Wonderingly, one of the men said to me: "But he is a Son of God, too."

Swami Vivekananda in his American lectures would often tell the people: "The lowliest worm is the brother of the Galilean [Christ]," and his pseudo-Christian hearers would run for the exits! Naturally they could not endure the truth that they were enslaving, killing, wearing, and eating the brothers of Christ and themselves. And now they are killing their own unborn and those whose hearts they want for transplants. What goes around truly does come around.

What do you think about astrology?

All that exists, despite the appearance of multiplicity, is really ONE in a very real and practical sense. And in every part the Whole is contained. Thus there is no possibility of separating ourselves from the universal life of creation except through transcendence. But until that transcendence occurs we must acknowledge our integral existence with all that "is." And part of that existence is the phenomenon of change wrought by the invisible tides of life.

Long before recorded history the wise observed that the human being was a miniature universe, a reflection of creation. Further observance revealed that changes in the external world–including the solar system–corresponded to changes in the individual's sphere of life. This was particularly noted in the matter of planetary movement. Thus it was discovered that the movements of the planets within the solar system corresponded to operations of biomagnetic and psychic forces within the individual person that were then reflected outward into the individual's environment or daily life routine.

The ancients understood that the planets were not the *causes* of the observed changes, but were merely indicators of forces operating deep within the magnetic levels of universal life. Further, the ancients understood that these magnetic fluxes produced a tendency toward certain conditions, or a state of favorability for the development of certain situations or conditions, but they did not believe that they were inexorable or unavoidable causes of those effects. The movements of the planets revealed the likelihood of certain effects, but not their inevitability. Therefore those who studied the movements of the planets were in no way fatalistic about their seeming foreshadowings. Rather, the movements of the stars were simply looked upon as indicators that certain times were more favorable for certain results and less favorable for others. And that is all. The fatalistic attitude that some people have mistakenly adopted in modern times was unknown.

The movements of the planets mostly indicate the character of prevailing biomagnetic influences–energies that are only slightly more subtle than purely physical forces. Most of the world's population is enmeshed in and controlled by such gross powers, although those who cultivate spiritual consciousness become less and less affected by those forces.

Consequently astrology can be used to comprehend what forces are moving within the collective psyche of "the masses." For example, we can certainly gauge the tendencies of national or international politics or economics by means of astrology. I well remember going to the First Temple and College of Astrology in Los Angeles every week to learn the world news of the coming week! In the class on Mundane Astrology, the astrological aspects of the previous week would be considered, and the accuracy of the predictions given at the previous class would be undeniably evident. Then, having seen that we had every reason to trust in the accuracy of her analysis, the instructor would proceed to reveal the major events of the next seven days. Only the most determined bigot could have failed to see that astrology was a viable science.

Astrology may be used to discover the hidden mechanisms of the personality. A wise parent should have a child's horoscope drawn up as soon after birth as possible, for it can be an invaluable guide to the parents in caring for their new charge. The horoscope will show the tendencies the child has brought over from its previous births and which are the seeds that are meant to germinate and come to fruition in the new life. But this is not meant to be accepted fatalistically or slavishly. Rather, the positive tendencies are to be cultivated to the optimum and the negative tendencies mitigated to the minimum.

What is going on with the channeling phenomenon that seems to expand almost daily? Do high beings of light ever speak through human beings? What is the value (if any) of their so-called "wisdom" and predictions? Are these False Prophets, like it speaks of in the Bible?

The question of "channeling" is not a simple one because under that single term there may occur several differing phenomena: 1) a conscious tapping into the knowledge of the Higher Self through which a person can "read" the cosmos; 2) direct inspiration from the Higher Self; 3) direct inspiration from another being; 4) mediumistic or shamanistic "control" by another entity; 5) simple fakery.

Let us take each one in turn and examine it.

Number One is rare because it takes a great degree of purification for the mind to be able to catch in an undistorted manner–and without interpretation interpolated by the "rational" mind–the subtle perceptions that take place on the level of the Higher Self. Those who have this ability do not make it public, so you can be sure that those who claim to do so really cannot! Moreover, no one who uses the "four soul killers"–meat, nicotine, alcohol, and mind-altering drugs–is capable of this at any time.

Number Two is possible, but only takes place within the context of the individual's spiritual life and is never "done" for others.

Number Three is very possible, but again when it is positive and reliable it takes place only for the assistance of the individual, and not for someone to communicate to another. Obsession by negative spirits and the psychic invasion of another's mind are both possible and greatly prevalent. One spiritual teacher of the East who has great experience with combatting negative psychic forces told a friend of mine that virtually every person living in the West–and the United States specifically–is obsessed to some degree by one or more negative entities. This is a terrible thought, but my personal observation confirms it. Those who make a public thing of relaying messages from invisible beings are likely harming both themselves and those who listen to them with faith.

Number Four is prevalent also and is *always* evil. You ask in your letter: "Do high beings of light ever speak through human beings?" The answer is: *Never.* For to do so the entity would have to invade and actually displace the individual, pushing him out of his body. This is a terrible thing to do, as it greatly harms the medium. Those great ones who have a message for humanity either appear objectively and speak their message, or they take human birth and live among us and teach us. But the lying or ignorant entities cannot–nor do they want to, for they have contempt for the human status, however noble their "channeled" words may be. A fundamental principle is enunciated by Saint Paul: "The spirits of the prophets are subject to the prophets" (I Corinthians 14:32). That is, a person with positive psychic abilities is always in control, and never relinquishes that control to anyone. A being that would seize control of another's body and will is never positive, but a being of darkness and destruction. This is without exception.

It is true that "tramp souls" do invade unsuspecting people, and even pretend to be great masters and figures from history (if they told their real identity the game would be up). They mix truth in with their error, using it as bait to convince those who are cautious that they are reliable. They continually speak "wisdom"–but what profit does it bring their hearers? It is not intellectual teaching we need, but practical instruction in spiritual development. A true master shows others how to become masters themselves rather than wasting their time with endless revelations that have no practical application. "Channeled" books and messages are classical examples of this useless verbiage.

There are various types of false prophets, and "channelers" are one type, though many of them are sincere people who, because of their own negative karmas, are themselves as deceived as their hearers.

Do you think Jesus is God or the Son of God, or God the Father or God the Son?

God is One. Yet from the spiritual viewpoint we also perceive a Trinity within the Unity. God in His transcendental, unknowable, inconceivable aspect is the "Father." That is, He is unknowable and inconceivable and incommunicable to the limited human intellect. He can be known directly, without the intermediary of any internal or external faculty through a union of love, for the soul has originally come from Him (the "Bosom of the Father") and must return to Him. We receive our being from Him—indeed, we are a part of Him, as the wave is part of the ocean, yet cannot claim to be the ocean. God, immanent in creation as its manifester and guiding consciousness, is the "Son." God, the dynamic power which manifests as the great wave of intelligent energy we know as the universe or "matter" is the Mother, the Holy Spirit. Yet, they are really One.

Jesus Christ was Adam, the first human being in this creation cycle. (See *Robe of Light*.) Having become one with God in his aspect as the "Son," he did not pass on into the Bosom of the Father, but came back to earth as an incarnation-reflection of the Son of God to repair the evil he had wrought as Adam. Yet, he himself said: "I and my Father are one" (John 10:30), and: "He that hath seen me hath seen the Father" (John 14:9). This is because the distinctions are only in our eyes. The Unity alone is real.

So, in brief we would say: Jesus Christ is God. We do not try to understand it, but rather strive to attain the same status he had. Then we will be it, and will not need to understand it.

Is the incarnation of God, such as was expressed through Jesus, an event that is singular throughout all of history, i.e., an event that took place once only? Or is it possible that God will assume another incarnation, even need to assume another, at another point in history?

First we should realize that an incarnation of God is not the infinite God born upon earth, but rather a totally liberated and perfected being–a siddha–who is born of his own will in human form. Since such a person is absolutely one with God, he can be called an incarnation of God.

In contrast to the dogmatizing of professional and amateur religionists, knowers of God assure us that there have been many incarnations of God upon the earth throughout the history of the human race. (What is more, incarnations of God occur in the higher worlds, as well.) And there shall be future divine incarnations as long as there is a human race. A person who feels that he cannot believe in an incarnation unless that incarnation is the one and only is like a man who cannot love his wife unless he is convinced she is the only female human being on the earth. Both views are foolishness.

Avatars (to use the Sanskrit term) do not come to earth for the vague purpose of somehow uplifting humanity and "saving" sinners. Rather, they come with the intention enunciated by Saint John the Beloved at the beginning of his Gospel: "To as many as received Him, to them gave He power to become the sons of God" (John 1:12). That is, an incarnation of God manifests upon the earth for the purpose of establishing a repository of spiritual power which will outlast his physical lifetime, and will bring salvation to future generations. Sometimes the avatar establishes a new religion upon the earth, and sometimes he regenerates a religion whose inner power has waned or even been lost. In the case of Jesus of Nazareth, the Christ, a storehouse of power–the Church–was established which was to be a haven for those adherents of the ancient mysteries of the Mediterranean world which had lost their deifying power. I use the word "deifying" because "salvation" is not having our sins forgiven or escaping a miserable afterlife in hell, but rather it is freedom–freedom from all ignorance, and therefore from all necessity of further birth-manifestations in this lowest of planes of existence and in all other higher planes of existence as well. Salvation is the return of the individual spirit into the bosom of the Father from whence it came, and within which it has existed eternally.

Since human beings are what they are, in time the spiritual power so brought to earth becomes dimmed, distorted, and (often) eventually lost. Therefore the avatars must come again and again to establish "the power to become the sons of God" among men.

Are there ever female incarnations (avatars)?

Except in extremely rare instances, divine incarnation usually takes place in a dual manifestation–that is, in both male and female forms. In the fourteenth century, in the controversy surrounding the Hesychast fathers of Mount Athos and their defender Saint Gregory Palamas, it was established as an irrevocable part of Eastern Christian theology that God, though one, has–from our standpoint at least–a dual nature: essence and energies. This teaching was not new to Christianity, but had never before needed official expression and approbation. In Hinduism this duality is also to be found–that is, that God consists of two aspects, divine consciousness and divine creative power–Purusha and Prakriti. For this reason, also in Hinduism, every male deity representing the infinite guiding consciousness behind the universe also has a female consort who represents the limitless field of conscious energy that is manifesting as the universe over which the Lord presides. Since the individual souls manifest and evolve within this great energy and are ultimately "born" out of it into the realm of pure consciousness, that energy field is called "Mother," as distinguished from the "Father" of pure consciousness. All creation is looked upon as both the Mother and Her evolutionary "womb." Thus, there are virtually as many incarnations of God in female form as there in male form. (Although rare, sometimes there has been an incarnation in female form without the male counterpart.)

In Christianity, this divine duality is manifested and symbolized through Jesus Christ and the Virgin Mary. Usually the male incarnation marries his female counterpart, but because of Jesus' unique spiritual mission—as well as the symbology which was to unfold through his life-drama—the divine power (also known as the Holy Spirit) was first born on earth and became his Virgin Mother.

The true purpose of divine incarnation is to show us our own face—to awaken us to the fact that we are ourselves incarnate gods—and to impart the power to manifest that truth.

I myself began using Buddhist meditation to enhance my own spiritual life as a Christian. At first I was afraid that I was being heretical, but the balance and joy I have gained has made my life so rich, and the sutras as well as the Hindu Upanishads are incredibly poetic and they do not contradict the Bible. I am defending myself so I obviously still feel a residue of guilt. But I love these books and I really enjoy meditating.

Since Jesus said that the kingdom of God is within, no inner search, according to a valid tradition, can possibly be heretical. Also, we have all practiced many religions from life to life and it is only right to feel an affinity for some if not all of the non-Christian traditions. We sometimes take up practices from those religions because of this intuitive familiarity.

Certainly the Hindu and Buddhist scriptures do not contradict the Bible, because Moses was an initiate of the Mysteries which originated in India, as was Jesus. Jesus quoted from the Bhagavad Gita, Upanishads, and Dhammapada in his teachings. Many verses that narrow-minded Christians like to quote (sometimes to prove that their religion alone is true) are directly from these sources. Some of the Psalms and the prophetic books of the Old Testament contain parallels to passages from the scriptures of India. As Saint Augustine wrote: "The identical thing that we now call the Christian religion existed among the ancients and has not been lacking from the beginning of the human race until the coming of Christ in the flesh, from which moment on the true religion, which already existed, began to be called Christian."

There has been a lot of talk about the "Second Coming" of Christ. But according to my study (and my limited understanding) my opinion for the last few years has been that the coming of Christ is an event more on the subjective level. The more we grow spiritually and become renewed and transformed, the Spirit of Christ grows within us, transforming the individual from the inside out. It is almost a metabolic change until even the very cells of our physical body are "Christified." This event is what I perceive to be the coming of the Lord. We [ourselves] are the next coming of Christ—the evolution of the spirit and soul and body of humanity—transforming us in the alchemists' sense from base lead or clay into gold, the divine nature of God. Is this a proper view? None of my friends agree with me.

Not only is your view "proper," it is one hundred percent correct, and your expression of it is really fine.

There are a some points I would like to expand on, however, that you might find meaningful.

The word translated "coming" is the Greek term *parousia* which means simply "presence," with the connotation of an advent. The first Coming of Christ was external and historical. But the sole purpose of that first Coming was to open the way that would in time lead to the true Second Parousia which is a completely individual, mystical experience of our own Christhood.

The descriptions given in the Bible of the "resurrection" and "judgement" are symbolic indications of the final process of transformation when, as you have said, the alchemy becomes complete and the lead of earthly life becomes transmuted into the gold of higher life, the original Paradisiacal status of the human being. And beyond that there is much more to come as we pass "from glory to glory."

When Jesus was asked if there were few that were saved (Luke 13:23), he said that indeed it was few only who were saved. But by salvation Christ meant this divine transmutation. Moreover, he did not say that only a few would be saved, but that in each generation only a few attained this condition, the others still being compelled to return through rebirth until they, too, became one of the saved few in a future generation.

Finally, it is true that Jesus Christ will come to earth again. But he will not drop out of the sky with a trumpet blast as the physically dead pop up out of the grave like toast as most Christians think. Rather, he will be born in Israel and this time be recognized as the Messiah.

A biblical passage which has long troubled me is that of the account of Jesus' casting of the devils into the swine, found in three of the Gospels. It troubles me on two accounts: One, I think that this and other such passages in the Bible seem to view animals as things and present a moral justification for the hideous

cruelties practiced upon animals; and, two, a God Whose love extends to only one species–ours–is not the God I know outside the Bible. This really has been a source of minor torment to me–it seems like some sort of fatal flaw in the character of Jesus–this uncaring attitude toward the pigs. Please comment on this.

I will make some observations on this incident in the life of Jesus, but they can only be speculations, for they deal with a person beyond my ability to gauge.

To exorcise evil spirits–that is, to expel them from a person or place– only to have them go somewhere else and perhaps work even worse things, is certainly not wise. All human beings have exorcistic powers that can be employed simply through their will. No special spiritual power is even required. Because of the weakened condition of human beings psychically as well as physically, this power is often not operative. Those with a little bit of spiritual or psychic power can indeed expel an evil entity, but their power stops at the mere expulsion. They have no control over where the entity will go and what it will then do. Great masters like Jesus, on the other hand, realize the need to safeguard the rest of the world, and therefore banish the exorcised spirits beyond the earth plane into that realm of chaos known as "the outer darkness." There the entities remain until, in the next cycle of creation, they will have a chance to normalize themselves and continue on their evolutionary journey.

The spirits knew that Jesus would not allow them to go where they pleased. Not wanting to be exiled into the outer darkness, they therefore begged him to let them go into the pigs that were grazing there. Why did they ask this? Because entities often obsess or possess animals and completely control their behavior. (They often pass into the bodies of those who eat the flesh of those animals, as well.) Thus they remain embodied–though in a non-human form–and continue to "live."

Why did Jesus allow them to go into the pigs? I will give my opinion, but it is only just that. First, by allowing the entities to pass into the pigs,

Jesus demonstrated that demons are real entities and not just superstitious fantasies or states of mental disorder, and that they can and do possess animals and humans. The resulting behavior of the animals when the entities passed into them was a proof both that there were many entities expelled from the man, and also that those entities affected the behavior of those they possessed. In this way Jesus graphically demonstrated the truth of the existence of evil spirits and their capacity to possess.

But there is more to it. The Torah forbade the eating of swine's flesh, and the raising of them for food was a blatant defiance of the Law. Since Israel was a theocracy, we could even say that such activity was illegal. These animals were being raised only for slaughter–and slaughter in the most cruel way, often being skinned alive. To save the animals from this fate and at the same time to prove the reality of spirit possession, Jesus permitted this.

Why did the pigs drown themselves? It is not easy for a soul to possess a body not specifically formed for its habitation. This is why obsession is more common than possession. No matter how intelligent an entity may be, when it intrudes itself into a body it rarely is able to maintain the body's normal bodily functions. This is one of the reasons possessing entities will possess and "dispossess" a human being, giving time for the legitimate soul to heal the damage caused by the invasion. In the New Testament we are told that people can become blind, deaf, or seized by muscular spasms when an entity is in possession. At the expulsion of the entity, the problem immediately leaves. Seizures similar to epilepsy are also manifestations of possession. That is, the legitimate soul is violently reacting inwardly and trying to itself cast out the invader. This conflict produces such spells. Sometimes these seizures are the reaction of the nervous and immune systems to the damage being caused by the intruder. Fevers can also be a response to possession.

Because the entities were obviously not able to control the central nervous system of the pigs, the animals became completely panicked and rushed into the water and drowned themselves. We must remember that pigs are highly intelligent creatures, and they may have known what they were doing. That is, they may have been deliberately drowning themselves to cast off the possession, just as some animals rush into water when they are infested with fleas or other such parasites. In fact, the pigs could have thought that they were experiencing such a physical infestation. However that may be, they were both freed from the possession and from the torturous death that was planned for them. And it is hoped that the swineherds took up a better profession.

A person like Jesus who literally sacrificed his life for the unworthy and the ungrateful was never being cruel or thoughtless in any of his actions. There is of course no reason why we should not inquire into such a person's motivations, however evolved he may be, since those motives may actually teach us spiritual and psychic lessons.

Would you say that all creation is God?

No, I would say the reverse: God is all creation. There is a very basic difference. God is not a sum total of "existing" objects, but the Sole Reality, creation being a momentary appearance for the purpose of our evolution, and destined to be transcended. But please notice, I say "*I* would say...." If you or anyone else wish to express it otherwise, fine, for no verbalization is capable of embracing the full range of What Is. Actually, both statements–all creation is God and God is all creation–are true. What is needed is the understanding that they are not complete and therefore must not be put forth as Absolute Truth. For they are equally as false as they are true, since they are mere intellectual concepts of the inconceivable.

Whenever I ponder an "is it true or not?" type of question, I always remember that Sri Ma Anandamayi, the great spiritual leader of India whom I was privileged to know and associate with for the last nineteen years of her physical embodiment, told her friends when they posed this type of question that in fact both views—like the Taoist symbol of Yin/Yang—contain the truth in seed form. But in conclusion she would always insist that there is a state of being in which such questions can no longer arise, and the attainment of that state is what should mostly occupy our thoughts rather than the puzzling out of the lesser dualities.

Do you believe that there have been other universes than this one in which we now are evolving?

Yes, I personally believe that there have been previous universes and that there will be future ones. The process never began, and it will never end. It simply *is*. God actually breathes himself out as the creation. In India it is likened to a spider spinning its web out of its own body substance. The universe is the Being of God. And from another viewpoint, it is merely a play of shadows on Light, like a motion picture upon a screen.

Do all beings evolve?

Absolutely, all beings sow and reap karma, including angels and archangels. I recommend that you read the chapter in Yogananda's *Autobiography of a Yogi* entitled "The Resurrection of Sri Yukteswar" where it is explained in detail.

Do you believe God is the all-powerful Person? That is, do you believe that God has also a personal feature, a more or less human form, but with all the powers?

God, being the source of all things and attributes, must of necessity possess all things and all attributes. God is totally PERSON. He is not merely "principle," or "being," or "reality," or any such abstractions—though he is the source of those things. In essence he is pure Consciousness. He IS what we ascribe to him rather than possessing traits as surface appearances or adjuncts (*upadhis* in Sanskrit). In other words—in as correct terminology as we can get: God is not omnipotent, omniscient or omnipresent. Rather, he *is* omnipotence, omniscience, and omnipresence. God does not rule or know all things—he is all things. Yet God is also No Thing. That is, he is the eternal subject, never really an object, though it may seem so to our defective spiritual "eyes."

God does not *have* name and form, he *is* name and form. When the purified soul directly has the vision of divine form, it is not to be considered in any way like our present mode of "seeing," nor is that which is perceived to be considered in any way like our earthly form.

The ultimate experience of God is only possible in perfect union of the soul with him. The soul has no senses—indeed needs none. The manner in which it perceives and delights in God is inconceivable to mortal minds. To even speak of either form or formlessness in relation to God is incorrect, as these are attributes which God transcends.

The goal of the soul is not to go to some perfect world which is like the earth except without defects, and there to eternally see God as an object. That is one stage on the path of evolution, but it is an elementary (though a sweet) one. The goal is to attain full union with the Lord, with no intermediary of time, space, or sense. The soul must become naked—that is, it must divest itself of all physical and psychic bodies and senses, and in its essence as pure spirit (and therefore pure consciousness) unite with the infinite source in the most intimate union of love. This is not the union of modern monism (which must not be mistaken for non-dualism which is quite different) in which all distinction is lost and the soul can think it has become the Lord. Rather, it is a union of love wherein the unity itself is a form of relationship, not annihilation.

If we could grasp the nature of this inmost, sacred state with our finite minds it would not be worth attaining. How those souls, made one with the Lord, perceive and communicate with him, living in his life as he lives in them, has never been stated. Nor can it be. To seek to define it is the height of intellectual egotism.

I hope this answer is clear, but I should point out that none of these views are dogmatic–only my personal understanding.

As we evolve, is God also evolving?

God being beyond change, I would not say that he is evolving. But since he has projected himself (or so it seems to our viewpoint) as the evolving universe, and since the evolving consciousnesses are part of his greater Life, then it can be said that he indeed is *experiencing* the process of evolution. But it is important for the individual to know that his evolution is more of a therapeutic appearance than an absolute reality. That is, all of this changing drama is really the dream of God.

Frankly, your writings have me confused. At one time they speak of God as non-dual, impersonal, and formless, and at other times God is spoken of in very anthropomorphic and personal terms. You also seemed to speak disparagingly of monism in a book

**review, but in several places in various publications you advocate
it. Am I really confused, or are you?**

Reading your question there immediately came to mind the response
once made to an inquirer by Sri Ma Anandamayi: "Have you now seen
that no answer is perfect in itself? Wherever there is the questioner and
the answerer, truth cannot be expressed." In other words, where there is
the sense of duality—and that includes the idea of truth and untruth—the
True cannot be either spoken or grasped. But let us analyze your difficulty.

Those who hold to the one-sided view that God is only formless and
disdain those who accept the fact that God is manifest in many—indeed
all—forms, are like the little children in the third grade who sneer at the
second-graders as "babies." After all, they read in the third primer, having
long ago left the second primer behind! Such childishness is rampant
in contemporary religion, especially among theologians—which is to be
expected since the intellect itself is hopelessly childish in its innate egoity.

That Which Is embraces both form and formlessness and exists
outside them both. God manifests as both with and without form in
order to communicate the Divine Essence to the evolving consciousness
according to its evolutionary status. To some, form is most immediately
communicable, and to others it is just the opposite. But we must realize that form and formless are dualities, one of the pairs of opposites
(dwandwas) which must eventually be transcended as the spirit evolves
beyond all relativity. And formlessness is *within* relativity, not *beyond* it,
for it is simply the opposite of form and cannot stand alone. Formlessness implies form—in fact, we cannot grasp the concept of formlessness
without the concept of form. The two are inextricably united, for they
are really one. To speak of accepting one and rejecting the other is as
absurd as attempting to divide heat from fire or wetness from water.

Form and formlessness are the two halves of merely one of the
principles of manifestation—i.e., relativity. However, since that which
manifests is God, then it naturally follows that God is thus both with

and without form to the consciousness that is yet within the realm of manifestation and relativity. Once that state is passed beyond by the perfected consciousness or spirit, the idea and experience of form and formless cannot arise, for no mode of contradiction or duality is any longer possible. In that illumined state neither acceptance nor rejection of anything, including philosophical concepts or principles, is possible, either.

Now, of course, some people do not like to use the term "God" because they feel it implies some limitations or conditioning. But, being limited by our language there really seems no alternative but to use that term. Obviously we are going to have to keep in mind as correct a concept as we can (realizing as well that no concept is complete or perfect) while using limiting terms–including the Vedantic terms such as Brahman or Satchidananda. Words are still just that: words. After all, we need not flatter ourselves, for fewer things are more limited than the intellect with which we love to so pontifically philosophize. This is why the wise remain silent. Wherever we find the noise of philosophical or theological controversy, there we may be sure ignorance is rampant and wisdom will never be triumphant.

No one can really understand these things except through direct experience that far exceeds the mind and intellect. And such experience is impossible within the human status except through perseverance in the practice of valid meditation.

What should be rejected is "unripe" non-dualism or monism which refuses to acknowledge the simple fact that the Sole Reality is immanent in relative existence-creation–indeed is Itself manifest and embodied in and through this relative creation. That being true, then it is certainly possible for It to manifest certain divine forms in order to stimulate the evolving consciousness to further awakening. If God can appear as a grasshopper or a mountain, then God can certainly appear as a "god" or "goddess." And since every particle of every atom maintains its existence and position simply through the conscious will and purview of God, then

God is actually more intensely personal than we can even conceive. And since it is God alone who is manifesting as all human beings through taking on all these forms, a certain degree of "anthropomorphism" is entirely admissible as long as it is held within the wider perspective that also embraces the divine transcendence of form.

How really silly to declare that God is appearing as all transient forms within the universe and then deny the existence and viability of those deific forms which the questing consciousnesses of all ages have perceived. To complacently agree to the existence of gnats and camels as temporarily viable realities–manifestations of the Real–and then shriek that all divine forms and manifestations are lies and inventions of "priestcraft" is to prove oneself a fool of the first order. Why is it only within the realm of religion that the experience of the individual becomes delusion to be rejected and fulminated against? Where now is the "all is One" and "everything reflects the Real" philosophizing upon which we preen our "advanced" selves? What kind of sophistication is that which solemnly affirms the reality and meaningfulness of a mosquito and its bite while denying any such status to the experience and objects of religion and mysticism? I leave it up to you to figure out the motive behind such spiritual and philosophical chicanery.

To sum it all up: God is both with form and formless. And God is also beyond both form and formlessness. Therefore all three: form, formless, and beyond both, are appropriate to affirm, while keeping in mind the realities of the other modes. It is when we declare that one or the other is the only truth–or the "highest truth" with the implication that the other two should be rejected out of hand–that we fall into error. Simplistic thinking in these matters is neither sophisticated nor beneficial. But such thinking is the bane–and the boast–of the Western mind.

What is life in the astral plane like?

There are many levels in the astral world, and they are all much more stable than the earth plane. Spending time in the astral plane is exactly like living within the earth plane, though in some of the higher astral worlds thought is more evidently a force. We are born into those worlds and work out karma in them just as we do here. Of course, there is much more learning done there and some people spend centuries in the astral equivalent of study. The lower astral worlds are so much like the earth that the people even live in buildings and there are changes in weather. In the higher worlds this is not so, and things remain more unvarying. Also, communication becomes increasingly non-verbal as we ascend to higher levels.

Many of the same things that are done on earth are also done in the astral worlds–negative as well as positive. You may remember that Yogananda in his autobiography speaks of wars going on in the astral planes with mantric power being used instead of bombs. The astral world may seem advantageous to our earthbound minds, but in reality it can be a terrible place, being both more intense and more binding than the earth plane.

It is very difficult for people to extricate themselves from astral involvement. This is why many people while incarnated on the earth are addicted to so-called astral travel. I knew one of Yogananda's personal secretaries whom he continually warned against this, but every night she would be "out and about." Many times she was almost destroyed by evil forces, and only the Master's intervention saved her.

Spiritual life can completely come to a standstill if our attention becomes overly focused on psychic and astral phenomena. One very psychic friend of mine told me that the first words she spoke to her guru were: "Can you get me off the astral?" Not all are so wise.

In one of your articles you mention "astral wanderers." A lady I know, who channels, is always talking about wanderers as if they were desirables. That is the only place I ever heard of wanderers, before I saw them mentioned in your book. In your book they seem to be most definitely undesirable. Could you please explain to me exactly what a "wanderer" is?

Not only are astral wanderers undesirable, so also is mediumistic channeling. Naturally, a person who traffics with such spirits will defend them as being good. This is the folly of all spiritualistic or shamanistic practices.

Some astral wanderers are discarnate human beings who, rather than accept their death and continue on their evolution, remain on the earth plane and try to contact human beings and ultimately enter their bodies–even if for only a short period. This is of course both foolish and unethical. Only the lowest, most ignorant, and materialistically-minded beings do this. And, frankly, only those of equally low vibrations (no matter how intelligent or philosophical they may be) wish to invite such beings into their auras or even into their bodies.

Other astral wanderers are entities not in the stream of normal earth evolution whatever, but beings who for some reason or other have wandered into our universe and gotten trapped here. Such entities are, as you can imagine, either very stupid or very evil (since only their karma could produce such a state), and also should be avoided. You will always find that those who use the Four Soul Killers and practice "psychic development" will come under the influence and domination of such beings. This is only to be expected, since their psychic energies are also of a low and deadening type.

What is your view concerning the disposal of a body when someone dies?

As you know, even though the body dies, we do not. Rather, we just step out of the body as we shed our clothing. Yet there is often a connection with our body according to our state of consciousness and (of course) our karma. This being so, relics of the saints convey the spiritual power of their former inhabitants and are very valuable indeed.

But whereas the departed saints affect their former bodies, those who have not attained the status of the saints may have the opposite experience–they are influenced by the condition of their bodies. In fact, many are still so connected with their bodies they remain earthbound and cannot pass on to the astral regions. This is very unfortunate. If, however, the body is dissolved in some manner, any ties with the body are also dissolved and the soul can pass on. This dissolving can take place after a long time of decay (which is why preserving the body is not wise), or by cremation. Cremation is a very wise thing, for it ensures that the departed cannot be bound to the body. Thus it releases them to pass on to higher worlds.

Though you did not ask about it, I would like to point out the importance of prayers for the departed to also help them in their further growth. The departed are aware of those prayers and the love that is expressed through them. Thus we continue through prayer to send our love to those who have physically left us. Moreover, prayers for the dead are a major help in the elimination of grief over the death of those dear to us.

How does someone really know what they want in life? It seems very confusing sometimes, and you can work really hard to achieve something you want very much only to find when you reach the goal or obtain the object you feel disappointment or decide you did not really want it.

How does a person know what they want in life? First we have to realize that we are composed of several layers, inside of which is an eternal spirit which alone is our true Self. But this real Self is covered over by the layers, each of which has its wants and attempts to overshadow all the other levels of our being in order to be the only voice heard. Our body wants comfort and pleasure. Our magnetic, emotional level wants happiness, love, peace, etc. Our lower, sensory mind wants lots of sense experience and distractions. Our higher, intellectual mind wants knowledge in the sense of facts and understanding of external realities. Our will wants power and skill to dominate. Our spirit wants *God*.

Since everything but spirit is merely its clothing, it is only sensible to let the spirit have its way–especially when we realize that the desires of our external levels are for transitory objects that, even if obtained, are swept away by the currents of karma and, ultimately, death. But God lasts forever. Therefore even when we do attain our lesser desires they turn out to be incapable of satisfying us in the long run.

Saint Augustine wrote that our hearts are ever restless until they rest in God. Before that, Jesus said, "Seek the kingdom of God first." And in our own times Sri Ma Anandamayi said: "In Him is everything; Him you must try to find."

It is of course true that we have come into this life with certain karmic destinies in relation to the external world and its population. But even here it is only the freeing of the spirit that can enable us to perfectly fulfill our destiny, whatever it might be.

We must cultivate a taste for God. In India, liver disorders are some-times treated with rock sugar. But to those with diseased livers sugar candy actually tastes bitter, so they do not like the remedy! It is the same with us: we have lost our affinity for the divine, which is our only destiny.

And how shall we develop that taste? Through meditation and a life of spiritual cultivation.

I recently came across a "yoga" system that involves leaving the body and ascending to the higher worlds as its practice. Are you familiar with this approach?

Yes. I think of it as the Up and Out school of meditation. (See *Dwelling in the Mirror*.) The idea that by simply going to higher worlds we will become enlightened is as ludicrous as to assume that by simply journeying to a university we will become educated. Rather, we have first to enter the primary grades, spend time studying there, and work our way upwards. What is necessary for us is to attain the necessary evolution required in this world for our graduation to the higher worlds. There we work on our evolution until qualified to move upward into even higher worlds. And so it goes, from rung to rung of the ladder until we can return to the Absolute from which we first came forth. "He that… climbeth up some other way, the same is a thief and a robber" (John 10:1), according to Jesus.

I recently read a question submitted to a meditation master. The inquirer said that whenever he meditates he leaves his body and floats up near the ceiling. He asked what he should do about this. The meditation master's answer was: "Go on through the ceiling." Will you comment on this?

It is extremely difficult, and therefore extremely rare, for an individual to leave the body before death. It is unfortunately true that some persons unnaturally force this ability, which carries over into subsequent lives so that a person leaves his body involuntarily while sleeping. I have known more than one person who has suffered in this life from this involuntary astral travel.

Am I saying that the man does not leave his body and float up to the ceiling? No; but I am saying that it is extremely unlikely. Is he hallucinating, then? Chances are not. Within our psychic bodies there are many points of perception. It is not at all uncommon for the beginning meditator's focus of consciousness to become shifted into one of his psychic bodies during meditation and thus to begin seeing through the "eyes" of that body—which can extend some distance beyond the physical body. It is this shift which also produces such sensations as expanding, rising, moving forward or backward, and such like. One of the most dramatic effects of this shift is for a person to experience himself as being many feet up in the air and to look down and see his body sitting below in meditation. For one who does not understand, this is naturally a very frightening experience. But it is nothing harmful at all. Therefore, it is most likely that the inquirer who thinks that he is floating up near the ceiling is actually moving into the awareness of his subtle bodies which extend out far beyond the physical body. In other words, he is experiencing one of his astral or causal bodies. This is actually quite normal, though not necessarily of any particular value. But he is not really outside his body.

It is also possible for the meditator to experience standing outside his body during the meditation period and even walking around and viewing it. He is not really doing so, but is simply looking through the "eyes" contained within his subtle levels. So if the inquiry had been directed to me, I would have explained it as I have now done, and assured the man that he was in no danger of flying away and getting lost in the cosmos. It is not so easy!

The second American to become a disciple of Paramhansa Yogananda was a young man named Warren Vickerman. "Vickie" became a highly developed yogi, and for many years led the Self-Realization Fellowship center in New York City. This naturally entailed his meeting many seekers and often becoming their advisor. Much like Yogananda's guru, Swami Yukteswar Giri, Vickie had little patience with nonsense, earthly or psychic. One day a woman came to him in great distress. "Oh! What shall I do? Every time I start to meditate I fly up astrally out of my body and hit my head on the ceiling!" Vickie looked at her with a glint in his eye and then said forcefully: "Lady, when you are in that state there *is* no ceiling!"

What are UFO's and are they connected with spiritual life in any way? I have heard people say that beings of light, be they Masters or whatever, will lift the "lightworkers" from the earth during cataclysmic earth changes. I don't know what to make of this idea or of how real the "contact" experience seems to be to those who claim to have had one.

There is no reason to disbelieve that there is intelligent life of many forms in the universe. As to whether or not UFO's are from other planets, I really cannot say, through it certainly is possible. Since each planet has its own scheme of evolution, one thing sure is that cross-pollination is not possible, therefore contact with these beings would be of little profit—perhaps even detrimental. What about those who tell of their contacts? I simply do not know. I have seen UFO phenomena myself, but it has never seemed relevant to me or my personal spiritual growth, so I have not pursued the subject. I do feel that many "contactees" are having psychic/astral experiences rather than actual physical contact. And all of the descriptions I have read (and that is a limited amount) seem either negative, false, or irrelevant.

It is remarkable that those who feel they have grown beyond the Fundamentalist Protestant teaching of "the Rapture" so unquestioningly accept the "beam me up Scotty" eschatology of the New Age! It is just another manifestation of the delusive insistence that an external force can intervene and save us from the consequences of our own doing. Karma is never evaded—it is either reaped or dissolved by us through interior illumination. The real "space brothers" we need to be interested in and involved with are the saints and angels of God whose work is to help us find our way through the labyrinth of earthly life and evolve beyond the necessity for rebirth.

When I listen to people on TV that talk to spirits that have passed on, they say that we chose to come back as who we are in this life, so that almost sounds like it was a script we chose to live out. That seems to be that it was all written and what happens is predisposed.

We do indeed determine what each life is going to be *in a general way*. For reincarnation does not stand alone. In fact, it is not an entity unto itself, but is the result of *karma*, the law that "whatsoever a man soweth, that shall he also reap" (Galatians 6:7). So every time we are about to reincarnate we look at our karmic balance sheet and decide just what karmas–good and bad–shall be reaped in the next life. It is rather like plotting a drama in which we are going to be the star. Having outlined the play, we then work on our costume: the kind of body we are going to have; and the sets: the kind of place we are going to live in, who our families are going to be, and what kind of people will surround us. But all this is just the framework. Within that framework our free will, and that of those involved in our life, determines most of what goes on with us–especially inside us. And since even the framework is of our own construction, that too is completely a matter of free will, actually. Destiny is simply the free will we have already set in motion.

The famous French playwright, Moliere, did not write out the dialogue of his plays. Instead he wrote the plot–divided into scenes and acts–on a big blackboard which the actors read and then went out and improvised. After each performance they discussed how it had gone and made changes in the plot outline and refined the dialogue. When they felt it was as good as it could be, it was all written down with stage directions and printed for others to act from. This is very much like our life as we live out performance after performance through reincarnation.

Let me give some examples of karma. If we are meant to be the renowned leader of a great army, it is a pretty safe bet that we will have to choose to be a man. And our male body will have to be healthy. If we are meant to fight on the side of good, then we will have to be born in a country whose policies are for the right things. And we will have to be born in a country that has a large army. And it will have to be that country's karma to engage in warfare. We will have to find the place to be born that can supply us with all this.

Now where does free will come in? Everywhere. Because what I have outlined is just the skeleton of a life. Each person has to fill in the spaces, and they usually are far more than the simple karmic bones.

Another thing about free will and destiny. We may be destined to go to Chicago, but we will choose how we go: bus, train, plane, car, or hitchhike, and if we hitchhike or drive we will decide what route we want to take. The road of karma has many–very many–branches, and we decide when we come to them which one to take. So we move freely within a predetermined framework. If we want to build a fence it can only be within the boundaries of the land we own. If we live on an island we can only travel within its boundaries. So we do have freedom, but it is not unlimited.

It also happens very often that our karma is not to *do* something, but to have the *chance* to do it. In some lives we may have the possibility to take up several professions, and we are completely free to choose from those. So we do a lot of I Will and I Won't within the framework of our karma. Those choices in their own turn create karma which will manifest in the future. When we look at it, we see ourselves as both caught in the machine of karma and at the same time as the free owner and operator of the karma. Ultimately, it is freedom that is the truth of the whole thing.

Yes, it is all predisposed–by us. Yet, as I have said, the predisposition is only a general outline. At every moment we fill in the details.

If that is the case, then we are automatically going to learn what we chose (unbeknownst to us at the time) to learn in this lifetime.

Unfortunately, learning what we should learn from life as it manifests our karma is not at all a guaranteed matter. That is where not only free will comes in, but also the ability to understand the lesson and the desire to get the right answer. Our karma gives us the chance to learn. It does not force us to learn.

Often we lose our free will and understanding as a result of spiritual ignorance–the state of darkened heart and mind. Lots of labels are put on this state such as "sin," "negativity," "challenges," and such like. But we do not need to know what to call it, we need to know how to get rid of it. And how do we do that? By the learning that comes from reincarnation!

Does this sound like chasing our own tail? It is. That is exactly what reincarnation is for us. The moment we wise up... reincarnation stops.

If we are choosing to come back and live this life to learn something, how do we know what it is?

How right you are! You have understood what nearly everybody misses: We have to figure out what we have come here to learn. Otherwise we fritter away life after life, meandering along getting nowhere.

You see, all that we need to know—why and how we got here and what to do now—is clearly known to the mind of our soul (spirit). But we are out of touch with our soul (a lot of people do not even know they have one) and consequently have not a clue. So we must awaken our soul consciousness. We have to know who and what we are before we can begin to have a glimmering about the who and what of God. When we really enter into the full awareness of our soul the awareness and knowledge of God will start coming about automatically. When we shut the doors of our mind and senses and turn deep within we will find the Great Secret: God.

I understand that it all works together for spiritual enlightenment, but how does the day-to-day process such as what type of job we have or our financial situation or our relationships with our friends and family come to play in the spiritual journey?

The day-to-day things are a result of karma—opportunities to work it out and learn from it. They are the classroom in which we learn (or fail) the karmic lessons.

There is an important word that rhymes with karma: *Dharma*. Dharma is often mistranslated as "religion" or "righteousness." There really is no way to translate it; for dharma means that way of life in which we shall most quickly come to the realization of our true Self and God (who is the Self of our Self). Dharma, like karma, is an individual matter, tailored for each one of us. It is the way by which we make sure that our karma moves us along in our growth into God. Dharma is the way of life (and thought) that takes us to the realization of our full spiritual potential.

With this perspective we can see that some jobs, people, situations, environment, and suchlike are in tune with dharma (dharmic), and some are against dharma (adharmic), and we have to use our free will to affirm the one and eliminate the other.

Do you think that souls that have warlike and violent tendencies reincarnate over and over because they are locked into a negative cycle?

The fact is, those who have *any* habitual patterns of behavior which they indulge will be dragged by them from incarnation to incarnation. Those who perceive the tendencies to those behavior patterns within themselves but refuse to indulge them, and work to eliminate them from their inner minds, will in time succeed and break the bondage they impose.

The only "habit" we should cultivate is that of lifting our consciousness to God in japa and meditation, for that frees us—not only from this world but ultimately from all worlds so we may reenter the transcendent Absolute from which we originally came.

What good does it do for us to reap karma if we are not aware what it is we are suffering for? For example, what help can an infant who is abused receive from reaping such negative karma if it does not realize what is going on?

Certainly, there is a point in our evolution where it is good to consciously understand what has caused the present sufferings–that is, if such understanding will truly facilitate our learning. (The reaping of karma is always for learning and growth–never for punishment or even reward.) Those who have a conscious spiritual life–a life of intentional spiritual discipline–will be shown such things when they need them. There will be no need to poke around on our own to discover the roots of the karma. Sometimes it is better that we not know on the conscious level. However, our true Self, the immortal spirit, the higher Self, is always aware of what is going on. Therefore every unit of karmic return is of ultimate benefit. Our job is to keep on treading the path and get beyond karma.

What effect does "repenting" have upon our karmic debts?

None whatsoever if it does not produce a resolve to spiritually elevate ourselves. True repentance, which is a definite and lasting reformation of life and thought, is necessary to ensure that we do not repeat the same mistaken action that produced the present karma. Feeling sorrow for a wrong action is beneficial only if it produces this reformation. Just being sad and depressed means nothing. In fact it is spiritually harmful. Nor is there any need to ask God for forgiveness. That is as silly as asking our parents to forgive us if we get burnt when we touch something hot, assuming that the pain will cease upon being told we are forgiven. Saying "forgive me" has value when it indicates that we are aware of our wrong and are determined not to repeat it. So it is good to tell both God and man that we are sorry and acknowledge our wrong–and set our will not to repeat it. Thus, while repenting does not affect our karmic debts incurred in the past, it can be a preventive measure for the future. And in the metaphysical realm an ounce of prevention is also worth more than a pound of cure.

You seem to accept that the Hindu/Buddhist concept of reincarnation is compatible with Christianity. How is this, and how is it that the Christian churches are apparently ignorant of this dramatic data?

Reincarnation is not an exclusively Hindu-Buddhist teaching, but has from the beginning been an integral part of Orthodox Judaism. Because this fact would imply that Christ and the Apostles would have held the belief in rebirth as Orthodox Jews, it has become a policy to toss around the red herring of "Hindu-Buddhist" whenever the ignorant have wished to combat the truth of reincarnation. (We met one bishop who thought Edgar Cayce had originated the concept of rebirth and so called all who believed in it "Cayce-ites." It seems that ignorance compounds itself.)

If you are interested in a historical study of reincarnation in both Judaism and Christianity, I recommend our publication *May A Christian Believe In Reincarnation?* The British Methodist minister Leslie Weatherhead has also written a booklet on the subject entitled *The Case for Reincarnation* that is still in print. There is another book entitled *Reincarnation For Christians* by John W. Sweeley that you might find significant as well. The three Weatherhead-Cranston anthologies on reincarnation also contain material from Christian writers. Another book is *Reincarnation In Christianity* by Dr. Geddes MacGregor, who I believe is a Presbyterian.

There is a great difference between what some Christians know and what they *say* they know. Some knowledge is simply swept under the convenient carpet of cowardly silence and some is outright denied.

One leading priest within a major Byzantine Orthodox jurisdiction within this country not only believes in reincarnation, but has engaged for years in research into methods of past-life recall. Our monastery has done research for him on the subject of reincarnation in early Christianity, and that research has been embodied in *May A Christian Believe In Reincarnation?* I am sorry to tell you that this very priest also publicly denounces reincarnation as incompatible with Orthodox Christianity!

I well remember discussions with a very learned Greek Orthodox theologian on the subject of reincarnation. Although he knew the truth of the matter, he continually took refuge in the assertion that "at this late date" it would be impossible to speak the truth since it was commonly held that an "infallible" Church Council had declared the beliefs in pre-existence of the soul—and therefore rebirth—to be false.

Another ploy besides attributing the concept of reincarnation to Hinduism and Buddhism is to attribute it to "the heretic" Origen. This is also quite convenient, as it draws attention from the fact that other Church Fathers also openly taught it.

My favorite comment on the subject of reincarnation is that given by the holy Roman Catholic Capuchin stigmatist-saint, Padre Pio. When one of his spiritual daughters was "told on" for believing in reincarnation, he told her accusers very firmly: "It does not matter what you believe about reincarnation. The only thing that matters is this: Are you seeking for God now?"

I read in a Christian magazine that reincarnation denies our individuality, and also that if we lived many times it would be impossible for us to know which body to resurrect in at the end of time. What is your response to this?

Frankly, I laughed! Nothing either you or I could ever say will change the opinion of those whose minds are so coarsened that they would put forth such objections. But if you want a verbal response I will give it.

The true individual is the immortal spirit that is inhabiting the body, which is nothing more than the vehicle or the clothing of that spirit. The objectors to reincarnation do not believe that when the body dies and turns to dust the individual has ceased to exist—their theology affirms that it indeed does continue its existence. How, then, can they say that the body is a determinant of individuality? Even they will admit that every seven years the body of each of us is totally replaced, that not a cell remains of the previous body. Therefore in the span of a single lifetime we live in several bodies and do not lose our individuality.

It is of course true that from life to life we differ in our personalities, but so do we differ within a single life as we move from infancy to childhood, to adulthood and onward. It is to be hoped that the individual continues to evolve—and therefore to change in outlook and thought—throughout the entire lifespan. That which holds all this together like the string within a strand of beads is the principle of pure consciousness—the spirit which, as has been said, is the only element of individuality, the body being only an expression of that individuality.

A perusal of the earliest Christian writings reveals that Christians originally believed that creation has never begun nor will ever cease to be, but goes on in continuous cycles—just as in Indian philosophy. This creation is not the first, nor is it the last. This was Christian teaching from the beginning. Those who believe otherwise have deviated from original Christianity. Does the fact of many creations deny the individuality of God? For creation is the body of God. Being made in the image of God, we, too, take on many bodies until we return into His infinite Bosom. But the individuality both of God and of His images never loses its integrity.

As far as the resurrection of the body is concerned, whether there is reincarnation or not, as Saint Paul declared: "Flesh and blood cannot inherit the kingdom of God" (I Corinthians 15:50). Therefore the concept of the resurrection of the body into an eternal state is alien to genuine Christian teaching, and the question of "which body?" is not a problem.

How would you distinguish or contrast Hindu (Sanatana) Dharma from other religions?

Dharma and religion are not the same, though religions may have dharmic characteristics and dharma may be expressed religiously. There is one dharma: the Sanatana Dharma of India. Other religions have random traits in consonance with Sanatana Dharma, but only accidentally, in a kind of hit-or-miss way. Therefore I would characterize them in two words: partial and confused. Sanatana Dharma possesses a legitimacy unknown to the others.

Just what part does doctrine or dogma play in spiritual life?

It is important to realize that all valid religion is a process of evolution, that only when religions degenerate do they become dogmatic structures. Later, if they survive and advance to total bankruptcy, they become social associations for mutual support and assurance on the most superficial levels, without a vestige of aspiration for higher consciousness. They become "communities" of self-congratulation, whose highest aspiration is to make each other feel secure in "belonging." That which the wise have sometimes called "the flight of the alone to the Alone" is alien to them.

Real religion is therapeutic and its purpose is transformation of consciousness. How the intellect thinks about or interprets it along the way is considered to be of little importance. Being thinking creatures, we definitely need a personal view, maybe even a cosmology, but it is utterly *personal*, and to attempt to get another person to accept our view is like trying to get them to wear our clothes while we are still in them. It does not work. You only end up with hypocrisy and religious wars.

Spiritual life is The Path in a very real sense. That is, it is a system of spiritual practices which produce results. Either you do them or you do not. How you philosophize or theologize is a matter of complete indifference. It is also just fine if you do not philosophize at all, but just keep on practicing. As they say in India: "Working, working, working: Done!" Walk the Path and the Goal will be reached.

One person may think that five miles up the road there is a mountain. Another may think that five miles up the road there is a plain. Fools fight over such differences. The wise simply walk on down the road and get there. Then they will know whether there is a mountain or a plain there or not. Chances are there will be a lake or a valley! And they will also realize that since they have many more miles to go beyond that point, it just does not matter after all. As a Pogo character once said: "Cut the philosophy and run!" One ancient writer likened true religion to the call of "Fire!" in a burning house. The response must be practical, not theoretical.

Isn't it necessary for us to distinguish between the exoteric and the esoteric elements of religion?

Absolutely not. For in an authentic religion all the elements are thoroughly esoteric, even though extending into exoteric manifestation. Therefore it is a grave error to attempt dividing the elements of a religion into the two classifications with the object of passing over or rejecting the exoteric and fixing attention on the esoteric remainder—or vice versa.

Please notice, however, that I qualified religion with the word *authentic*. There are indeed religious systems in the world whose worthlessness is demonstrated by the very fact that they have no esoteric character to any degree. On the other hand, there are systems—religious, philosophical, and occult/esoteric—whose utter worthlessness is equally demonstrated by the fact that they have no exoteric manifestations of their esoteric principles. That is, they have no practical side for demonstration or realization of those principles.

Just as all living beings in this relative creation are combined of both visible and invisible elements, so a living religion—or, more correctly, a religion that leads to higher life (i.e., consciousness)—is constituted of both interior insights and exterior practices. Yet, as has been said, their character is essentially esoteric.

Dion Fortune, the greatest public occultist of the last century, pointed out that esoteric science intuits the occult principle and then demonstrates it through methodology that either manifests it overtly in the physical plane or imparts direct intuitional knowledge of the principle to the practitioners on the inner levels of their consciousness.

Thus, many supposedly external rules and observances are mistakenly interpreted and perhaps even rejected. But when the intuition illumined by meditation and esoteric development is brought to play in their consideration they are seen to be thoroughly esoteric and even "inward."

This is forcibly brought out in *The Gnosis of the Ten Commandments and the Beatitudes* in which they are shown to be guidelines for those who are developing their innate spiritual powers.

In any viable religion, the inculcation and development of the esoteric viewpoint is the primary requirement. Although the esoteric understanding will develop through the years as the aspirant, through meditation, garners his own insight through practical experience of the invisible realities and their visible indications, yet the set of the sails must be founded on esoteric principles from the beginning. Otherwise religion degenerates into a system of rules calculated to please or displease a testy deity who dispenses reward and punishment along the purely subjective lines of egoic whimsy. Such a religion must inevitably be rejected by intelligent investigators and its stultifying effect must be shaken off.

It is to be hoped, however, that those who so free themselves from ignorant religion will not come to the conclusion that all religion is ignorant and dispensable. It is a limited intellect indeed which decides that simply because one object proves to be defective all similar objects are likewise faulty or inadequate. Yet many who pride themselves on their intelligence make such an absurd conclusion continually. To conclude that our experience or knowledge of one or two sects within a vaster religion—itself only one of many religions in the world—renders us knowledgeous of religion in general or capable of accepting or rejecting religion out of hand is to display a narrowness of intellect that is ill suited to the search for truth.

Sometimes I wonder: Do I have to give up everything in my life? Is the solution to be totally secluded from the world?

The answer is Yes—but in your heart. Through meditation, all the clutter that we call "ours" and "us" begins to be cleared out of our hearts, and God begins to fill in the empty spaces. After a while we will always be alone with God, no matter what the body is doing. When we look at the lives of saints we find that their lives were usually filled with more activity than ordinary people, that they were more involved with "goings on" than was usual. But that was only the external situation. In their inmost heart they were ever with God. Therefore they never got burned out or fed up with all the whirl around them. For amidst it all, they were resting in loving communion with God.

Yogananda's guru said: "Everything in the future is bound to improve if you are making an effort now." If we fill our moments with the remembrance of God and meditate faithfully, everything else will take care of itself. There is no need to puzzle over the future. Just as in our growing up we automatically shed the ways of childhood, so as we grow interiorly the externals will adjust accordingly. However it is good for us to realize what the implications of spiritual quest may be. The secret is: those who are willing to pay the price, whatever it might be, and determine to do so at the beginning are usually not asked to.

I understand your perplexity in seeing how labyrinthine karmic implications are and the amazing nuances involved in the struggle for freedom. But it is very interesting: just after reading your letter I opened a magazine and found this quotation:

> Do your best.
> Leave the rest.
> Angels do no more.

That is certainly the answer to all questions in life, spiritual or otherwise, the only "catch" being that we must be sure we really are doing our best.

What is the purpose of "spiritual practice"?

Everything is Consciousness, but when it is unmoving we call it spirit, and when it moves (vibrates) we call it energy. Spiritual practices are methods which develop the individual's consciousness and its potential states. That is, spiritual practice awakens, develops, and attunes the inmost consciousness of the individual. The basic intention of spiritual practice is to transmute the consciousness from humanity to divinity, passing through the infinite variety of evolutionary states that lie between those two poles. Since the process is direct and pragmatic, it does not manifest as externalized powers or displays. I do not mean by this that the aspirant does not experience change, but the changes are mostly internal and usually apparent only to the practitioner.

My mother gave me your *Spiritual Benefits of a Vegetarian Diet* booklet. I am currently a meat-eater whose attempts at spiritual growth and meditation have been difficult and the information you have provided has shown me how to overcome those difficulties. But I have some questions: 1) Could I experience withdrawal symptoms when my "bodies" start expelling the toxins from eating meat? If so, what should I expect? 2) How long does it take for these toxins to be expelled from my bodies? When could I expect to be free of these negative influences?

No one I know has ever had withdrawal problems upon becoming a vegetarian. It might be that someone in their fifties or sixties would have some reaction from so long a time of eating meat, but I have known several who did not. One thing is sure: there is no need to work up to being a vegetarian by slowly eliminating meat from the diet. The best thing is to stop instantly. Some people say that if the body is used to meat the switch to vegetarian should not be all at once. That is as silly as saying that if our body is used to drinking polluted water we should quit gradually. After all, meat is not like heroin to an addict, or like whiskey to an alcoholic. It is addicting, but only psychologically. It has been my observation that a definite (perceptible) change for the better occurs six months after becoming a vegetarian, that is after abstaining absolutely from meat, fish, and eggs. Then after three more years a dramatic difference is experienced. Naturally, the improvement is happening all along, but these times are like plateaus we reach in the purification of our bodies. Interestingly enough, in the Eastern Christian monastic tradition an aspirant is a postulant for six months and a novice for three more years before becoming a permanent monastic. There must be a connection somewhere.

Doesn't the Genesis account of the sacrifices of Cain and Abel contradict the position of vegetarians?

Here is the incident you refer to: "And Adam knew Eve his wife; and she conceived, and bare Cain, and said, I have gotten a man from the Lord. And she again bare his brother Abel. And Abel was a keeper of sheep, but Cain was a tiller of the ground. And in process of time it came to pass, that Cain brought of the fruit of the ground an offering unto the Lord. And Abel, he also brought of the firstlings of his flock and of the fat thereof. And the Lord had respect unto Abel and to his offering: But unto Cain and to his offering he had not respect" (Genesis 4:1-5).

Where in this account of Cain and Abel's sacrifice is there any mention of eating whatsoever–either of vegetables or of animals?

It is obvious that the acceptability or unacceptability of the sacrifices was a matter of the inner disposition of those who offered. Considering that later on non-animal food substances were daily offerings in the Temple, it would not be logical to conclude from this story that animal offering is acceptable and vegetable offering is not. (Though that, too, would have absolutely nothing to do with the principles of vegetarianism.)

Nor can it reasonably be concluded from the Genesis account that the animals offered by Abel were killed. Rather, they were dedicated to the service of God–just as the Essenes insisted upon doing at the time of Jesus.

The killing of animals and the eating of their flesh was absolutely unknown to Adam, Eve, and their children. Only later in the spiritual degeneracy of the human race did the hideous practice of flesh-eating arise.

It is interesting to see that carnivores consistently see only what they like in their reading of Genesis, and completely ignore the explicit statements that vegetarianism was the divinely ordained diet for both humans and animals: "And God said, Behold, I have given you every herb bearing seed, which is upon the face of all the earth, and every tree, in the which is the fruit of a tree yielding seed; *to you it shall be for meat.* And to every beast of the earth, and to every fowl of the air, and to every thing that creepeth upon the earth, wherein there is life, *I have given every green herb for meat:* and it was so" (Genesis 1:29, 30).

Humans are not natural flesh-eaters. To be so is to violate the divine pattern.

Some people think that Saint Paul's saying that false spiritual teachers would be "forbidding to marry, and commanding to abstain from meats, which God hath created to be received with thanksgiving" (I Timothy 4:3), is a condemnation of monastic life and vegetarianism. What do you think?

I think they need to hear the words of Jesus: "Ye do err, not knowing the scriptures, nor the power of God" (Matthew 22:29). And those who pay attention to their ludicrous distortions of the Bible need to heed some other words of Saint Paul: "From such turn away" (II Timothy 3:5).

Even a little good sense should show that this verse has nothing whatsoever to do with monastic life. In Christianity today monastics are found in the Eastern Orthodox, Roman Catholic, Anglican, and some European Evangelical Churches. (In the Evangelical churches the monastics are known as deacons and deaconesses.) None of these churches prohibit marriage, so such an accusation cannot be brought against them.

A person does not become a monastic because he has been forbidden to marry. Rather, he takes up monastic life to fulfill spiritual aspirations, the intensity of which preclude marriage–just as do certain secular careers. Both the Lord Jesus and Saint Paul speak highly of the celibate life as a worthy offering unto God.

Jesus said: "There are some eunuchs, which were so born from their mother's womb: and there are some eunuchs, which were made eunuchs of men: and there be eunuchs, which have made themselves eunuchs for the kingdom of heaven's sake. He that is able to receive it, let him receive it" (Matthew 19:12).

And Saint Paul: "It is good for a man not to touch a woman.... For I would that all men were even as I myself.... I say therefore to the unmarried and widows, It is good for them if they abide even as I.... He that is unmarried careth for the things that belong to the Lord, how he may please the Lord: But he that is married careth for the things that are of the world, how he may please his wife. There is difference also between a wife and a virgin. The unmarried woman careth for the things of the Lord, that she may be holy both in body and in spirit: but she that is married careth for the things of the world, how she may please her husband" (I Corinthians 7:1, 7, 8, 32-34).

As is usual with such ignoramuses, the word "meat" is taken to mean animal flesh, whereas the word *maton* used by Saint Paul (who was writing in Greek) simply means "foods." And the food "which God hath created to be received with thanksgiving" is clearly described in the Book of Genesis where God tells Adam: "Behold, I have given you every herb bearing seed, which is upon the face of all the earth and every tree, in the which is the fruit of a tree yielding seed; to you it shall be for meat" (Genesis 1:29, 30). Those who cannot understand this simply do not wish to do so.

But Saint Paul was talking about something. What was it? He was speaking of those who would try to introduce into the Christian Church some very ancient ideas of those who were dualistic in their philosophy. Such persons usually believed that either the entire creation was produced by an evil power, or that some of the things to be found within creation had been placed there by evil forces. Such persons believed that some vegetables had been created by the Satanic power and that to eat them was to become tainted by evil powers and even to come under their control. They especially abhorred all root vegetables since they grew in the darkness and not in the light. (Some said that potatoes were all right to eat since when cut open they were found to be "light"–white–inside. You can draw your own conclusions about this type of thinking.) Others preached against the supposed evils of eating beans. And so the list went. It was the incursion of these ideas into Christianity which Saint Paul was warning against.

All this simply goes to show that the Bible in the hands of some people becomes an instrument of utter foolishness.

In the Gospel of Thomas saying 12 says: "The disciples said to Jesus: We know that you will depart from us; who is it who will be great over us? Jesus said to them: Wherever you have come, you will go to James the Just, for whose sake heaven and earth came into being." Does your group have an affinity with James the Just?

This requires more of a historical explanation than a commentary.

Originally Christianity was intended to be communal after the pattern of the Essenes. That did not last long, unfortunately, though the Christians of Egypt managed better than those in Jerusalem.

The Sons of Thunder, Saint James and Saint John (Mark 3:17), were the two leading figures in the original Christian Church. Saint James was not only the bishop of Jerusalem, he was also the spiritual head of the communities made up of families. Saint John, his brother, was the spiritual head of the communities made up of the unmarried. But the Apostles all looked to Saint James for spiritual direction until his martyrdom by Herod (Acts 12:2). The epistle which he wrote to all the Christian communities is found in the New Testament. There is also a very valuable text found in the Nag Hammadi Library entitled: *The Secret Book of James*.

Hopefully all esoteric Christians have an affinity with Saint James, usually referred to as The Great.

You seem to believe that Sanatana Dharma, the Eternal Truth, is found only in India's philosophy, but my study has led me to believe that Sanatana Dharma is in all religions. Do you deny that?

I do not deny that statements in agreement with Sanatana Dharma can be found in most religions–and even perhaps all. But that means very little.

For example, if a complete and fully functioning automobile could be found only in one country of the world, but automobile parts were scattered all over the globe and would be found in all countries, could you really say that automobiles were found everywhere? Only if you had a very poor grasp or definition of automobiles. You do not have an auto if you do not have the whole thing. India alone has had–or does have–the full picture. Other religions have only fragments–and a fragment is not a picture at all. Instead of automobiles, let's think of a picture. Even if millions had a fragment of a picture, would you say: They all have the picture? Not unless you have a strange idea of what a picture is.

There is truth in all religions. That fundamentally is true, but let's say that there was an eastern-style bazaar where diamonds were sold. Heaps of diamonds–or what was claimed to be diamonds–were set there for sale. And what if someone comes to you and says: "Diamonds are in all these piles, but I must tell you that only one is one hundred percent diamonds. The others have anywhere from two percent to ninety percent diamonds. But they all have diamonds!" Would you then go about at random buying "diamonds" from them all? I hope not. Every heap having some diamonds cannot give those heaps an equal value. And any sensible person would seek out the hundred percent heap and buy from there. Shankara, the greatest philosopher in recorded history, said: "The philosophical concepts that are commonly known in India have not even been dreamed of outside India." I believe that myself because I have seen it to be so.

Since the core of every person's existence is the divine Self (Atman), it is only natural that some eternal truths would be intuited at different times in different places throughout the world. Further, there were great teachers in the West such as Pythagoras and Apollonius of Tyana who went to India and lived there for some years learning Sanatana Dharma and then returned to West and taught what they had learned–and often were rebuked for having gone to India and then teaching its wisdom in the West. Nevertheless their influence affected to various degrees those lands in which they taught as time went on.

Do you accept the Nicene Creed as a statement of truth?

No. The Nicene Creed (as well as the Apostles' Creed and the Athanasian Creed) is a product of degenerate and deluded Churchianity, a mixture of fact and fiction.

Certainly I accept the truth stated in the Nicene Creed that there is one God which manifests in a triune manner and that the goal of life is to attain conscious, divine immortality in the highest world of perfected beings (siddhas), far beyond the paltry "heaven" of most of the world's religions. Other than that it is, as I say, a mishmash of misunderstood truth and outright fiction, the product of spiritual ignorance.

I especially do not accept the idea that Jesus is God, the creator of the world. Jesus was/is a siddha in the tradition of Sanatana Dharma, not Judaism. In his conversation with the king of Kashmir he told him: "I was born in a distant land *where there is no truth.*" This demonstrates that Jesus did not believe in the religion he was born into. That is why Jesus returned to India: to be with and live truth–Sanatana Dharma.

It seems clear to me that your beliefs are those of Hinduism. What makes you a Christian?

In one sense–nothing. In another sense, a great deal.

A worthwhile religion consists of two elements: beliefs (philosophy) and rituals, including formal worship.

As far as beliefs are concerned I do not have a single one that is not part of Sanatana Dharma. I have no distinctive "Christian" belief whatever. And neither did Jesus, who was a Sanatana Dharma missionary and a member of the Nath Yogi Sampradaya. Just as a follower of Shankara is a Sanatana Dharmi automatically, in the same way anyone who follows the true teachings of Jesus is a Sanatana Dharmi–it cannot be otherwise.

It is ritual–including worship–which "makes" me a Christian. During my first pilgrimage to India I met and became very close friends with a great yoga siddha, Sri Dattabal of Kohlapur. In one of our conversations he told me with marked gravity that although he did not want to discourage me, he felt impelled to tell me that when I returned to the West it would be very difficult–and perhaps even impossible–for me to retain the spiritual energy (shakti) I had received in India. And if I did not retain it I would not be able to maintain a viable sadhana. I took his words very seriously and began pondering how I could manage living in the West without losing what I had gained in India.

A few months before going to India I had discovered the Roman Catholic Church and its rituals, especially the Mass. Although raised a fundamentalist Protestant and having heard and read a lot of anti-Catholic propaganda, since my mind had been opened by yoga sadhana I could perceive the very real spiritual power which the rites conveyed, even though the beliefs were not acceptable. Upon returning from India I discovered that I had developed a surprising ability: I could feel the presence of a Catholic church a mile or more away and could go right to it. I filed my impressions away, but after nearly ten years, during five of which I established and headed an ashram under the direct personal supervision of Anandamayi Ma, I realized that we needed the power and protection the sacraments created by Jesus provided to ensure our spiritual survival outside the divine atmosphere of India. The same conclusions had inspired two leaders of the Theosophical Society, James Wedgwood and Charles Leadbeater, to found the Liberal Catholic Church in 1916, reworking the traditional rituals to conform to the principles of Sanatana Dharma. Learning about this I contacted a Liberal Catholic bishop who bestowed holy orders on me and two other ashramites, eventually consecrating me a bishop. When I reported on all this to Anandamayi Ma and asked if I had done right, she expressed her full approval and told me: "You must realize that the will of God is being done through you."

One day the doorbell of the ashram rang, and the monk who answered came to tell me that a bishop of the Saint Thomas Christian Church had come to meet me. Thus we established contact with the Mother Church in India. Saint Thomas Christianity is exactly this: The teachings of the rishis of India and classical yoga sadhana along with the rituals Jesus ordered for the West who lacked the samskara rites available in India. (Please see *The Yoga of the Sacraments*.) But the belief and outlook and purpose are that of classical Sanatana Dharma. We use the term "Original Christianity" because we want to get it across to those who visit our website that Jesus' original teachings were those of Sanatana Dharma exclusively. Contemporary Christianity often has nothing to do with Jesus except the spurious use of his name. Those who read and understand the material posted on our website will realize that our position is simply this: You cannot follow the teachings of Jesus outside of Sanatana Dharma, because they are nothing but Sanatana Dharma. Jesus learned his wisdom from the sages of India and so must those who would follow him.

For more information about this aspect of our monastery, please read *The Christ of India*.

Is there such a thing as a Saint Thomas Christian Creed?

Actually we do not think of it as such, but I suppose the Creed we recite in the Mass could be called a Saint Thomas Christian Creed:

We believe in God, the undivided Unity, embracing all in oneness.

We believe in the Holy and all-glorious Trinity, Who pervades the whole universe, Who dwells also in the spirit of man.

We believe in Jesus Christ, the Lord of love and wisdom, first among His brethren, Who leads us to the glory of the Father, Who is Himself the way, the truth, and the life.

We believe in the law of good which rules the world and by which one day all His sons shall reach the feet of the Father, however far they stray.

We strive towards the ancient narrow path that leads to life eternal. So shall His blessing rest on us and peace forevermore. Amen.

It is, however, not our composition, but was printed in the fourth edition of the *Liberal Catholic Liturgy*, and we adapted and adopted it—as we did the Mass rite.

One thing should be pointed out, though. Jesus is described as "the way, the truth, and the life." This does not mean that Jesus is the *only* way, truth and life, but that his living example and teachings open the way, truth and life to those who become what he was. The same is true of Rama, Krishna, Buddha and other great teachers of India.

What is the true nature of a human being? To me humans seem all confusion and very little else.

To our external sight your conclusions seem very right. But the confusion is only external—incidental. Beneath the appearance of confusion is the reality of the true Self within every sentient being. And that is why in the Bhagavad Gita Krishna advises Arjuna (and us, as well): "Become a yogi." Yoga clears the mind (manas) and intellect (buddhi) and opens the individual's consciousness to see Reality both within and without.

The real part of each human being is an eternal spirit, free from all bonds and defects. When through yoga practice all the levels of a person become purified, then the inner light shines forth and confusion is ended.

So not only is a human being not really confusion, he is not a sinner, either. Sin is not the nature of anyone. Just as a person covered with mud is not mud, so those who have fallen into evil ways are not really evil but deluded, and delusion is not permanent in anyone.

Is there no teacher or master that was unique in the world's history?

Just as no two snowflakes are alike, in the same way every person is unique in their manifestation. Each master teacher has a distinctive approach suited to the needs of those he is destined to teach. But no master is greater or better or more beneficial than another.

Jesus alone rose from the dead by his own spiritual power.

Not so. Many great masters have manifested in physical bodies after their death. A disciple of Hariakhan Baba caught smallpox while on pilgrimage to Kailash with Baba. Baba transferred the smallpox to his body, died and was cremated by the disciple. When the disciple came back down from the Himalayas he found Hariakhan Baba giving satsang at a devotee's house! In *Autobiography of a Yogi* other examples of resurrection are given.

According to the *Nathanamavali*, a history of the Nath Yogi Sampradaya to which Jesus belonged: "Isha Natha [Jesus] came to India at the age of fourteen. After this he returned to his own country and began preaching. Soon after, his brutish and materialistic countrymen conspired against him and had him crucified. After crucifixion, or perhaps even before it, Isha Natha entered samadhi by means of yoga. [Yogis often leave their bodies in samadhi, so it is not amiss to say that Jesus did indeed "die" on the cross.]

"Seeing him thus, the Jews presumed he was dead, and buried him in a tomb. At that very moment however, one of his gurus, the great Chetan Natha, happened to be in profound meditation in the lower reaches of the Himalayas, and he saw in a vision the tortures which Isha Natha was undergoing. He therefore made his body lighter than air and passed over to the land of Israel.

"The day of his arrival was marked with thunder and lightning, for the gods were angry with the Jews, and the whole world trembled. When Chetan Natha arrived, he took the body of Isha Natha from the tomb, woke him from his samadhi, and later led him off to the sacred land of the Aryans. Isha Natha then established an ashram in the lower regions of the Himalayas and he established the cult of the lingam there." ("The cult of the lingam" refers to the Shaivite branch of Hinduism.) From this we see that the spiritual power of the master Chetan Nath had a part in the resurrection of Jesus.

To understand the true nature and purpose of Jesus, read *The Christ of India* and *The Aquarian Gospel of Jesus the Christ*.

Don't human beings need a Savior?

Yes and no. All human beings need some catalyst for spiritual awakening. It may be a book, a spoken sentence or a highly evolved person. But at the same time the only savior that is absolutely necessary is our own illumined Self. Someone can lead us or awaken us to the possibility of higher life and consciousness, but we must save ourselves by attaining that life and consciousness. No one can—or need—do it for us.

When does the soul come into being?

The soul and the spirit are not the same. The soul is the astral and causal bodies of the human being. The spirit is the spark of divine consciousness that is the real person. The soul is subtle vibration manifested as several layers or bodies inhabited and enlivened by the spirit.

The spirit is eternal, part of God and without beginning or end. It is never born nor does it die. Rather, its bodies, the soul, undergo birth and death. The soul comes into being when the spirit begins the journey of evolution through reincarnation.

To someone who asked about a book written by a psychic which he questioned.

Your assessment of ——————'s book is completely right. I personally believe nothing he said or wrote that was unique to him.

Psychism is a poor basis for anything, including religion and spiritual philosophy. Unfortunately psychics trust themselves rather than scrutinizing everything they think they perceive. Often they see correctly, but only partially and therefore draw wrong conclusions. Also, they fail to realize that certain realms and subjects may be beyond their capacity to fully or correctly perceive.

Only the self-realized are fully trustworthy, but we are going to have to decide who is self-realized! So we must to some degree trust ourselves.

As Krishna said: "Therefore become a yogi."

If someone has a clairvoyant skill on the level of a siddhi, is it an impediment to one's progress if indulged in? Or is this a God-given talent that can be put to use for humanity if it can be used constructively? In your experience is it difficult to strike a balance or should one focus on clarifying Awareness in the knowledge that all things are added at the proper time?

Since our sole purpose for existing is the attainment of liberation through conscious union with God, that is what must be the center of our life. Such a centering is impossible if there are any distractions, and psychic matters are distractions. They are also on a very low level when compared with our true goal. I have never known of a psychic ability that did not eventually prove faulty and therefore misleading and distracting as well.

When someone evolves to a certain point, spiritual clairvoyance, which is not at all psychic clairvoyance, arises naturally. Even then, the wise yogi keeps focused on the goal of complete liberation. However in some cases the occasional–very rare–use of spiritual clairvoyance may be used. However it will only deal with the spiritual life of the individual and will only be directed to their liberation. In other words it will only relate to the process of sadhana–nothing else. Only after enlightenment can spiritual clairvoyance be safely exercised, and then only at the will of God. In great Masters such as Yogananda and Sivananda this "clairvoyance" is really divine consciousness, a glimmer of omniscience.

People, including yogis, can wander for countless lifetimes in the psychic realms, whether in or out of the body. Just as a rocket only has the necessary fuel to reach the target, so the human being has only the requisite shakti (inner power) to reach union with Brahman. If any of that power is used for another purpose, no matter how benevolent or altruistic, another lifetime will be wasted and the wheel of rebirth will keep turning.

What is the nature of God: personal, impersonal, both equally, or is one of the two primary?

God is only personal or impersonal in relation to a consciousness immersed in the duality of samsara. God is beyond the two, just as God is beyond samsara. So those in samsara will consider God either personal or impersonal, and being samsarins will no doubt wrangle with or disdain one another for holding a wrong view. Those who have gone beyond duality will be beyond personal/impersonal, and will keep silence—just as does Brahman.

What is the nature of spiritual practice/sadhana/yoga?

The only purpose of yoga sadhana is to realize the Self, both the individual and cosmic, the jivatman and the Paramatman. Therefore it must be exclusively adhyatmic in nature. *A Brief Sanskrit Glossary* defines adhyatmic: "pertaining to the Self (Atman), individual and Supreme." A practice centered on an external "god" such as Shiva, Durga, Ganesha, etc., which is really only a symbol or portrayal of one or more aspects of God, or on an avatar such as Rama and Krishna, is by its and their nature partial and therefore limited and cannot lead to Self-realization and liberation in the Infinite. Gods and avatars only exist for us in samsara. Parabrahman, the Supreme, is beyond samsara and cannot be revealed through concentration or worship on either gods or avatars. To realize God we must get beyond all that which God is beyond.

Is meditation and pranayama sufficient?

Meditation and pranayama should be one single sadhana, not two separate things. Repetition of a mantra in time with the breath should be our practice in both meditation and outside meditation. The Upanishads declare that the two spiritual powers we possess are breath and sound. This is explained in our publication *Soham Yoga*.

Is bhakti of a deity necessary?

As already pointed out, a deity or a symbolic form of God is partial and therefore limited, whereas our goal is to realize our eternal Self within the Infinite, the Self of our Self.

Jnana and bhakti are states, not practices or "yogas" (sadhana). Shankara in his writings says that bhakti is total dedication to the search for God-realization and liberation, and that jnana is God-realization, the state of liberation itself. Bhakti means dedication to an ideal or a purpose—in this case realization and liberation. Swami Sivananda often said: "Emotion is not devotion."

In Chapter Six of *Raja Yoga* by Swami Vivekananda, he says about much of the "bhakti" in India:

> "All over the world there have been dancing and jumping and howling sects, who spread like infection when they begin to sing and dance and preach; they also are a sort of hypnotists. They exercise a singular control for the time being over sensitive persons, alas! often, in the long run, to degenerate whole races. Ay, it is healthier for the individual or the race to remain wicked

than be made apparently good by such morbid extraneous control. One's heart sinks to think of the amount of injury done to humanity by such irresponsible yet well-meaning religious fanatics. They little know that the minds which attain to sudden spiritual upheaval under their suggestions, with music and prayers, are simply making themselves passive, morbid, and powerless, and opening themselves to any other suggestion, be it ever so evil. Little do these ignorant, deluded persons dream that whilst they are congratulating themselves upon their miraculous power to transform human hearts, which power they think was poured upon them by some Being above the clouds, they are sowing the seeds of future decay, of crime, of lunacy, and of death. Therefore, beware of everything that takes away your freedom. Know that it is dangerous, and avoid it by all the means in your power."

What is ideal for a daily practice?

The meditation and the continual japa of Soham as found in my book *Soham Yoga.*

To someone who asked about the composition of the New Testament and its authority.

Most scriptures are, as Sri Ramakrishna said, a mixture of sand and sugar, so we have to take the sugar and leave the sand. That is true of the entire Bible, as well. For the authentic teachings of Jesus I go to *The Aquarian Gospel of Jesus the Christ* by Levi Dowling and the writings of

Paramhansa Yogananda, especially *The Second Coming of Christ*. I personally consider the Bhagavad Gita to be all sugar and the only truly comprehensive scripture on spiritual life. Further, I believe Jesus to have studied the Gita and taught is principles when he returned to Israel. (See *The Christ of India*.)

Can you explain the chakras to me?

Just as the outer universe is a complex of many interrelated points such as suns and planets, in the same way the material and subtle bodies of the yogi—which reflect and react on one another—are a network of life energy points known as chakras. Chakras are points in the bodies into which the universal life force (vishwaprana) flows. Without that constant inflow the bodies would become dormant and disintegrate—would die. The chakras are both entrances and exits for the cosmic life power as well as reservoirs of that power and points of intelligent direction of the power. There are many subsidiary satellites of the chakras called adharas. Adharas are reservoirs of pranic energies, storage units for the energies that flow into the subtle bodies through the chakras, and therefore can be (and often are) mistaken for a chakra.

The Nath Yogi tradition teaches that there are nine major chakras:

1) The Muladhara, located at the base of the spine
2) The Swadhishthana, located in the spine a little less than midway between the base of the spine and the area opposite the navel.
3) The Manipura, located in the spine at the point opposite the navel.
4) The Anahata, located in the spine opposite the midpoint of the sternum bone.
5) The Vishuddha chakra, located in the spine opposite the hollow of the throat.

6) The Talu chakra, located at the root of the palate (opposite the tip of the nose).

7) The Ajna chakra, located at the point between the eyebrows–the "third eye."

8) The Nirvana chakra, located in the midst of the brain: opposite the middle of the forehead, directly beneath the crown of the head.

9) The Brahmarandhra chakra, located at the crown of the head.

The nature and function of the nine chakras

1) **Base (Muladhara) chakra.** The Muladhara chakra deals with the purely physical, atomic structure of the body. Therefore its energies deal with healing, correcting and empowering the very cells and organs of the body. Positive energies of this chakra manifest as insight into all material phenomena and independence of them; negative energies manifest as totally material perceptions and impulses toward avid attachment to material things and disbelief in anything higher than matter.

2) **Swadhishthana chakra.** The Swadhishthana chakra deals with neurological energies, emotions and desires, including sex/lust. It involves all that is self-centered and egotistical in a person. Through its purification are corrected those areas of our physical and emotional life. It also deals with the fluids in the body including the lymph and blood when there is an abnormality there. Positive energies of this chakra manifest as gentleness, sensitivity to others' feelings, helpfulness and even self-sacrifice; negative energies manifest as negative emotions such as anger, resentment, hatred, jealousy, envy and–most of all–lust.

3) **Navel (Manipura) chakra.** The Manipura chakra deals with the metabolism and the assimilative powers of the body. It, too, relates to desires, especially the desire to acquire, control and encompass. It relates to the digestive system as well. So those are the aspects

of a person that correction of this chakra can affect. Positive energies of this chakra manifest as strength of will and purpose and a highly developed sense of order and right conduct; negative energies manifest as greed, possessiveness, negative ambition and materialistic involvements.

4) **Heart (Anahata) chakra.** The Anahata chakra deals with metabolism and controls the cardio-pulmonary system. It too deals with feelings, but feelings of higher affection and altruism. (It is still in the lower levels, so do not mistake its movements for true or spiritual love or devotion to God.) It also deals with the faculty of sight and therefore basic perception as well as lesser intuition. It has a lot to do with the immune and circulatory systems and controls the thymus gland in the center of the chest. Positive energies of this chakra manifest as loving-kindness, generosity, and unselfish actions for the benefit of others; negative energies manifest as the desire to dominate others and to use them for selfish advantage.

5) **Throat (Vishuddha) chakra.** The Vishuddha chakra deals with intellectual development and the power of speech. The thyroid is controlled by it also. The will is also involved to some extent. Higher intuition comes into play here to some extent, as well. Positive energies of this chakra manifest as wise, uplifting and healing speech, words that have the power to manifest what is being spoken; negative energies manifest as foolish, meaningless words, lies, manipulative and negative, harmful speech.

6) **Talu chakra.** The Talu chakra is a kind of switching station as on a railway. Subtle transmuting energies and the Kundalini move up the spine from the Muladhara to the Vishuddha chakra. Then they need to move forward and reach the Ajna chakra. In the centuries since knowledge of the Talu chakra was almost lost, sadhakas throughout India have expressed frustration with the fact that the energies rise to the Vishuddha and will not move to the Ajna. This is because the way the subtle bodies are constituted the Talu chakra must be prepared

and activated before the energies can move forward to the front of the head. But that has usually not been known. I personally have heard of several people making this complaint and known one man who sought advice from many renowned yogis over the years but received no help.

7) **Third eye (Ajna) chakra.** The Ajna chakra controls, coordinates and partakes of all the functions of those beneath it. It particularly deals with spiritual intuition and spiritual will. Positive energies of this chakra manifest as clear intuition, spiritual perceptions and spiritual will power; negative energies manifest as chaotic or negative psychic experiences as well as whimsical, capricious and negative applications of will.

8) **Nirvana chakra.** The Nirvana chakra is the center in which liberation (moksha) is attained and experienced. Without knowledge of this chakra there is a problem in the liberating energies moving from the front of the head back and upward to the Brahmarandhra chakra through which the yogi's spirit rises to merge with the Absolute. Like the Talu chakra, the Nirvana chakra must be prepared and activated before the energies can so move. The Nirvana Chakra is also called the Jalandhara chakra. Jalandhara means "Holder of the Net" in the sense of perfect mastery of both the subtle energy network of nadis and chakras and of samsara itself, the "net" in which all sentient beings are caught until the Nirvana Chakra is reached in full awareness. Jalandhara also means: "holder of the aggregation," as it also controls the seven chakras beneath it.

9) **Crown chakra.** The energies of the Sushumna crown chakra are purely spiritual and unconditioned by any influences other than our finite spirit and the Infinite Spirit from which we derive our very existence. So there is never any trouble there. It need only be reached and empowered by the Kundalini to establish the precedence of these holy powers over the lower levels of our existence.

These nine chakras are the actual nine gates of the body spoken about in the ancient scriptures (see Bhagavad Gita 5:13), not the nine openings found in the body. The nine chakras are major factors in the subtle energy system of a human being, the ruling power centers, though there are a great number of minor chakras throughout the gross and subtle bodies of each one of us.

Do you believe in or know to exist the masters that the Theosophists (and I. K. Taimni) talked about?

There is too much evidence of the reality of the Masters from the testimonial of so many of the early Theosophists to not believe in their existence at the time of Blavatsky and for at least some time later.

I find the claim that they were vastly superior in knowledge to anyone else living at that time in India bordering on the irresponsible, because no one person could have known all the great yogis of the entire Indian subcontinent. And what would have qualified them to know this? Nor have I seen anything in such sources as *The Mahatma Letters* to suppose that they had knowledge equal to the leading yogis of India, much less superior.

Furthermore, can it be assumed that they are living today (something not impossible to many great yogis) or have left their bodies yet remain in contact with qualified aspirants? Is there evidence that the Himalayan Brotherhood itself still exists? And the most important: Is it relevant to us?

I am always uneasy about those who claim to have hidden or invisible masters. Yet, though I may not readily believe, it would be irresponsible of me to deny the possibility, for I would have no basis for that.

Both Vyasa and Shankara, along with many other great teachers, such as Patanjali, have told us that the ultimate master is Ishwara and that the practice of yoga itself becomes the teacher of those who diligently apply themselves to sadhana. This I believe.

༄༅

If there is only one consciousness it would seem that any distinction would be unreal. Is it only ego and mind that form false personality and distinction?

It is very crucial to avoid all simplistic interpretations of Indian philosophy. "Brahman alone is real, all else is unreal" has to be understood, not just cited. Certainly only Brahman is real, but Brahman has projected this entire field of relative existence and placed us within it to evolve and expand our scope of awareness until it is such that we can participate in the infinity of Brahman. Paramhansa Yogananda said that God (Ishwara) is the Cosmic Dreamer and we are co-dreamers with him. Maya is continually being mentioned by some as though it were "the Devil," but Maya is the consciousness of Ishwara manifesting as the cosmos. We can think of it as a kind of training film. That is why it is called Yogamaya. Just as a motion picture is only light on a screen, in the same way the entire range of creation is an image in the Mind of God. And it is being shown to us for the development of our consciousness. So it is not amiss to say that it is both real and unreal. Even a hallucination or misperception is a real mental phenomenon.

Personality and distinction are necessities for our evolution. It is identification with them and clinging to them as fundamental realities that are the problem. We have jumped out of the boat into the water and drowned. We are presently in a school for developing consciousness, and until we develop our consciousness to the requisite level we keep coming back over and over. The entire school system is temporary and meant to be used and then transcended. At the moment it exists for us and refusal to accept it gets us nowhere.

To understand this the Gita should be carefully studied. Several times the Gita cites the Sankhya philosophy which is the original philosophy of India and the basis of Yoga. The very term Yoga-Vedanta is a contradiction. It is only the Advaita Vedantins that keep getting their feet tangled up in relativity because their philosophy does not tally with the experience of anyone. They even have had to come up with the absurd proposition that we should believe in non-duality yet live as though there is duality. If something does not survive the testing-ground of life it has no value and may even do harm. Yogananda warned people not to get "philosophical indigestion." Through many years I have seen a great deal of foolish and evil ideas justified by adherents of an undigested non-dual philosophy. Thomas Riley Marshall, Vice President under Woodrow Wilson, once said: "What this country needs is a good ten-cent cigar." I doubt that it does, but this I do know: No one needs a simplistic ten-cent philosophy, no matter how sophisticated it sounds or how complexly and insistently it has been expounded for centuries.

To an Indian friend who had to give up a deep personal attachment and was profoundly grieved.

Please accept my deepest sympathy and concern over your sorrow.

Peace and fulfillment are only to be found within, for God is there. However difficult it may be due to agitation of mind and heart, please meditate. Whatever mantra or Name of God you prefer, cling to its japa throughout the day and in meditation. This is your lifeline.

When intensely sad, it is often better to leave the house and walk about for a while. Visit temples and pray. Attend satsangs and participate in them. Do not be alone too much.

This is very simple advice, but I assure you it not only helps, but when followed unbrokenly it can heal and bring peace to the heart.

Is Lord Shiva the God of Israel? If so, how should I properly worship Him?

Shiva is Yogeshwar, the Lord of Yogis. His true worship is not of any image or symbol, but is the practice of meditation.

I need help to pray. I try to be importunate and pray every day (as Lord Jesus said). But lately I have realized my prayers do not seem to work.

What is real prayer? In Sanskrit the word is *upasana*, which means to draw near or even sit near. In the Bible the word is *prosevke*, which means the same thing. Certainly we can speak to God what is in our hearts, but the most effective prayer is meditation and japa.

Through meditation and japa our mind and heart become purified and we become able to cope with the daily assaults of the world and our own restless mind. Meditation also puts us beyond the reach of much that may otherwise bother us. The mind becomes stronger and we become able to remain calm and endure. This is especially true in times of grief. We can choose either to immerse our minds in God or immerse them in our pain. I am not speaking theory–this is my experience, including at the death of loved ones.

There is nothing wrong in asking God for help or even for what we need materially, but Jesus said: "Seek ye first the kingdom of God, and his righteousness; and all these things shall be added unto you" (Matthew 6:33). Then we will not just have some perishable situation or things, but we will have God!

**And it troubles me that all these years I have prayed and perhaps
God has not paid any attention.**

Since "the Lord lives in the heart of every creature" (Bhagavad Gita
18:61), he knows all our anxieties and sorrows. He never ignores us,
but all the many aspects of our life, especially our karmas, determine
their results. Again, we must take refuge in God literally by meditation
and a life that is in harmony with our meditation. Often we cause our
own suffering, but desire, fear and mental confusion keep us from
realizing that.

**I ask for strength, purity/clarity of heart and mind, courage, to
teach me to meditate and gain forgiveness of sins.**

This is certainly the right prayer. And meditation is the highest remedy,
though we must examine our lives and minds and see if we are holding
to something that is hindering us.

**I realize I'm doubtful when I pray as I feel God would not listen
to me or hates me and that I don't pray with faith.**

Do not give up. Certainly God hears and cares. Have faith in both
God and yourself.

I pray entreatingly. I pray to Shiv-ji, Lord Krishna, Lord Jesus, Mahavatar Baba-ji and Divine Mother.

This is good, but sadhana is the best.

I try to say mantras and prayers of repentance. I rarely get comforted. I feel very alone and helpless. I am going through a very difficult time and although this is not the first time I have been troubled, I'm trying to pray to get help. I even ask God what I can do to help myself so that He doesn't have to do much. But I get nothing. I want to know what I can do to pray better; more effectively.

Meditation is the only answer. Meditate with single-minded determination. Carefully read and apply the teachings of the Gita, the great source of wisdom. Paramhansa Yogananda used to say: "A saint is a sinner that never gave up." There is also the saying: "A diamond is a piece of coal that did not give up."

Yogananda said that the most important thing in his autobiography was the statement by his guru, Sri Yukteswar: "Forget the past. The vanished lives of all men are dark with many shames. Human conduct is ever unreliable until anchored in the Divine. Everything in future will improve if you are making a spiritual effort now."

I am reaching out to God with all my strength and heart and I'm getting nothing.

Yogananda told about a man in India who wanted to love God, and since he had heard that a person should shed tears of love for God, he put chili powder in his eyes so they would flow with tears. Fortunately a saint knew what he was doing and came to him and told him: "Dear brother, if you did not already love God, you would not be willing to undergo such pain. Please understand this." To keep calling on God when suffering is proof that you are not far from God. How many people in this world would do so?

If I have such bad past karma (maybe a reason why my prayers aren't working) then what can I do to redeem myself so that God would pay some attention to me? I don't want miracles, just some comfort.

I know it sounds repetitious, but interior cultivation is the only lasting remedy. Please be sure that I understand your suffering. Such experience is not new to me, and I can assure you that by persevering you will win the battle and attain blessedness. This I can tell you: meditation is the highest activity a human being can engage in, for it creates tremendous spiritual karma that unfailingly manifests in time.

Again, please read the Gita. Also read Chapter Two of *Autobiography of a Yogi*: "My Mother's Death and the Mystic Amulet." A mantra was the "heart" of the amulet, and by doing intense and prolonged japa and meditation with that mantra, Yogananda "daily traveled far on the wings of his amulet."

To a friend who sent a long quotation from an Indian who had made a fortune running and eventually selling a string of hatha yoga centers. After selling them, she began notifying people of the "demonic evil" of yoga in any form, and raving on and on in the style of ignorant, fundamentalist "Christian" bigots about yoga and dharma.

You cannot reason with insanity, hatred and bigotry. Nor is there any value in refuting attacks based on them. Such people are, as Saint Jude said, "raging waves of the sea, foaming out their own shame" (Jude 13). As the great Master Yogananda used to say in relation to such people: "You go after God," and leave them behind in the dark. Eventually they will come to the light, also.

Do you have anything further to add to Trailanga Swami's story that may not have been written by Master Yogananda in his autobiography?

Yes, I do. First, three things that Yogacharya Oliver Black told to me when I spent all day with him in the fall of 1968. Yoganandaji had himself told these things to Mr. Black.

Trailanga Swami liked to tantalize the British police in Benares. Of course, they were scandalized at his nudity, so they were always trying to arrest him for it. He really liked having them run after him, for though he weighed a great deal, he could go very fast, but would always run only an arm's length away from them. Eventually he would take a street that led to the Ganges, and just as they thought they would catch hold of him he would leap far out into the Ganges. There he would either just sit on the water, remaining stationary even through the river was flowing very swiftly, or when the water was clear he would sink to the bottom and sit in meditation. Whichever he did, he would remain there for days with the police taking shifts to watch and eventually arrest him. And then he would disappear! Eventually it would start all over.

In *Autobiography of a Yogi*, Yoganandaji tells of times when Trailangaji would be locked in a jail cell and then after a while be seen walking along the roof. But there was a variation on that. Just like in the Middle Ages, there were stout wooden "cages" at the juncture of streets where the police would put criminals to be mocked and pelted with rocks and whatever the cowardly populace had to hand. Since he was so fat, they would have a hard time jamming Trailanga Swami in one of those cages, and when they did, his fat body would bulge out through the slats. But after a while he would suddenly be sitting on top of the cage, and not inside. When the police would start climbing up to grab him, he would jump out into the street, and the whole chase scene would be repeated.

Having decided that I would not be shocked at the account, Mr. Black then told me that often Trailanga Swami would stand in the Ganges and make his genitals as large as a fire hose and spray the pilgrims (and police) with the same force as a fire hose. But it was not urine, it was marvelous perfume! He would also go into a Shiva temple and either urinate on the linga or urinate in his hand and then pour it over the linga. Of course, the priests and worshippers went wild, but it would be discovered that it was heavenly perfume, and not urine at all.

At the beginning of 1968, Swami Kriyananda was scheduled to teach a two-week seminar on yoga at the University of the Pacific in Stockton, California. In time he realized that he would not be able to do the seminar, so he asked me to go in his place. At the end of the first week Swamiji came to the afternoon session and showed us slides of India which he had taken. (He also sang bhajans for us, including *Gokula Chandra*, accompanying himself on the tanboura.) One of the slides showed the temple in Trailanga Swami's Benares ashram. The central object was a life-size marble statue of the Swami, but to the side and standing on the floor was a half-relief sculpture of the goddess Kali. Although it was not in any way an artistic production, something about it fascinated me. I remarked on it to Swamiji, and he told me that one day Trailanga Swami had been in another part of the ashram conversing with a disciple. At one point, the Kali image, having come to life, walked into the room where they were seated and held a conversation with Trailanga Swami, then walked out, returned to the temple and became stone again. The disciple was absolutely stunned and speechless. But Trailangaji simply said to him: "So now what have you got?" meaning that no experience, however amazing, was of any value whatsoever if it did not impart wisdom or meaningful change to the aspirant.

Finally, I can tell you that you can purchase a book on Amazon: *Trailanga Swami and Shankari Mataji* by Swami Paramananda Saraswati. Shankari Mataji was a disciple of Trailanga Swami. Yoganandaji briefly wrote about her in his autobiography and included her photograph. The material in the book is mostly her memories of Trailangaji which she personally told the author.

I am in a slight spiritual/religious quandary about the topic mentioned in Ephesians 1:7: "In Christ we are set free by the blood of his death," etc. I feel this is such an easy way out versus cleaning up my act and ridding all past karmic sludge via lifetimes of evolving through higher and higher spiritual levels, I hope!

Anyway, it seems like one philosophy says we must all evolve and thus purify ourselves and this Bible quote says Christ's blood via His death forgives our sins??? Please help me understand.

First, it must always be kept in mind that the New Testament has been heavily edited to make it conform to the theology of the fourth century state religion which called itself Christianity.

But, let's look at the King James Version which is still the most accurate, though it has outdated language: "In whom [Christ] we have redemption through his blood...."

The word translated "redemption" is *apolutrosis*, which means deliverance and liberation–to be set free. This is the very meaning of the Sanskrit word *moksha*, usually translated "liberation." So the ideal is the same.

Jesus of Nazareth, having lived with the masters of India and attained liberation through perfect union with the universal Christ–Ishwara, the personal aspect of God (also called "the Son of God)–was thereby a Christ.

Jesus said: "Except ye eat the flesh of the Son of man, and drink his blood, ye have no life in you" (John 6:53, 56). The "flesh" of Jesus Christ is his outer life of perfect holiness, and his "blood" is his inner, Christ Consciousness. It is this alone that liberates anyone–as Jesus himself was liberated through Christ. The word *aima*, translated "blood" not only means the physical blood of a living creature, but the seat or center of life itself. "For the life of the flesh is in the blood" (Leviticus 17:11). It is the Christ Life that redeems us and procures for us the forgiveness of sins that is mentioned next in the verse from Ephesians. And guess what? The word here translated "forgiveness" is *aphesis,* which like *apolutrosis* also means release, deliverance and liberty: moksha.

A final point: It is not in the present-day New Testament that we find the truth about Jesus, his nature and his teachings, but the *Aquarian Gospel of Jesus the Christ* by Levi Dowling.

**Can Soham only take one so far in the direction of Self-reali-
zation? Should Soham be let go of at a certain point, or is the
practice retained? Can a still and silent mind be achieved if there
is still Soham with the breath even if it is very subtle? In my practice the intonations of Soham have softened and become like a
wisp of smoke that is almost indistinguishable and inseparable
from the breath–even indistinguishable from the breath.**

In the scriptures that deal with yoga and meditation, such as are
cited in *Soham Yoga*, Soham is declared to be both Brahman and the
Self. Self-realization is the realization of Soham as the Self and Brahman–the individual Self (jivatman) and the Supreme Self (Paramatman).
Soham is itself the revelation of Brahman and the Self. Therefore there
is no question of letting go of Soham in meditation. Rather, as you have
experienced for yourself, in meditation (and outside as well) the japa
of Soham becomes increasingly subtle just as you have described. And
in time that is experienced not just as the movement of the breath, but
as consciousness itself. For Consciousness and Sound are discovered to
be the same, as Purusha and Prakriti are the same, not two. Therefore
the yogic treatises tell us that the breath is continually sounding Soham
because the two are one.

**While being with Soham and the breath I have also focussed on
letting go of thoughts, feelings, etc. Obviously, there is a way to
go in that practice and I am seeking your advice.**

There is no need to think of letting go of thoughts, feelings, memories
and suchlike. Instead just relax into the mental sound of your intonations

of Soham and let Soham fill your entire awareness.

I hope you will occasionally reread or skim through *Soham Yoga* to keep these ideas vivid in your mind.

In the beginning of *Robe of Light* the separateness of God and the individual soul is stated and, if I understood correctly, the possibility of the soul to partake in the consciousness of God, but always being separate from Him. Is my understanding correct if I conclude from this that you are saying that perfect union with God is not possible? Or does it mean that it is not possible unless the individual ceases to exist?

The individual spirit is never separated from God, but is nevertheless distinct from God. We are always one with God, but there is a difference: God is always infinite, we are always finite. Although we do not "become God" in the sense of being infinite and no longer individuals, we can participate in certain aspects of the Divine Consciousness. The how of that is what *Robe of Light* is all About.

Union with God is not only possible, separation from God is impossible. Equally impossible is the cessation of the individual spirit.

Our problem is that we do not realize or experience the eternal order of things. The words of the Prodigal Son's father could easily be the words of God to the individual spirit: "Son, thou art ever with me, and all that I have is thine" (Luke 15:31).

My second question is about the meaning of Jesus Christ's life for all of humanity. How exactly was his mission important for us? I know *Robe of Light* deals with precisely that issue, but

does that mean that before Christ incarnated, it was impossible for a normal human being to become enlightened? Or more difficult?

The great Master Teachers such as Jesus have a twofold meaning: a universal meaning for all human beings as a manifestation of spiritual perfection which all can draw inspiration from, and a personal meaning for all those for whose benefit they specifically were incarnated at a certain time at a certain place.

What, then, is the meaning of Jesus' paying back the debt for "original sin" and the concrete consequences for a truth-seeker today versus a seeker in 1000 B.C.?

Jesus as a person is unique among teachers because of his having been Adam and therefore with a meaningful karmic connection with a great many people, but that does not make him superior to the other avatars, or even indispensable. As Yogananda often said, we must come to realize that on the highest level there is no difference between one master and another.

Jesus' incarnation and crucifixion was for the expiation of his personal karmic debt–not to God, but to that segment of humanity in this creation cycle that had been affected by his past negative actions and influence. Yet all humanity has been benefitted by his incarnation to different degrees and in different ways to some extent. However, if Jesus (or Krishna or Buddha, etc.) had not been born, human beings would still have managed because of their innate divine nature. Every great Master is unique, but not absolutely necessary for anyone. By that I mean that there is no one whose "salvation" depends on a Master without whom they cannot attain liberation (which is what salvation is). Yet, just as individuals from life to life come into association with those with whom they have past karma or present affinity, so it is with the great Wayshowers.

However, the only requisite for a human being is the attainment of conscious union with God as a result of evolution of their consciousness. Great Souls come into the world for that purpose, and although in the divine plan there are those who have an affinity for one of them, there is no one savior for all or even for an individual.

I want to ask you if you know how one can communicate with family members that have passed on, and if you can offer any pointers in that direction.

It is very important–necessary, actually–that after a certain time in earthly incarnation the human being leaves the body and spends time in an astral world so the previous life experiences can be assimilated into the individual's psyche. And equally important is the rest and rejuvenation of the person's astral and causal bodies so in the next life the person will be born in an appropriate body that will be charged with the life force needed for that life. This vital cycle must go on uninterruptedly after death for the sake of what we might call "reincarnational health."

Two things interrupt and interfere with that needed preparation for a next life.

1. Being drawn back from the astral world into this world (though in an astral body) and focused on the past life in its various aspects that the evolving individual needs to leave behind and move forward and prepare for the next life. It is like a level in school. When it is over, it is over and should be moved beyond.

Contact by the departed with loved ones after death can cause anguish at seeing their sorrow over the departed's absence, and can even in time cause them to be earthbound and unable to go back into the astral world where they should be. As a result they can become wandering spirits, tormented by their inability to communicate with "the living."

2. The desire to be with and able to communicate with embodied people can cause them to reincarnate too soon without have gotten the rest and regeneration their subtle bodies needed. As a result in the next life they will be weak in health and susceptible to many physical problems and ailments.

The universe is a school which has rules, and those who ignore or break the rules run into difficulties. They are not punished, they just undergo the consequences of not following that which is designed for their continued welfare and happiness in whatever world they may be.

When loved ones leave this world they can experience real distress and mental anguish at the sorrow of those they leave behind, since for a short while they can feel the emotions of the mourners. Therefore those who love them should do their best not to sink into grief, but should rather think of the departed with love and appreciation and pray deeply for the progress of that dear one's soul. Prayers for the departed are effective means to uplift and free the departed to prepare for the subsequent life.

There is nothing wrong in vividly remembering those who have left the earth plane, but always with love and blessing and prayers for their continued progress. Their absence is sad for us, but they have not died, just gone to another dimension. But a selfish desire to pull them back and be with them as before death is very harmful to us and them.

Freedom to grow is needed in every world in which we may be born and evolve. We must let them go. They belong to God and to the cosmos. Jerry Jampolsky was right: Love is Letting Go.

To someone who asked how Jesus could have a personal karmic debt requiring the crucifixion for its expiation if he had become Christ and was in total conscious union with the Absolute.

This was part of the Great Sacrifice made by Jesus. Definitely he had no compulsory karma whatsoever. But he willingly retained the karmic debt in order to facilitate his mission as a World Savior. He could have just consumed that karma and let the world continue to muddle through, but did not.

Masters are able to retain karma to use as a kind of karmic thread, a means by which they can more easily reincarnate back in this world.

For example, Master Yogananda had decided in detail upon his next earthly life in India when he will wander by the Ganges with just a few chosen disciples. For a year prior to his mahasamadhi he had occasionally been warning his disciples that he would be leaving this world in the near future. Naturally, most of them just could not take it in, one of the reasons being that he scheduled an ocean voyage to India and designated the disciples who would be going with him. For some years he had basically lived without eating. He had a little clear plastic "satchel" in which he took nuts and fruit with him during the work on Lake Shrine. And that he mostly gave to the workers, who found that a tiny mouthful stopped all hunger and thirst and gave them the energy for the day's hard work. But toward the end of his remaining time he began only eating elaborate Indian food, giving great attention to its preparation. Much of his time before the Indian Consulate's visit at whose banquet he planned to leave his body was spent perfecting various Indian bazaar dishes for his honored guest, particularly singharas (samosas). In over thirty years in America he had never been able to duplicate them exactly like those in Calcutta, but at last he succeeded.

By using his karma at will, not being under its power at all, he created a karmic force in that last year which would facilitate his return. For no matter how trivial a desire, decision or action, if unfulfilled or undissolved it will bring a person back to incarnation. (A great nineteenth-century master, Sri Brahma Chaitanya of Gondawali, Maharashtra, told of a little girl who had been brought back to rebirth solely because she wanted a necklace! When she gave it to him, silently indicating that she was offering it to God, she left her body after a few days.)

It was the same with Jesus. Neither karma nor karmic debt mean to the Masters what it means for us.

I understood that one of the blessings of transcendent meditation was that progressive superconscious states burned off the impurities of mind, the karmic tendencies and latencies–our impulses for action-reaction. To the extent that the mind is established in superconscious levels, is not karma effectively overcome?

Yes. But completely at the will of the master yogi, who can rearrange things as they go on according to his divine consciousness. But never under compulsion or coercion.

Is Karma such an absolute Law that must be totally met? I ask this because Karma seems a more nuanced expression of universal law than we realize and perhaps does not function quite in the way we imagine.

Karma is Consciousness, just like everything else.

Is there not a Law of Grace–reflecting our spiritual state–that progressively dissolves karma as we evolve?

Evolution dissolves karma as we evolve. And that itself is Grace. Please realize this: We can never understand Masters and how they accomplish their divine mission in this world until we become Masters ourselves.

Can someone today have had "no" past lives? Could this be the start of lives?

We have many, many reincarnations in lower life forms before we ever reach human form. (See *Robe of Light*.) By the time we are (primitive) human beings we have no doubt been around for more than one creation cycle. So all human beings have a very long history behind them.

What if someone can't recall a past life/lives? How do they unblock this?

There is a very good reason for people not remembering their past lives, lest they get stuck in one and not move on and thereby retard their progress. So if someone draws a blank in trying to remember, it is better to drop the idea for a while and return to it occasionally to see if the blank remains. When the time is right, the memory will be available.

Sometimes people have lived on other planets in intelligent life forms very different from ours, so even if they remember, it either makes no sense to them or they do not believe it. It is not common, but it does happen.

Why do some people feel shame and embarrassment over the memory of a past life? Is this normal and why are people ashamed?

That is so subjective and personal that there is no simple answer for it. Certainly, a person might get a glimmer of a life that somewhere had an unpleasant or "shameful" element and feel shame and embarrassment even if that aspect has not surfaced consciously. It is good to be cautious at such times, perhaps waiting a while and then trying again.

I once remembered quite a bit about a childhood in a life three centuries ago. It made no sense to me: I lived alone with my mother in a large house and never saw anyone else but an elderly woman who was some kind of servant that came each day. When I was about ten years of age, I did meet two other boys my age. We became friends and often spent time together in a forest, but I never saw their homes or anyone connected with them. In my early teens my mother died and then no one at all came near our house, and to escape starvation I wandered until I found a road and walked to a large city where I made a very poor living.

One day when pondering the peculiarity of that life I understood: I must have been an illegitimate child of someone who kept my mother and me hidden away and my existence was strictly kept secret. Since the lapse of three centuries made me indifferent to such a life, I might have felt ashamed if the impressions of the social ideas of that time were still in my subconscious.

Is it possible to consider all humans as God?

All that exists is part of God, though in a way that the ordinary mind cannot conceive. Everything is God; yet only God is God–all else is "god." When perfect liberation (purna moksha) is attained, the individual jiva is a perfect reflection/manifestation of Shiva. Yet the jiva is always finite and Shiva is always infinite. Paramhansa Yogananda said that we should never say "I am God," but we can say: "God is manifesting as and through me."

Did Jesus Christ actually "absorb and cancel" the karmic debt of the world's people and all sentient beings for all past, present and future offenses?

No, he did not. For proof of that, take a look at the world! Is it karma-free? Has suffering ended? And deliberate evil? Of course not. If life is the best teacher, then I can only assume that these "Bible-believing" Christians have been skipping class for a lot of lifetimes.

What *did* Jesus do? "Behold, I have set before thee an open door" (Revelation 3:8). That is why in the Creed of our Sunday worship we say: "We strive towards the ancient narrow path that leads to life eternal."

He opened (revealed) the way to ascend to God—not just get rid of bad karma. Unfortunately, Christianity has destroyed and distorted that way. But since Jesus learned it in India we can find it still there, for India is a far more reliable source for understanding Jesus' teachings than the many warring churches can ever be.

That is why the masters of India sent Paramhansa Yogananda into the West to present authentic Christianity—which is really Sanatana Dharma, for Jesus was neither Jewish nor Christian in his religion but an authentic follower of Dharma. That is why he told the king of Kashmir:

> "O King, I hail from a land far away, *where there is no truth, and evil knows no limits*. I appeared in the country of the mlecchas as

Isha Masiha [Jesus Messiah/Christ] and I suffered at their hands. For I said unto them, 'Remove all mental and bodily impurities. Remember the Name of our Lord God. Meditate upon Him Whose abode is in the center of the sun.' There in the land of mleccha darkness, I taught love, truth, and purity of heart. I asked human beings to serve the Lord. But I suffered at the hands of the wicked and the guilty. In truth, O King, all power rests with the Lord, Who is in the center of the sun. And the elements, and the cosmos, and the sun, and God Himself, are forever."

This is pure Vedic Dharma. (See *The Christ of India* for the complete conversation of Jesus with the king of Kashmir after his resurrection and return to India.)

Thus, the puzzle for me is, I assume I still must do my part to resolve all my own karmic "pile"? This is puzzling for me and probably many others if Jesus Christ "took" it all.

But he did not "take" anything. That is why he said in Revelation 3:21: "To him that *overcometh* will I grant to sit with me in my throne, *even as I also overcame*, and am set down with my Father in his throne." We, too, have to overcome, just as did Jesus. This is the real teaching of Jesus.

Please define "He could have just consumed that karma..." in your blogpost.

Jesus could have just "worked off" or neutralized his karma, but he used it as a means to help others. However, he only helped them–he did not "save" them. Each one of us must do that for ourselves. And he showed the way.

This subject also leads to arguments with Christians who say: "Why do I need to reincarnate to pay off my sins via rebirth if Jesus Christ paid the price for me?"

How do you argue with falsehood? It is a lie: Jesus "paid" nothing for us. We ourselves must pay it all. Karma is clearly outlined by Saint Paul: "Be not deceived; God is not mocked: for whatsoever a man soweth, that shall he also reap" (Galatians 6:7). If Jesus enabled us to not reap what we have sown, then he would be the greatest mocker of God along with us. Certainly the karma of negative action can be neutralized by the karma of positive action–but that is all in our hands. That is why Zacchaeus "said unto the Lord;… *if I have taken any thing from any man by false accusation, I restore him fourfold*" (Luke 19:8). That way he cancelled his karmic debts. Jesus did not do it for him.

Faith is not only worthless, it is destructive when it is placed in something that is not true. Sincerity counts for nothing when we are deluded.

I just cannot lie back like a slouch and ride on the Christian riff that all is paid and all I have to do is cruise right into Heaven.

Of course you cannot. You are a rational human being who knows better, because it does not work that way as these "believers" find out after death and in future lives.

In India which is mostly worshipped: God with form (Saguna Brahman) or God without form (Nirguna Brahman)? Do you think that to worship the Personal God is better than to worship the Formless God?

Certainly in India Saguna Brahman is worshipped more than Nirguna Brahman. But we must not forget that Saguna and Nirguna mean with qualities (guna) and without qualities, not just with form and without form–though that is included. As usual it is good to turn to the Bhagavad Gita in this matter. There we find this in the twelfth chapter:

"Arjuna said: The constantly steadfast who worship you with devotion, and those who worship the eternal Unmanifest–which of them has the better understanding of yoga? The Holy Lord said: Those who are ever steadfast, who worship me, fixing their minds on me, endowed with supreme faith, I consider them to be the best versed in yoga. But those who worship the Imper-ishable, the Undefinable, the Unmanifested, the Omnipresent (All-pervading), Inconceivable, Unchanging, Unmoving, the Constant–controlling all the senses, even-minded everywhere, happy in the welfare of all beings–they attain to me also. Greater is the effort of those whose minds are set on the Unmanifest, for the Unmanifest as a goal is truly difficult for the embodied ones to reach. But those who, renouncing all actions in me, intent on me as the highest [goal] worship me, meditating on me with single-minded Yoga–of those whose consciousness has entered into me, I am soon the deliverer from the ocean of mortal samsara. Keep your mind on me alone, causing your intellect to enter into me. Thenceforward, without doubt, you shall dwell in me" (12:1-8).

Are Lord Krishna and Rama both the Personal God?

Brahman is one, being both Saguna and Nirguna, and also beyond those distinctions. The same is true of every individual jiva as well. So whether we consider an avatara to be Brahman Itself or a perfectly liberated being, a siddha (as do the Sankhyas), the same applies.

But They [Krishna and Rama] are not physically here in this world anymore. Why even until now do so many people worship Lord Krishna and Lord Sri Rama?

Again we find the answer in the Gita–in part of the section I have just cited. Krishna himself says:

"But those who, renouncing all actions in me, intent on me as the highest [goal] worship me, meditating on me with single-minded Yoga–of those whose consciousness has entered into me, I am soon the deliverer from the ocean of mortal samsara."

Sri Krishna and Sri Rama are eternal as are we. Just as they delivered those who took refuge in them when they were here on earth, so they deliver their sharanagatis even now. Thousands of years have proven this to be true.

Of the Trimurti–Brahma, Vishnu and Shiva–which one is superior?

As you know, Brahma is reverenced but not worshipped, and both Vishnu and Shiva are worshipped throughout India. Since Vishnu and Shiva are manifestations or forms of the one God, they are equal. Only ignorance makes them seem different–and ignorance is a poor basis for worship and devotion.

How do those who worship the Impersonal God (Nirguna Brahman) imagine Him for the purpose of concentration? Or is it not necessary to imagine any form of God during worship of Him?

It is very necessary to realize that there are not two Brahmans, Saguna and Nirguna. Rather there is only Brahman who to us in relative existence appears dual in aspect: with qualities (guna) and without qualities (nirguna).

Naturally, there would be no mental image of Nirguna Brahman, but according to the scriptures, the japa and meditation of Soham unites us to Brahman in total being, nirguna and saguna.

In the oldest upanishad, the Isha Upanishad, the sixteenth verse says: *Yo sav asau purushah; soman asmi*–I am that Purusha [Spirit-Self]: I am Soham. In Sanskrit Soham means "I Am That," but at the core of every sentient being Soham exists as the Self–*is* the Self. Therefore the seer of the upanishad concludes: "I am Soham." *Soham asmi*–"I am That I am"–is exactly what God told Moses was his Name (Exodus 3:14).

In the next oldest Upanishad, the Brihadaranyaka Upanishad, we are told: "In the beginning this (world) was only the Self [Atman], in the shape

284 Satsang with the Abbot

of a person. Looking around he saw nothing else than the Self. He first said, I am Soham [*Soham asmi*]" (1:4:1). Thus, Soham is the "first speaking" of the Absolute Itself: the expression of the knowledge and knowing of the Self. We, too, are Soham. Later in the Upanishad (5.15.2), the identical words are said as in the verse cited previously from the Isha Upanishad.

At the beginning of the Maha Vakya Upanishad, Brahma the Creator is said to have declared: "The personal knowledge that this Sun is Brahman is got by chanting the Ajapa Gayatri: Soham." At the end of the upanishad Brahma says that those who invoke this Gayatri will have the realization: "I am that sun who is the ethereal light. I am that Shiva who is that sun of Knowledge. I am the supremely pure [vishuddha] light of the Atman. I am all the light that we know."

"Solely by the mantra Soham joined to the inhalation and exhalation, the jiva perceives the supreme Brahman" (Narada Parivrajaka Upanishad 6:4).

"The Supreme Swan [Paramhansa–the Self] is Soham" (Nirvana Upanishad 2). The two syllables *So* and *Ham* are the two wings by means of which the swan-spirit flies back to Spirit.

"Soham is the seed-mantra, the essence, of the Sun" (Surya Upanishad).

"This mantra [Soham] which is called Ajapa Gayatri will give salvation to all yogis. Just mental repetition of this mantra will help one get rid of all sins. There are no practices as holy as this, no japa which is equivalent to this, and no wisdom equivalent to this and in the future there shall be nothing equivalent to it. This Ajapa Gayatri which rises from the Kundalini supports the soul. This is the greatest among the sciences of the soul" (Yoga Chudamani Upanishad 33-35).

"The breath goes out with the sound 'ham' and goes in with the word 'so'.... This chanting of the mantra 'Soham, Soham' [in time with the breath], is called Mantra Yoga" (Yoga Shikha Upanishad 1.5).

"The Gayatri called Ajapa [Soham] is the giver of liberation to the sages; by merely repeating it mentally one is released from all sin" (Garuda Purana 15:70).

"Know this [Soham] to be the Paramatman" (Jnanarvana Tantra).

"The body is the temple of God. Let the jiva worship with 'Soham' (Kularnava Tantra).

"The living soul knows itself to be 'Soham'" (Yoga Vashishtha, Utpatti Khanda 3:64:9).

"The breath of every person in entering makes the sound of 'sah' and in coming out, that of 'ham.' These two sounds make Soham. Throughout a day and a night there are twenty-one thousand and six hundred such respirations. Every living being performs this japa unconsciously, but constantly. This is called ajapa gayatri. All jivas are constantly and unconsciously reciting this ajapa mantra, only for a fixed number of times every day. But a yogi should recite this consciously" (Gheranda Samhita 5:84, 90).

"One constantly meditates: 'Soham'" (Yogavishaya of Minanath [Matsyendranath] 29).

For much more on this, see Chapter Three of *Soham Yoga*.

You write in a Q&A section that Jesus did no such thing as pay for our sins. If that is the case, why does he say in Mark 10:45 that he came to give his life as a ransom for many? Or even more to the point, in Matthew 26:28 he says "This is my blood of the covenant, which is poured out for many for the forgiveness of sins."

One problem we have is that fact that the "original Greek" texts date from sometime after the beginning of the fourth century and have been made to conform to the theology of the Nicene or Constantinian version of Christianity. Even the Aramaic text was corrupted after this time and the Peshitta text was imposed on the Aramaic-speaking churches. (Lamsa's so-called "original" text is the Peshitta. In the (Aramaic) Cureton Gospels we have the nearest to the original, but the "translation" published in 1894 is little more than a paraphrase of the King James gospels. One of our monks who was a linguist translated all four into English, but after his death the computer disk on which they were found was damaged by a company we gave it over to for transcription. We do have the gospel of John and Luke and hope to post them on our website in the future. But we cannot be sure there was not some meddling with those texts, though they are much older than the Greek.

The root of the problem goes right back to just after the departure of Jesus from Israel to return to India. (See *The Christ of India* on our website.) In the ancient book of Kashmiri history, the *Bhavishya Maha Purana*, there is the following account of the meeting of a king of Kashmir with Jesus sometime after his return: "When the king of the Sakas came to the Himalayas, he saw a dignified person of golden complexion wearing a long white robe. Astonished to see this foreigner, he asked, 'Who are you?' The dignified person replied in a pleasant manner: 'Know me as Son of God [Isha Putram], or Born of a Virgin [Kumarigarbhasangbhawam]. Being given to truth and penances, I preached the Dharma to the mlecchas…. O King, I hail from a land far away, where there is no truth, and evil knows no limits. I appeared in the country of the mlecchas as Isha Masiha [Jesus Messiah/Christ] and I suffered at their hands. For I said unto them, '"Remove all mental and bodily impurities. Remember the Name of our Lord God. Meditate upon Him Whose abode is in the center of the sun."' There in the land of mleccha darkness, I taught love, truth, and purity of heart. I asked human beings to serve the Lord. But I suffered at the hands of the wicked and the guilty. In truth, O King, all power rests with the Lord, Who is in the center of the sun. And the elements, and the cosmos, and the sun, and God Himself, are forever. Perfect, pure, and blissful, God is always in my heart. Thus my Name has been established as Isha Masiha.' After having heard the pious words from the lips of this distinguished person, the king felt peaceful, made obeisance to him, and returned" (*Bhavishya Maha Purana* 3.2.9-31. The word "mleccha" means a foreigner, a non-Indian.)

Here we see that what Jesus says he taught in Israel was not the religion called Christianity that we have today, but that of India. Especially
significant is Jesus' statement that "I hail from a land far away, *where
there is no truth, and evil knows no limits.*" This is certainly no endorse-
ment of the Judaism of that day as being a true religion. Yet we find
from the book of Acts that the apostles and their converts were meeting
daily in the Temple of Jerusalem and conformed so fully to the very
religion Jesus has repudiated at the age of twelve, that they even made
male converts be circumcised!

Part of the intrusion of the old beliefs and ways into the beliefs of
Christianity was the insistence on the former legitimacy of blood sacrifice. See the ninth chapter of the book of Hebrews where we find such
an insane statement as: "Without shedding of blood is no remission
[of sins]" (Hebrews 9:22). Therefore Jesus had to be declared a perfect
blood sacrifice to appease the wrath of a justly angered God. And things
unraveled from there. This is why Jesus said in the Greek text: "Many
will say to me in that day, Lord, Lord, have we not prophesied in thy
name? and in thy name have cast out devils? and in thy name done
many wonderful works? And then will I profess unto them, I never knew
you: depart from me, ye that work iniquity" (Matthew 7:22-23). In the
Aquarian Gospel there is even more of a point put on those words: "And
when the judgement hour shall come a host of men will enter pleadings
for themselves and think to buy the favor of the judge with words. And
they will say, Lo, we have wrought a multitude of works in the Omnific
name, have we not prophesied? Have we not cured all manner of disease?
Have we not cast the evil spirits out of those obsessed? And then the
judge will say, I know you not. You rendered service unto God in words
when in your heart you worshipped Beelzebub. The evil one may use
the powers of life, and do a multitude of mighty works. Depart from
me, you workers of iniquity" (101:24-28).

Certainly Jesus is a world-savior, but not in the way of the gross and
ignorant theology of the churches. And he did show the way to eternal

life, but Christianity began destroying it from the very first. Which is also why Jesus asked: "When the Son of man cometh, shall he find faith on the earth?" (Luke 18:8).

How do we find the authentic teachings of Jesus? In the very same place where he got them: India. The religion he brought from India back to Israel was and is based on the Upanishads, the Bhagavad Gita and the Yoga Sutras from which he quoted. If we learn and adopt that religion then we are the disciples of Christ. Not otherwise.

I would like to understand the perception of Jesus' life better. I don't know if you would like to comment but I'd appreciate it.

The best place to start is the *Aquarian Gospel* by Levi Dowling. In both the Introduction and the text the difference between "The Christ" and "a Christ" (as was Jesus) is explained.

Paramhansa Yogananda's *Autobiography of a Yogi* (first edition) and *The Second Coming of Christ* give the true nature and teachings of Jesus. PDFs of both books can be downloaded from our ocoy.org website. However, the two-volume edition from SRF contains material from other publications of Yogananda added by Sri Mrinilini Mata when she edited it, so I recommend you get a copy of that as well if you do not already have it.

Jesus Christ and Yoga by Shyam Sundar Goswami also gives the insights of a yogi into the nature and mission of Jesus who was a master yogi and a member of the Nath Yogi Order.

The kindest thing I can say about Rudolf Steiner's ideas is that they are thoroughly unsound. The idea that he was a Christian mystic is so false that it is not even laughable–just shameless.

Every Master is unique and makes a unique contribution to the world by his life and teaching. Max Heindel in *The Rosicrucian Cosmo*

Conception explains the uniqueness of Jesus to the world without any sectarianism or exclusiveness.

The following is taken from a condemnatory review of The Gospel of Thomas for Awakening *that was posted on the Amazon page where it can be ordered. It is extremely revealing about the attitude toward and the concept of God held by the reviewer—and most of contemporary Christianity.*

No other person ever raised himself from the dead after three days in the grave.

As a child I encountered this argument and being ignorant accepted it. Later on when I learned what had been going on in the real world outside the blind and narrow world of Churchianity I realized it was errant nonsense.

Throughout history there have been masters in the Eastern religions—Hinduism, Buddhism and Taoism—that have manifested themselves in living physical bodies after their physical death. For example: Shyama Charan Lahiri Mahasaya, Swami Sri Yukteswar Giri and Paramhansa Yogananda. My friend Durgaprasad Sahai was present when Swami Keshavananda, a disciple of Lahiri Mahasaya written about in *Autobiography of a Yogi*, manifested in physical form in Benares. He told me about it in detail. I myself saw the Raja of Solan in a physical body in Brindaban two or three years after his death.

These masters did not retain the physical body after their various appearances to others. But if that is desired as proof there is the well-known and proven example of Sri Hariakhan Baba in the twentieth century. Baba went with one of his disciples on pilgrimage to Kailash.

At one point the disciple got smallpox and was dying. Hariakhan Baba took the disease on his body and died of it. The disciple had his body cremated and, grieving, went to Almora to inform his fellow devotees of Baba's death. At the edge of Almora he came to a shop of a devotee in order to tell him the sad news. "Why are you not with Baba?" asked the man, and said he was at a certain devotee's house. When the disciple hurried there he found Hariakhan Baba there in his resurrected physical body in which he lived for more years.

And what about those that have never even died? Are they not more free from the bonds of death than someone who dies and resurrects? In India today there are deathless masters such as Ashwatthama (from the days of the Mahabharata War), Agastya Muni and Mahavatar Babaji of *Autobiography of a Yogi*. I personally know three people who met Babaji, and know others whose gurus knew him well and told them many things about him.

And since when is physical embodiment a proof of immortality? The body is not the spirit. No one ever really dies.

Furthermore, according to the *Nathanamavali* (see *The Christ of India*) Jesus was raised from the dead by his guru, Sri Chetan Nath of the Nath Yogi Order.

No other person lived a perfect, sinless life, and can grant eternal life to anyone who will repent of their sins, embrace him and believe on him in their spirit.

Now how could anyone know that unless they knew every human being that ever lived?

I met a missionary in India who insisted on this nonsense. I reminded him that Jesus said: "He that believeth on me, the works that I do shall he do also" (John 14 12). Since we were in Calcutta I told him about the many times those in helpless moral conditions (some hopelessly addicted to drugs) came to Sri Ramakrishna who was living in the Dakshineshwar Kali Temple and begged for his help. He would simply touch them and they would instantly be freed from their bondage. I also told him of yogis I had met in America and India who could do the same thing. "Can you do that?" I asked. "No," he answered. "Then who are the true Christians–them or you, according to Jesus?" I asked. And he had no answer.

A very close friend of mine committed a terrible evil which from that moment on blighted her life. For some years she was burdened with the effects of her deed. One time we were both in India and I urged her to go that very day to her guru and plead for help. The next time I saw her the change was instantly evident: the terrible cloud had been dispelled. I told her so, and she told me that her guru had simply touched her with both hands and moved them throughout her aura. "I felt all that awful guilt and the damage it had done to me dissolving away, and I left completely free," she said. And she remained so.

Over and over I have seen great yogis deliver people at a glance. Many times I have witnessed profound spiritual release and healing occur when people have simply entered the place where the yogis were and stood looking at them, often with tears of relief and joy streaming down their faces. One woman I knew could not recover from the death of her father, so she came from Europe to India to see her father's guru. "If I just tell him my grief, he will help me," she told me. And I well remember the morning she returned from seeing the yogi. She was radiant with joy, completely free from sorrow.

As Yogananda wrote in his autobiography, there are many Yogi-Christs in India. I have known some. And they could raise the dead, heal the sick and cleanse lepers like Jesus, too.

That is Jesus' marvilous [sic] gift to us. Eternal life, if we can believe in him and accept his free gift. Thank you Lord Jesus!

Why thank the Lord Jesus if it is *your* faith that enables you to be saved? You say: "*If* we can *believe* in him and *accept*." Even as a Fundamentalist I saw the absurdity of my salvation being determined by my own emotional response to Jesus. Why would that be the condition of my salvation? Then I would be the cause of my salvation, and not him. (Later on I learned from reading Indian spiritual writings that this was the actual truth. Thank you, India!)

What has faith to do with the reality of something? In 1962 I was instantly healed of fever and a terrible ulcer in my throat by Swami Krishnananda of Krishnanagar in rural Bengal. (Swamiji was a disciple of Sri Ma Sarada Devi, the virgin wife of Sri Ramakrishna.) I just could not believe I was healed. I not only believed that the ulcer was still there, I kept swallowing very hard to get it to start hurting again. But it did not. I had been healed. Faith had nothing to do with it.

To deny the Lord Jesus Christ as the Son of God is blasphemous and if one does not repent of such heresey [sic] in this life damnation is in your future.

What a terrible belief about God: that he is such a psychotic failure that if his handiwork goes wrong and does not do as he wants it to he will either destroy it or torture it for eternity in unquenchable fire. Some savior! Some love!

I would like to ask all who believe as does this reviewer: Who do you really believe in: God or Godzilla?

Reading Abbot Burke's *The Christ of India*, (all in all a great book) I am a bit confused as to the disposition of Saint Thomas Christians on the matter of God. At one point, he states that they are Unitarian and at other times asserts they are Trinitarian, both practically and esoterically. Which is it?

It is both, because God is both Unity and Trinity. We must realize that since human beings are only on the first rung of the evolutionary ladder, the material universe, they really cannot comprehend the divine nature as it is, since it is beyond conception—but not beyond direct experience. As a result, we must speak of it in terms common to this world.

God is beyond all conception, and therefore is beyond both Unity and Trinity as we think of it. Yet in speaking of the possibility of interaction between humans and God and the ultimate realization of their oneness, we have to speak as well as we can, though only approximately. God is absolutely One, yet in relating to us manifests in a triune manner. And since God never changes, he must be essentially One and Three simultaneously, otherwise it could not happen. Yet, since even the concepts of one and three are from our side only, he is neither one nor three.

A child beginning to talk really does not have the mental development to understand what his mother and father really are as human beings. But they respond to his addressing them, even if he does not articulate "mother" or "father" clearly. In the same way, our reaching out to comprehend through language is an act of will which does lead us onward to increasing understanding and then transcendence of that limited comprehension into "open vision direct and instant" (Bhagavad Gita 9:1) which is beyond words. And in that vision we get beyond them, too.

To someone who, referring to the foregoing answer asked why it had to be one and three and not four, five, six, or any number.

You are absolutely right. Any number that applies to an aspect of God is perfectly legitimate. Here is an interesting section from the Upanishads regarding this.

"Then Vidagdha Sakalya asked him: How many gods are there, Yajnavalkya? He answered, in accord with the following nivid (invocation of the gods): As many as are mentioned in the nivid of the hymn of praise to the Vishwedevas, namely, three hundred and three, and three thousand and three. Yes, he said, but how many gods are there, Yajnavalkya? Thirty three. Yes, he said, but how many gods are there, Yajnavalkya? Six. Yes, said he, but how many gods are there, Yajnavalkya? Three. Yes, said he, but how many gods are there, Yajnavalkya? Two. Yes, said he, but how many gods are there, Yajnavalkya? One and a half. Yes, said he, but how many gods are there, Yajnavalkya? One. Yes, said he." (Brihadaranyaka Upanishad 3.9.1)

God is not like an egg or an apple that you can count him, so he is not really one, either. As the ancient sages of India have told us over and over, he is all and he is no thing. Therefore he is every number and no number.

The only ones who really understand this are the siddhas, the perfected yogis.

In reply to someone who had read *Robe of Light* which discusses the importance of both Jesus and Mary in the history of the human race as the reincarnations of Adam and Eve. He asked what the function and role of other great historical spiritual figures

has been in relationship to the advent and mission of Jesus and Mary. Particularly he asked about Buddha in relation to them.

Many times I cite the teaching of Yogananda on various topics, and his words here are relevant. In one of his recorded talks he expresses the need for us to realize that all the masters who have appeared on earth are of equal status—that there is no difference between them as far as their spiritual level is concerned. Some have had wider influence in the world and some less, but that is no indication of their value.

There is no way that a person can live in India and not be affected by many great masters of the past such as Krishna, Rama, Buddha and Shankara. Certainly they would have influenced Jesus, and contemporary masters also had a marked effect. For example, Yogananda said that the Three Wise Men were Mahavatar Babaji, Shyama Charan Lahiri Mahasaya and Swami Sri Yukteswar, and that when Jesus went to India he studied with them.

Each liberated being is a product of many influences, including many teachers and masters. No one master stands completely on his own independently. Every one who is saved has many saviors along the way up the evolutionary ladder. As Yogananda said, no master is greater than another. Each one is unique and yet in essence all are the same—as are we who are destined to one day be masters ourselves.

I have a question arising from your teaching of meditation. You have written: "Meditation is the process of centering our awareness in the principle of pure consciousness which is our essential being." I wanted to check the meaning of that as the terms can be applied variously and it can sound abstract.

So in real terms is that the practice of attending with my conscious (thinking-feeling) mind, i.e. my consciousness, to stay

attentive within the field of my greater awareness which has a more spacious and rarefied character. And from here the Presence of the Divine may arise. I hope you follow my explanation, is this correct?

When Sri Ramakrishna was asked, "What is the Self?" he replied: "The witness of the mind." That is, the witnessing consciousness is the Self. When in a calm and relaxed manner we fix our awareness on Soham and the effects its japa and meditation produce, we are being ourselves. That pure consciousness which is experiencing is our Self. The Kena Upanishad defines the Self as "the Ear of the ear, the Mind of the mind, the Speech of speech, the Life of life and the Eye of the eye" (1:2). That is why meditation is so simple. As Vyasa and Shankara said in their commentaries on the Yoga Sutras, meditation is witnessing a stream of identical thoughts.

To someone who asked for more about Warren Vickerman, the second American to become a disciple of Paramhansa Yogananda.

The very first person I had a conversation with at the Hollywood SRF Center was Annie Vickerman, the wife of Warren Vickerman ("Vickie"). She was taking care of the little octagonal bookstore. We became good friends and in later conversations she occasionally told me some things about him.

A young man of deep introspection, Vickie came to realize that the breath is the foundation of the mind, and that the restless, uncontrolled breath is the great obstacle to deep spiritual perception. Though living in New York City, he somehow learned that a Swami Yogananda was living and teaching in Boston. Intuitively feeling that the swami held the key to his dilemma, he managed to find his address and went, unannounced, to Boston. As he was walking up toward the house in which Yogananda was saying, the Master came out onto the porch. Stopping right where he was, Vickie asked: "Can you help me to get rid of the breath?" Yoganandaji smiled and said: "Come right on in!" And he did, and became his second disciple in America.

Yoganandaji often stayed with the Vickermans in New York. Vickie was an excellent cook, so the two of them often spent hours in the kitchen cooking up Indian specialities and creating new ones. Whenever Annie (who could not cook at all) entered the precincts she was immediately shooed out and the door closed as the experts continued their culinary conquests.

Warren was serious about finding God and expected other yogis to be the same. Neither could he be fooled by talk. A man visited the Vickermans one day and Annie listened to him recite his spiritual experiences and insights to Vickie. Immensely impressed, when the man left Annie told Vickie: "That was remarkable, wasn't it?" "It was all lies, not a word of truth in it," was Vickie's brief retort. "How do you know?" asked a bewildered Annie. Sitting down, Vickie quietly said: "Because I was watching his heart chakra the whole time." So much for that!

Vickie became a highly developed yogi, and for many years led the Self-Realization Fellowship center in New York City. This naturally entailed his meeting many seekers and often becoming their advisor. Much like Yogananda's guru, Swami Sri Yukteswar Giri, Vickie had little patience with nonsense, earthly or psychic. One day a woman came to him in great distress. "Oh! What shall I do? Every time I start to meditate I fly up astrally out of my body and hit my head on the ceiling!" Vickie looked at her with a glint in his eye and then said forcefully: "Lady, when you are in that state there *is* no ceiling!"

One day Annie came across a modern language translation of the Bible. She read out to Vickie the part in Revelation about Saint John's vision of Jesus standing in the midst of seven golden candlesticks (in the King James Version). The translators used the term "lampstands" which they felt modern people could relate to. Vickie's comment was: "My God, it sounds like Saint John's vision took place in Macy's Department Store!"

Vickie meditated nearly all night sitting on his twin bed. Annie would be in the other bed reading. Just before Vickie began to meditate, he would open the drawer in the table beside his bed and bring out a handful of Almond Joy candy bars that Annie loved. Tossing them over to her, he would say: "Here, enjoy yourself." And she did. Eating the Almond Joys, she watched as he went deeper and deeper into meditation, entering samadhi without breath or heartbeat and sometimes levitating off the bed. And that was how she fell asleep every night.

Vickie owned a carpet company that made very high quality carpet, so he donated and had carpet installed throughout the Mount Washington headquarters and the Hollywood Church. It was a deep blue color and still in use when I lived next door to the church in 1961 and 1962.

Now, even though you did not ask, let me tell you about Annie herself whom I have always admired greatly.

Annie was born into the topmost stratum of New York City society known as the Four Hundred. Famous people whom even I had heard about or seen on television were her close friends. Her best friends were Wanda and Wally Toscanini, the daughters of Arturo Toscanini the great conductor. Three to four nights of every week she would have dinner with the Toscanini family, and it was always spaghetti, at the demand of the Maestro.

In 1924, Swami Yogananda came to New York and spoke in Carnegie Hall. Annie went to hear him and became his faithful disciple. The life of the Four Hundred was the only life Annie knew, but when many of the Four Hundred derided and denounced the Swami, Annie cut nearly all her social ties and made his disciples her only close friends.

After Vickie's death she moved to Hollywood and lived just around the corner from the SRF Center. She single-handedly managed the bookstore and often filled in as cashier in the cafe Yoganandaji had created. In later years she lived in Encinitas near the hermitage.

Truly it can be said of Annie: God and Guru were her life.

Epilogue: In my first conversation with Annie, which took place in the bookstore, she told me something that I now pass on to you, as it is from the Master himself.

More than once when talking with Vickie and Annie, Master Yogananda told them: "In three generations you won't even know I came to this country." When they asked him what, then, was the use of his coming here, he replied: "I have planted the seed and it will grow. My work will go on, even if sometimes my name will not even be mentioned."

(Swami Kriyananda wrote that the Master often said to those at Mount Washington: "When I am gone you all will change everything." In a letter to Rajasi, regarding himself and the organization after his departure from this world, he wrote: "They will go their way and I will go mine.")

Someone told me that the Indian scriptures say if householder yogis only engage in sexual relations at night they are actually brahmacharis. Is this so?

I have come across this in some "scriptural" books myself more than once through the years. Nevertheless, this statement is not only false, it is foul. Do not believe it. I have read the dharma shastras on the rules for the grihasta life and they are far more stringent, I can assure you.

But since you mention "householder yogis," let me assure you that all such talk is usually just empty air. Three men are held up as examples of "householder yogis" to the world: Sri Ramakrishna, his disciple Durgacharan Nag and Shyama Charan Lahiri Mahasaya. Let us look at their examples, which are holy indeed.

Sri Ramakrishna was first of all a monk, a member of the Puri branch of the Swami Order. Ramakrishna was his monastic name. His family and the owner of the Dakshineshwar Kali Temple decided that celibacy had made his brain overheated and that if his brahmacharya would be broken then he would be "normal." So first of all, the owner of the temple took him to a house of prostitution in Calcutta and left him there until "it" would be done. When he went back he found Sri Ramakrishna seated in samadhi while being worshipped by the prostitutes who upbraided him for daring to attempt defilement of such a holy man. His family had gotten him married for the same nefarious purpose, but the bride was a child at the time. So after the Calcutta failure it was decided to send Sarada Devi, his now-adult wife, to live with him in the temple and end his brahmacharya. What they did not know was her exalted spiritual status. One night he asked her: "Have you come here to bring my mind down to the lower planes?" "Why would I?" she replied, and they lived together in unbroken virginity. He worshipped her as Kali and she worshipped him as Kali. After his mahasamadhi she carried on his work as a supreme jnani and yogeshwari. Read their biographies and their spiritual discourses, especially *The Gospel of Sri Ramakrishna,* and decide who in India or America are really householder yogis.

Durgacharan Nag declared to his parents that he wished to never marry, but they lied to him and told him that he need not break his virginity—just get married and live with his wife in celibacy. Being a pure soul and of impeccable honesty he could not conceive of the real intentions of his mother and father. So he married and through the years endured the complaining, haranguing and demanding of his parents and his wife that he break brahmacharya and have children. But he held firm and left this world still a brahmachari. Swami Vivekananda said that he had travelled throughout India and the world and had never met anyone the spiritual equal of Nag Mahasaya.

Yogiraj Shyama Charan Lahiri Mahasaya was secularly employed, married and had children when he met his guru, Mahavatar Babaji, in the Himalayas. There he became a yogi, and from that time onward lived in perpetual celibacy with his wife. For twenty-five years afterward he worked in a government office, returning to his home to spend the entire night in deep meditation, and most of the days when the office was closed. After his retirement he spent night and day in his small room where he received disciples and spiritual inquirers. You can read in Chapter Thirty-One of *Autobiography of a Yogi* about his wife complaining to him regarding this "neglect" of his family. One of his children died while he was discoursing on spiritual subjects with his visitors. When the wailing from the upper floor announced the death, someone asked if they should leave. "They are doing their work and we are doing ours," was his calm remark, and continued his teaching. Such are the ways of a true householder yogi.

As I say, these three are continually cited by those who have no intention of following their actual example. And I can add two more: the parents of Paramhansa Yogananda. Regarding these two great yogi-saints, Yoganandaji wrote: "Early in their married life, my parents became disciples of a great master, Lahiri Mahasaya of Benares. This contact strengthened Father's naturally ascetical temperament. Mother made a remarkable admission to my eldest sister Roma: 'Your father and myself live together as man and wife only once a year, for the purpose of having children.'" That Yogananda would reveal this to the world shows how important he thought this information would be to serious married yogis.

How outrageous that these virgin and celibate holy men and woman would be the excuse for "yogis" to live a selfish and materially-conscious married life the same as any desire-controlled ignoramuses who live for their own interests and gain. They are not yogis but bhogis, those who live for their own enjoyment and self-satisfaction.

I have read much of your site and *The Christ of India* and am interested in the dharmic approach taken by the Saint Thomas school—most of which seems natural to me.

While there is documentation on Hindu acceptance and worship of Christ, how can a follower of Christ respectfully and meaningfully engage with Hindu aspects, from specific helpers such as Ganesha to omnipotent archetypes like Shiva?

I attend a Tamil Mariamman temple from time to time and experience no inconsistency but am still reserved in my engagement.

Any pointers will be much appreciated.

Sanatana Dharma did not come out of the mind and ideas of some individual who then persuaded others to follow him. Rather, it is a revelation given to many sages (rishis), who were master yogis, in their superconscious experience. That is why there is no founder claimed by Sanatana Dharma. Also, that revelation can be confirmed by yogis who purify themselves and become able to enter the same superconscious state.

Sanatana Dharma is based on realization, not intellectual philosophy. Consequently, only the adept yogi can really understand its nature and meaning. Yoga Sadhana is the key to really "becoming" a Sanatana Dharma. I say this from experience. There were many aspects of Sanatana Dharma that upon first encounter seemed utterly silly to me. But as I persisted in meditation and yogic discipline I literally saw the reality and value of them.

I will share with you some experiences I had.

One day I went with some yogi friends to the now extinct Wil Wright's Ice Cream Parlor in Westwood, California. In a niche to one side of the door there was a white marble statue with the head of an elephant. One of my friends pointed to it and said: "That is the Indian

Elephant-headed God, Ganesha. I don't know what it's doing here." Neither did I, for I was thinking: "Elephant-headed God! Whoever thought that up? How stupid." But some weeks later in meditation I saw Ganesha and knew he really was a form of God. And more than that: I loved him. I not only believed in him, I got an image of him and put it on my meditation altar.

I was completely disgusted with the idea of the Goddess Kali. I thought it was horrible. Then one night in meditation during a tremendous rain storm I saw the Devi dancing in the storm, stamping her feet with great vigor on the earth. And I understood. The next day I took an anti-Hindu book I had bought long before becoming a yogi, cut out the picture of Kali, threw the book in the garbage and kept the picture with me at all times. How I loved worshipping in the Kali temples when I went to India!

I read that Krishna was blue. I figured that was symbolic, but when I saw Krishna, Shyam Sundara the Beautiful Dark One, he was blue. Not like the blue of many modern pictures and images, but a dark, dusky blue. Some months later I saw a dark storm cloud in the sky that was the exact color I had seen in my vision. And quite some time later I learned from a Gujarati friend that Krishna is sometimes called Ghanashyam—dark like a cloud.

Later on I read that Rama was green. In the perspective of the foregoing experiences I was not so quick to reject it, but then I remembered that the skin of Europeans and Americans actually contain green pigment. So perhaps Rama just had a lot of that pigment in his skin for some reason and was "greenish." But when I saw Rama his skin was an exquisite light green. Some time after I read a description of Rama as being green like a young blade of grass—exactly as in my vision.

As Krishna says in the Bhagavad Gita: "Therefore be a yogi" (6:46).

To someone who wished I would write anything I might know about Mahavatar Babaji that is not in *Autobiography of a Yogi*.

I will tell you what others told me in India about Babaji.

Dr. Mukherji

Within a week of my landing in India in 1962, I was staying at the Anandamayi Ashram in Ranchi, less than a mile from the Yogoda Satsanga Ashram. "My" room was the free homeopathic dispensary in the daytime and my bedroom at night. It was wonderful. I was in India!

The dispensary was run by Dr. Mukherji, a disciple of Swami Purnananda who was a direct disciple of Babaji. In our conversations he told me some things that I gladly pass on.

As recorded in *Autobiography of a Yogi*, the disciples of Lahiri Mahasaya called Babaji by several names: Mahamuni Babaji Maharaj, Maha Yogi, Trambak Baba and Shiva Baba. Purnananda and many of his fellow-disciples of Babaji simply called him Babaji Brahmananda. That appeals to me the most.

Babaji is not as inaccessible as many people think. He does not just roam in solitude in the Himalayas with only a handful of disciples with him. And though comparatively speaking few people stay with him, there is a small trickle of aspirants who come to spend some time with him.

Swami Purnananda stayed with Babaji more than one time in the Himalayas, sometimes for years. He told Dr. Mukherji that the famous Devendranath Tagore (see the *Gospel of Sri Ramakrishna*), a Bengali philosopher and religious reformer, was a disciple of Babaji and spent quite some time with him in the Himalayas. When his even more famous son, Rabindranath Tagore, was in his teens Devendranath sent him to live with Babaji for three years.

Other disciples, other yoga sadhanas

There is also a misperception about Babaji and his spiritual mission. It is assumed that he only had one disciple "in the world," Lahiri Mahasaya. What I have written here shows this is not true. Furthermore, it is believed that Kriya Yoga is the only practice favored by Babaji. But there are two of his disciples whose teaching contradict this.

Vijay Krishna Goswami

The renowned Bengali saint, Vijay Krishna Goswami (also in the *Gospel of Sri Ramakrishna*) was a disciple of Babaji. He was of the Vaishnava philosophy and taught to his disciples and the public in general the continual repetition and singing of the Maha (Great) Mantra that is found in the Kalisantara Upanishad:

> Hare Rama, Hare Rama,
> Rama, Rama, Hare Hare.
> Hare Krishna, Hare Krishna,
> Krishna, Krishna, Hare Hare.

I can tell you an amusing story about Babaji's rescuing Vijay from his shrewish wife—at least for a while. Vijay and his wife were in Brindaban where Krishna lived until the age of twelve. Vijay's wife was always complaining about his ascetic ways and all the time he spent spreading the message (for which Babaji had commissioned him) of the Maha Mantra and the time spent with his disciples—much like the wife of Babaji's disciple, Lahiri Mahasaya. After days and days of this fussing, as his wife was continuing on and on with her complaints, Vijay silently prayed: "Gurudeva, please free me from this misery!" Immediately his wife found herself in the Himalayas with Babaji and his holy band. She remained there a while and then walked all the way back to Brindaban, arriving there six months after her disappearance. She was much more docile after that.

Neem Karoli Baba

Another very famous disciple, also not a Kriya teacher, was Neem Karoli Baba who lived to be over three hundred and fifty years old, and was reputed to be an incarnation of Hanuman, the great devotee of Lord Rama, an avatar who lived in Indian thousands of years ago. For three and a half centuries Neem Karoli Baba taught people to continually repeat the sacred mantra Ram—the name of Rama. (Many yogis of India repeat Ram, but do not consider it the name of the avatar, but a name of the Absolute Itself. Interestingly, Ram is also a Hebrew name of God.) Several books have been written about Sri Neem Karoli Baba. I only saw him once, and every moment I looked at him I was literally drunk with bliss.

Finally I want to tell you about three people I have met that saw Babaji.

An attorney

One was a supreme court lawyer living in New Delhi. He had never heard of Babaji, but one time when on pilgrimage to Varanasi, he was sitting in the evening at Dasashwamedh Ghat. An extraordinarily beautiful woman came up to him and simply said: "Follow me." He did not know it, but this was Babaji's sister, about whom Yogananda wrote in *Autobiography of a Yogi*. He followed her through dark narrow alleyways and then down narrow stairs into an underground cave. Only a single light was burning there, and by its light he saw a young man with bright red hair sitting there in meditation. The woman motioned for him to sit. When he asked who the man was, she only said: "Great Babaji," and indicated he should not speak. He sat there an hour or so looking at the radiant figure before him. Then in silence the woman signaled he should stand up and follow her. She led him back to Dasashwamedh Ghat and left without a word. Only a day or so after he returned to New Delhi he came across *Autobiography of a Yogi* and saw the picture of Babaji which was just like the yogi he had seen. Many times he went back to Varanasi seeking Babaji or his sister, but was not successful.

A woman-yogi friend

I met the above lawyer in the home of a woman who had also met Babaji. From her I learned the following.

When Babaji met Lahiri Mahasaya near Ranikhet, he took him to a cave where they had been together in Lahiri Baba's previous life. That is commonly known as "Babaji's cave."

But Babaji has several caves, and one has a most peculiar character. It is located in a dense forest populated by many ferocious tigers and other dangerous animals. When someone becomes lost in that forest toward nightfall one of Babaji's disciples comes and leads him to that cave. According to what the lost person is accustomed to at home, that is what he finds in the cave. Poor people find it very sparse, others find it simply furnished and well-to-do people find it luxuriously furnished–with carpets, chairs, tables and a comfortable bed. Each one is given the kind of food he would usually have at home. In the morning the disciple shows him the way out of the jungle. Some people meet Babaji himself in the cave, but some others do not.

My friend and three others went high into the Himalayas to find that particular cave in hope of seeing Babaji. They stayed in a simple guest house near the forest. One day as night was about to fall, they suddenly heard tremendous roaring of a tiger that seemed to be very near them. Remembering the way they had entered the forest, they began running as fast as they could, desperately praying to Babaji to protect them. The guest house was some miles away, but they reached in it twenty to thirty minutes! This was a miracle and a miraculous escape by Babaji's blessing, they were confident.

Every day they went out searching. But after a few days my friend became very ill and ran a high fever. She urged the others to go on and continue their search for the cave, which they reluctantly did. After some time a radiant figure came in through the open door of her room. His features were not easy to see because rays of light were shining from his body, but he looked to her exactly like Babaji's picture, and he had reddish hair in a knot on his head in the style of the ancient sages rather than hanging down as in his picture. He sat and had a long conversation with her on spiritual matters. (She never told me what was said.) Then he said: "The others are coming, so I will leave now." He started for the door and melted away from her sight.

For the next three or four days the same thing happened. But the time was running out for the other pilgrims and they had to return to their jobs. So my friend told them to go ahead and she would try to get to the railway station several miles away in some manner. This they did not want to do, but she insisted, and the next day they left.

That afternoon, the radiant yogi returned as usual, but told her that she must leave and get treatment in Delhi, otherwise she would die. "But I can't walk," she protested. "Then I will carry you on my back," he said. And so he did. He carried her luggage and she held on around his neck and away they went. In another miraculously short time they were at the station. The yogi put her in a compartment, said farewell, and was gone.

As she sat waiting for the train to start, she began to pray: "O Master Babaji, if this was really you who visited me and brought me here, come back and let me see you and be sure." Nothing happened. The train started up, and as it gained speed leaving the station, suddenly Babaji was there standing on the platform. Her heart leaped up and she tried to get up and leave the train, but it was going too fast.

The next station was quite a distance away, but she prayed: "O Babaji, please come to the next station. Then I will know it is really you I have seen." She was so invigorated by her desire that she was able to feebly get up and out of the train when the train stopped at the station. She went up and down the platform looking, looking and looking here and there. But saw nothing. The conductor blew his whistle and she hurried back to the train but stood in the door looking out, planning to jump out onto the platform if Babaji appeared. The train was picking up speed, and when it was going so fast it was impossible for anyone to get out of the train, suddenly Babaji was there, standing and looking at her. Then she knew the deathless master had truly come to her and saved her life. She and her son told me this just as I have now related it to you.

A yogi-friend

The preceding two accounts were told to me during my first pilgrimage to India. Early on in my second pilgrimage I was staying at Sivanandashram in Rishikesh in the Himalayan foothills. There I met a very well-known and respected young yogi of North India and spent much time with him. One afternoon he began asking me about Babaji, and if he ever left the Himalayas. I told him that he definitely did and came down to the plains at the feet of the Himalayas. "Well, I saw him in the Lucknow train station only a week ago," he told me. Then he described to me how he had seen a young man with long, bright red hair waiting on the platform of the Lucknow station with several other men. All were simply dressed like Himalayan yogis. "I could not quit looking at him," the young monk told me. "I have never seen anyone like him in my life. I knew this had to be a great soul. When the northbound train came, he got into a third-class coach with the others, and as the train left the station I realized that this must be the Babaji of Yogananda's autobiography. The thought had not occurred to me before. I believe he kept me from realizing who he was until it was too late to approach him."

So that is what little I know.

To the same person who wanted me to share what I know about Yoganandaji's highly advanced disciple, Yogacharya Oliver Black.

In 1968 I was able to go to Detroit for an SRF Sunday service at the Art Institute conducted by Yogacharya Black, and the entire next day I spent with him at his home. He spoke of many interesting things, but here are those I remember that related to his association with Paramhansa Yogananda and his yoga practice.

The first time he went to California to be with Yogananda, they were at Encinitas. The Master led him from the hermitage to the Golden Lotus Temple on the edge of the cliff overlooking the ocean. (Later the sea eroded the foot of the cliff and the temple fell into the ocean, and only the steps remained.) The temple was a miniature of the Taj Mahal with a tower at each corner. At the top of each tower was a one-room suite. Master Yogananda pointed to one and explained that it was used by him. Another was for Rajasi Janakananda, and another for Dr. Lewis. Then he pointed to the fourth tower and said: "This one is for you. Whenever you come here this is where you will stay." Mr. Black was astonished at this, wondering why the Master would show him such generosity. But his later life as a disciple certainly demonstrated why. (He did not say that–I did!)

The next day was Sunday and he naturally was at the service conducted by Yoganandaji. He told me that as Yogananda was speaking he saw a figure he somehow knew was a Himalayan yogi standing just behind the Master. The yogi's long black hair was streaming back behind him as though being blown by a strong wind. More surprising, the yogi was moving his mouth exactly like the Master, though no sound was coming out. Yogacharya decided that the yogi was speaking through Yoganandaji, but after a bit realized that the yogi *was* Yogananda as Mr. Black had known him in a previous life, and the Master was showing this to him.

Since we are "at" Encinitas in this narrative, I want to tell you something more than one disciple of Yoganandaji told me about Oliver Black. Whenever he stayed at Encinitas with the Master, he would take him every day for a drive, considering this was his way to show his appreciation for the great guru's blessing in his life. One day as they were going to the car for the drive, it began to rain heavily. Mr. Black was disappointed that he would not be able to take his guru for a drive that day.

But Yoganandaji went out of the building and around to the passenger side of the car, looked up and instantly there was no rain and the sun began shining brightly. Then he looked at Yogacharya and quietly said: "Just for you, Oliver, just for you." And so it was.

Mr. Black owned a factory that made auto parts used by the various automobile manufacturers in Detroit. The economy had recovered from the crash of 1929 and everyone was optimistic. But in mid-1937 he realized one night in meditation that another crash was coming, though not as severe. Early the next morning he called in his chief executive and gave him a check from the Chrysler Corporation for thirty-eight thousand dollars. "Charter a plane right away and fly to New York and cash this check. Bring the money back here to me, today," he told him. The man looked at the check and said: "This check is on the Chase Manhattan Bank—there's no better in the country!" "Do what I tell you. Tomorrow you will know why," Mr. Black assured him. The next day the crash came and that check would have been worthless.

All through the depression, from 1929 onward, Mr. Black made a great deal of money solely through good business moves that were prompted by his intuition developed through meditation. There was an even more profitable aspect to his meditation. He told me that sometimes he would start seeing visions in meditation that made no sense to him at all. First it would be a short vision and then be repeated, getting longer each time. Then other visions would come, and as he pondered them he would suddenly understand their meaning and would have a clue to an invention of some kind. Since he had not even graduated from high school, he no technical understanding, so he would find some expert and explain his ideas. Each time they would be declared viable and he would eventually sell the invention for a great deal of money. He invented the vertical take-off plane, but the Air Force stole the idea and claimed it as their own. He was in litigation over it for years, including at the time he told me about it. But: You Can't Fight City Hall. So nothing came of it. He invented a 3-D camera that put the viewer into the picture. Kodak offered twenty-four thousand dollars, and he told them they knew it was worth many times more. But they kept hoping he would accept their first offer, and he did not. After one series of visions he made a drawing of something he did not even know the nature of, but he knew the parts that would go into it, and that it was supposed to fly. He took it to the Department of Aeronautics at Wayne State University and showed it to one of the senior staff. "Do you know what this is?" the man demanded. "No. I came here for you to tell me," was Mr. Black's reply. "You have invented a flying saucer. This thing will do everything saucers are reported capable of doing. For example, it can change directions in an instant. And even more amazing: all the parts to assemble one are available right now! One could be made tomorrow." At the time he told me of this, he was beginning to present it to companies that made "flying machines." That, too, was not bought by anyone. He told me about some visions he was having that were very strange and really made no sense. The next time I saw him about a year later he told me that the invention had to do with motel beds, and he was in negotiation to sell it. Later I learned from a member of his SRF center that he sold it for tens of thousands of dollars.

Since we are on high finance, here is something about Babaji and Big Business. Mr. Black was on the board of one of the big automotive corporations in Detroit. (I believe it was General Motors.) There was another board member that at every meeting would bring up something he was displeased about and complain and carry on for a long time. Every one would sit there and wait until he shut up and then the meeting would proceed, nothing being done about his silly complaint. One day Mr. Black went a couple of hours before the board meeting and decided to meditate in the board room. As he was meditating, he prayed: "Babaji, all of us are so sick of hearing this man fuss and fuss, wasting our time, at every meeting. Will you please do something to stop him?" The meeting proceeded as usual, and at one point the grouch got up and began. But he did not get through even a sentence. Suddenly he stopped speaking and got a look of terror on his face, then flopped back down into his chair and did not speak during the rest of the meeting. And never afterward did he bring up his pet gripe. "So it pays to talk to Babaji," laughed Mr. Black as he finished the account.

Master Yogananda asked the Yogacharya to keep in frequent contact with him, to write or telephone often. But for some reason he never did, only rarely communicating with the guru. After a few years of this, one morning as he sat on the floor of his meditation room meditating, he opened his eyes and saw Yoganandaji sitting right in front of him! He was sure it was not a vision but a physical materialization. Yoganandaji was sitting with his back to Mr. Black. His long hair was in a kind of bun at the back of his neck and he was wearing a really ratty old bathrobe (Mr. Black's words). Oliver waited for the Master to speak or do something, but he then clearly got the impression that his guru was displeased with his non-communication and so had his back to him. After looking at the guru's back for a while, he closed his eyes and resumed meditating. After meditation, when he knew he could get through to Mount Washington headquarters on the telephone, he put in a person-to-person call to Faye Wright, the future president of Self-Realization Fellowship (then to be known as Sri Daya Mata). "Tell me," he asked her as soon as she came on the phone, "does Master ever put his hair in a kind of bun on the back of his neck?" "He does it sometimes in his room when others aren't around," she told him. "Well, tell me this. Does he ever wear an old, beat-up bathrobe?" "Oh! That old thing!" she exclaimed. "He has been wearing that in meditation for years. It is so awful that we keep threatening to take and burn it. Why are you asking?" So he told her. And from then on kept in frequent contact with his Master.

In 1969, after returning from India, I was able to pass through Detroit and again go for the Sunday service at the Art Institute. This Sunday for the first time there was going to be a cafeteria lunch after the service so people could speak and listen to Yogacharya Black on a more personal and informal basis. People were asking questions and he was answering, but my memory has only retained one. The subject of sex and "marital relations" came up. Mr. Black began to laugh. He turned to me (I was sitting next to him on his left hand) and asked: "Shall I tell them what Master said about this? Shall I tell them?" "Yes! Yes!" I answered. "Really? Do you want me to tell them? Do you want me to tell you?" he repeated, turning back to them, continuing to chuckle. "All right, then. You asked about it. Master said, 'It is nothing more than the joining of two sewers'!" Stunned silence. Stunned consternation. I studied the faces of all those around us and found their expressions and reactions most interesting. Some were overtly angry, even outraged. Others were smiling in agreement. And others were intensely deadpan so no one would know they were the hardest hit. But Mr. Black simply sat there, quietly chuckling to himself and occasionally looking askance at me and continuing to chuckle.

That was the last time I saw him, though I continued to get news of him occasionally.

In writing the previous sentence I remembered something that I had been told about Yogacharya Oliver in 1961, that I want to include. At the previous triennial convocation at the SRF Lake Shrine, Mr. Black had spoken. Many of the audience were amazed and awed to see that throughout his talk all four of the great Masters–Babaji, Lahiri Mahasaya, Sri Yukteswarji and Paramhansaji–appeared behind him in turn. One would appear, and immediately upon his fading away, another would appear. This continued over and over as long as he spoke. I think this was a message from the Masters about this beloved disciple's inner unity with them.

There is more information about Oliver Black in *Conversations with Yogananda*, by Swami Kriyananda.

To someone who wrote and asked me what was my inner sense of Oliver Black and his presence.

A friend of mine was once travelling with an Indian yogi in Canada. Seeing his "strange" clothes, a little girl came up to him and asked: "What are you?" The yogi smiled at her and answered: "Oh, just what I'm supposed to be."

Oliver Black was just what he was supposed to be. Totally natural and totally supernatural. Many of Master Yogananda's disciples were just like that, also.

Where do evil spirits come from? The Christian Bible acknowledges them–Legion, for example (Mark 5:9; Luke 8:30).

It is important to understand that in all relative existence there are only the Supreme Spirit, God (Brahman), and the seemingly infinite number of individual spirits (jivas). The individual spirits live within God, with whom they are eternally one, yet distinct from him in a manner only the perfectly liberated spirits can comprehend.

There are not different kinds of spirits, but as spirits enter into relative existence and begin evolving through higher and higher forms, there is differentiation in the energies of which their various bodies are composed. For example, the body of a bird and the body of a human being are vastly different, but the spirit in those bodies are the same: pure consciousness. I recommend you read *Robe of Light* on our website for a detailed explanation of this and its purpose.

There are spirits that harm human beings but have no wish to harm. Some of these are spirits that wander into the world from other dimensions and wreak havoc, but with no negative intention. They just do not understand the world in which they find themselves and are not aware of the effect they are having on human beings. Also very undeveloped spirits without understanding may harm human beings because they do not understand the nature of a human being. Undines, water spirits, often inspire swimmers to swim far out into the ocean in a kind of euphoric trance and then not be able to swim back, so they drown. The undines want the humans to join them and live in the water. But their influence causes them to die. Salamanders (fire spirits), sylphs (air spirits) and gnomes (earth spirits) do the same. The subconscious minds of some human beings perceive their "call" to join them in water, fire, air or earth. Those who respond and consequently die are considered suicides, but they are not. Both they and the spirits are victims of their ignorance and incomprehension.

A spirit may become flawed in its evolution and become corrupted, twisted and negative. Then we say it is evil, though the spirit is never evil, only its bodies, which include the mind and will. Evil spirits are often degraded human beings and sometimes more powerful beings that have sunk down from higher worlds because of their evil vibration which impelled them downwards.

Evil spirits cannot endure high vibration. Those who continually keep their vibrations high through spiritual practice will not be harmed by evil spirits. One of my meditation students lived in the most haunted place I have ever been, and some of the spirits were really evil. Two week later I visited there again and every spirit was gone, just from the vibrations created by the daily meditation of the student.

If everything is made by and from God, why does Satan exist as a spirit?

Free will is a fundamental condition of all spirits. Those who set their wills to evil become "demons." Lucifer, the fallen archangel, is one of these. He is the most powerful evil spirit operative in the earth plane (solar system).

Satan is not a spirit, though often confused with Lucifer. Satan is a negative, delusive force in the universe which vibrates in opposition to upward evolution and "works" to entrap deluded human beings. It is a conglomerate of aeons of negative energies emitted by negative entities and events (such as war). Since everything is essentially consciousness, the Satanic force operates in a kind of blindly intelligent manner and can seem to be a person, but that is a mirage, a mere seeming.

As with evil spirits, high spiritual vibrations dispel Satanic influence and those leading a spiritual life need not give either Lucifer or Satan a thought, though it is good to be aware that they may intervene in the life and minds of ignorant human beings around us.

Can you be reincarnated if you donate organs or get cremated? Or does the physical body not come into it at all–is it just our soul and spiritual self?

Human beings are made of many layers. When we die we leave both the physical body and an energy body behind–which is why the hair and fingernails of dead people continue to grow for a while.

If things go as they should, we leave those lesser bodies behind without a thought and go on with our higher bodies (which contain both the memories and conditionings of our previous lives) to another existence in the higher worlds, after which we again reincarnate, taking on new energy and material bodies. The situation of the bodies we leave behind does not at all affect us. Occasionally there are exceptions but they are very rare.

Although I don't have a problem understanding all the concepts of Vedanta, the minute I reflect upon the Christian Bible it seems to all confuse me. I find the teachings so different, although they must be the same.

It is the Bible that is confused because it (the New Testament) has been edited to conform to the theology of the new state religion called Christianity at the beginning of the fourth century. The original teachings of Jesus were those of Sanatana Dharma which he learned in India. Please see *The Christ of India* on our website. (Also available as a book.)

I understand that beyond everything there is only Brahman. The Bible does talk about the devil, and possession. Vedanta won't address the issue.

In India they are very conversant with evil spirits and exorcism. Sri Ramakrishna had many experiences with various kinds of spirits. Once he went to a place where there were earthbound spirits. They told him his presence tormented them and asked him to leave, which he did.

Please do not equate Vedanta with Sanatana Dharma. Vedanta is just one of the orthodox systems of philosophy within Sanatana Dharma. And Advaita is only one form of Vedanta. There are also Dwaita and

Vishishtadwaita Vedanta. Vedanta Society is another thing, altogether, being the Western branch of the Ramakrishna Mission which is just one of thousands of spiritual institutions in India, though certainly one of the largest.

You say "A spirit may become flawed in its evolution." How can a spirit, essentially Brahman, become corrupt?

I said: "A spirit may become flawed in its evolution and become corrupted, twisted and negative. Then we say it is evil, though *the spirit is never evil, only its bodies, which include the mind and will.*"

When the Christian Bible talks about the Revelation for example, the fight between good and evil, it leads us to believe there is a devil and that he can manipulate people and occupy their body and that we will be on one side or the other at the end of time. It talks about evil spirits as though there really is an opposite force which could lead us to hell.

Certainly there is a force which works against our development and liberation. It is called the play of Maya. You may recall that Sri Ramakrishna saw in a vision two men come out of his body—one dark and one light. They were the papa (evil) purusha and the punya (righteous) purusha, the forces of light and darkness in each person. The punya purusha struck the papa purusha with a trident and killed him. Then the punya purusha merged back into Sri Ramakrishna's body. This must be understood in the context of Sanatana Dharma, not that of Christianity (Churchianity) and its mistaken views.

Vedanta, I don't think, believes in hell. Why not? How can the Christian Bible be opposing to Vedanta? I'm trying to match them up in some way to make sense of it, but I'm failing. For 2 years I've tried and still cannot understand the disparity.

Sanatana Dharma believes in the existence of numberless heavens and hells whose character differs according to the karma of individuals when they enter the astral world.

Again, Jesus was a Sanatana Dharmi, not a follower of Judaism or Christianity. Furthermore, all religions are not the same and they most certainly are not one in essence. They differ greatly in degree of truth understanding. Some are destructive in their effect even if their intentions are to "save" people. Only Sanatana Dharma believes in the divine nature of the Self (Atman), for example, and that is a very basic concept that affects every other aspect of Sanatana Dharma. All religions may have a common basis, but only Sanatana Dharma knows what it is.

Sri Ramakrishna said this: "The Hindu religion alone is the Sanatana Dharma. The various creeds you hear of nowadays have come into existence through the will of God and will disappear again through His will. They will not last forever.... The Hindu religion has always existed and will always exist" (Nikhilananda translation of *The Gospel of Sri Ramakrishna*, under the heading of Monday, October 20, 1884).

Is it possible that people like Hitler can have such a corrupted soul that they come back to earth to haunt people? Is this a corrupted soul?

Many evil people become trapped in the earth plane and harm people. They are then called "demons." Such are certainly corrupted in their subtle energy levels. But in time their eternal, divine status will assert itself. They will have a tremendous amount of karma to undergo and overcome. They will have to do as much good to humanity as they did evil. It will take a long time, perhaps creation cycles, but they will turn back. Eternal alienation from God is impossible for anyone, since we are all rooted in the very Being of God: gods within God.

When a disaster strikes, for example the holocaust, how can it be that all those people deserved that? Vedanta says we only get what we deserve. It does seem strange to me that all those people who deserve what they got just happened to be in the same place at the same time.

Why should it be strange? The universe is a perfect evolution machine, and karma is a major factor. Group karma operates as precisely as individual karma. In *May a Christian Believe in Reincarnation?* I have cited the words of the great Rabbi Hillel, a contemporary of Jesus, in the *Daily Prayer Book*, edited by Philip Birnbaum (Hebrew Publishing Company, New York). In the second chapter of the section entitled: *Ethics of the Fathers*, the seventh section says: "He [Hillel] saw a skull floating on the surface of the water. He said to it: Because you drowned others, others have drowned you; and those who have drowned you shall themselves be drowned." The persecuted have been persecutors in previous lives, and the present persecutors shall be the persecuted in the future. We may think the world is flawed, but it is seen as perfect when we hold the profound overview of the Indian rishis.

Vedanta also believes in re-birth until you reach moksha or liberation, but the Bible teaches us that we go to heaven or hell. Am I right to compare to try to make sense?

After each birth we go to a world very much like this one, or to a miserable one (a hell) or a happier one (a heaven), all according to the nuances of our karma. It is not true that there is only one life, or that anyone can go to hell forever. If you compare the views of Sanatana Dharma and those of the Bible in these matters you can only conclude that one is true and the other is false.

In my writings I quote from the Bible to show that a great deal of it escaped the deformation of those who reworked it to reflect "official" Christianity, and that it demonstrates the original, fully oriental (Indian) character of Jesus and his teachings. A person who wishes to follow Jesus must follow him to India. I recommend that you read *The Second Coming of Christ* by Paramhansa Yogananda.

My confusion is with the opposites. If I chose either Christianity or Vedanta maybe I wouldn't have this problem. But I have experienced both and now it has become a problem for me, and I love both.

A very dear friend of mine was a niece of Edith Gray, a Canadian who went to India and became a disciple of Sri Ma Sarada Devi. My friend showed me a copy of a letter written to Miss Gray by Swami Saradananda at the time Holy Mother was in Benares. Miss Gray had asked why it was she was sometimes more attracted to Jesus and at other times more attracted to Sri Ramakrishna. Saradanandaji wrote to her that this was very natural, and that Sri Ramakrishna had told him that he (Saradananda) and some of the other disciples had been disciples of Jesus.

We should love all God's messengers to humanity such as Rama, Krishna, Buddha, Ramakrishna and Jesus. And insofar as they convey the true teachings of those great ones, we can respect the religions that bear their names. But we must also be like the wise ant who can take sugar and leave the white sand behind. In *The Gospel of Sri Ramakrishna*, Sri Ramakrishna says: "Books—I mean the scriptures—contain a mixture of sand and sugar. The sadhu takes the sugar, leaving aside the sand. He takes only the essence." We must do the same.

You say, "Free will is a fundamental condition of all spirits. Those who set their wills to evil become 'demons.'" I totally agree, but does Vedanta?

Sanatana Dharma certainly does, as is seen by the sixteenth chapter of the Bhagavad Gita. It brings us inestimable good to read a chapter of the Gita daily.

Please would you help me, or direct me to some understanding. Why don't I understand when I love and adore God so much?

You do understand, but you are trying to fit or see everything according to the things which those who claim to be authorities have told you.

This is a common affliction of those who are in the West and attempting to adopt the wisdom of the East. They see one thing but have been told to think/say it is something else. Books and teachers from the East often say things that may sound good as platitudes and "positive thinking," but do not conform to reality, and therefore are not a viable philosophy at all. We must always keep our sugar-from-sand intelligence working. And if others do not like it, that is their problem.

As Paramhansa Nityananda, one of the nineteenth and twentieth centuries greatest yogis, told people: "You were born with a brain, not a book." We must be honest in our conclusions at all times. There is nothing at all wrong in concluding that something is mistaken, no matter who is saying or doing it. Consider how Swami Vivekananda never at any time failed to speak how he saw and felt. He even told Sri Ramakrishna he considered him deluded! Sri Ramakrishna often said that one could attain liberation if they always spoke the truth. And Swamiji's truthfulness and assertion of what he saw as truth led him onward to the Truth. He said: "Awake! Arise!" He did not say: "Listen; accept; believe and obey."

Although we are ourselves Brahman, is there a main God when we pray? Does this mean that there isn't an actual God in the sky as it were?

Brahman has a threefold manifestation: (1) transcending creation and impersonal, (2) pervading creation and personal and (3) cosmic creative energy. This is the Trinity, One but Three. God within creation as its manifester and guide is Ishwara, the personal aspect of God. When we pray, we pray to Ishwara, whatever name we might use. So God does hear and answer prayer. God is everywhere, so he is "in the sky" but also in us.

"The devoted dwell with Him, they know Him always there in the heart" (Bhagavad Gita 5:17).

"The Lord lives in the heart of every creature" (Bhagavad Gita 18:61).

To a friend who had questions about right and wrong and my position on certain questions regarding the personal conduct of others.

Although Original Christianity (Sanatana Dharma) has beliefs, it has no dogmas. That is, there is nothing a person *must* believe or think about something.

Faith/belief is according to the evolutionary level and character of each person. That is why the Bhagavad Gita says: "The faith of each one is according to his nature. A man consists of his faith—he is what his faith is" (17:3). Therefore no one should be coerced as to their personal beliefs—including those who think people should be so coerced. Keep quiet and let people alone is a good rule to follow.

Beliefs, like actions, are according to a person's individual status. We need not be involved in those of others. "Offering actions to Brahman, having abandoned attachment, he [the wise aspirant] acts untainted by evil as a lotus leaf is not wetted by water" (5:10). We are in the water of earthly life, but we should not get wet and bogged down in it. We should stay in our own individual pond and stay out of others'.

A cornerstone of evolution is working out things for ourselves. Religion (not dharma) tries to make people dependent on them for their ideas and actions, but that is stagnating and often destructive. Everyone must cope with their mental and material karma. Some choose to correct their negativity, some to suppress it and others to express it. That is the way things are.

Freedom is necessary for growth, and that includes the freedom to accept or reject something. One summer when we were living in the desert, we decided to move for the hot months to a higher altitude. Just a short drive from our monastery we found in the mountains an ideal place that had a sign saying it was for rent. We called the phone number and the owner refused to rent to us because he was an atheist and we were monks. We did not argue, nor even consider protesting his "discrimination" against us. It was his house and his principle. He did right–and we did right by respecting his feelings and finding another place to rent.

What is the most authentic document of Jesus' teaching? The Gospel of Thomas? Are there others you would point to?

The Gospel of Thomas seems to be the most authentic. Certainly the four Gospels of the Bible contain his teachings, but mixed in with untrustworthy elements. Still, they should be read with the understanding that the sugar must be separated from the sand, as Sri Ramakrishna said about all scriptures.

The Second Coming of Christ by Yogananda is invaluable in understanding Jesus' teachings, as is his autobiography and the books of his public talks.

The Aquarian Gospel of Jesus the Christ is a remarkable document that does not claim to be infallible, but is also invaluable in understanding Jesus and the difference between THE Christ and A Christ.

The Unknown Life of Jesus Christ seems to be very much conformed to the idea of the narrators. Still, it is good to look into.

In *The Christ of India* the quotation from the Bhavishya Mahapurana is short but certainly authentic. There we see what Jesus thought of the religion of his land of birth and his definite adoption of Sanatana Dharma.

Jesus the man taught that the Universal (Christ Consciousness) pervades all of our visible and invisible (manifest and unmanifest) universe and that Christ Consciousness pervades all and is All including the body, mind and actions of the perceived individual which is a spark of the Absolute (Father). Correct?

Definitely.

Why is monastic life chosen over engagement in society where the influence of the Christ Consciousness awakened in the monks can influence the consciousness of society?

The purpose of monastic life is to intensely develop and evolve the consciousness without hindrance. Our website, which embodies hundreds of hours of work, and continues to expand, reaches far more people than any other form of activity ever could.

Consciousness is not just imparted by physical contact, but by the unseen unity with all.

Is the story of the historical Jesus also an allegory of the journey of the Soul to merge with God? If so could you elucidate or point the direction?

The lives of all great masters who after perfect realization return to the earth as avatars are certainly portrayals of esoteric truths, mostly in symbol. The life of Jesus and the early life of Krishna are mystic portrayals of the soul's journey to God-realization.

It would require a book to explain the meaning of their lives, and perhaps one day I will manage to write one.

How do the teachings of Advaita, Veda, Upanishads, Bhagavad Gita, Ramayana fit with St. Thomas Christianity? Western Christianity? Eastern Orthodoxy? Catholicism?

The vital question is, how do those religious expressions fit with Sanatana Dharma? The degree of their agreement with Sanatana Dharma is the degree of their validity. Sanatana Dharma is the touchstone of all religious philosophy and practice.

The healings and miracles of Christ have been done by yogis before Christ and after. What does this mean and are these siddhis part of St. Thomas Christianity?

The meaning of Jesus' miracles is simply that he, too was a yogi—and more, a perfectly realized master, an avatar. Since real Saint Thomas Christianity is the Sanatana Dharma taught by Jesus, certainly those siddhis have manifested. The pinnacle of the church in India was Saint Gregorios of Parumala, whose shrine is visited by thousand of Christians, Hindus and Moslems every day. His miracles are continuous. And Saint Gregorios was committed to the restoration of Dharma to the Saint Thomas Christian community.

Can a householder be a Saint Thomas Christian?

Certainly. Millions have been and are.

How can a St. Thomas Christian participate in Satsang?

That is a completely individual matter, but should not be limited to Christian groups.

Many believe Jesus taught in Kashmir and in fact is entombed in a Shrine in Kashmir. Some ancient Kashmiri texts point to Jesus in Kashmir, do you think this tomb is the tomb of Jesus?

No. The tomb from which he resurrected in Jerusalem is one of the major centers of spiritual power in the world. But when his earthly life was over in India he released the atoms of his body into light. There was nothing to bury.

What is the advantage of a pilgrimage to the Holy Land or Kerala? If "the Kingdom of God is within you," Why travel?

The world is not the same everywhere. Each place has a distinctive vibration. Certainly the vibrations of a cowboy bar, a prison, a hospital or a holy shrine are not the same. There are centers of spiritual power on the earth, and visiting and meditating there is more effective than in an ordinary place. In India there are certain areas called tapobhumis where yoga practice requires must less time for success than elsewhere.

Yogis have always valued pilgrimage, but not wandering all the time. My sannyasa guru told me that he once was completely without peace due to some very negative things that had been done to him. No matter how much he meditated, he just could not regain his spiritual balance. So he decided to go on pilgrimage. At each place he visited, he experienced benefit, but still there was an undercurrent of inner unrest. Then he went to the Sri Ramanashram in Tiruvanamalai and went into the hall where for decades Sri Ramana Maharshi had spent most of his days and nights giving darshan to people. "The moment I sat down and closed my eyes, total peace arose in me, and I was healed permanently of the spiritual wounds within," he told me. "I can tell you that Ramana Maharshi is living in subtle body in that hall. I know."

Finding everything within is the ideal, but only the very adept yogi is able to do that.

If ALL that is, IS GOD, then this aspect of God is writing to HIMSELF. The reply comes from HIMSELF. The only perceived separation is Illusion. We are one in Christ and God, the Father....

Anyone can say or think this, but if it is not experienced in a continuous state of consciousness, then for all practical purposes it is not true. After awhile the mind begins telling itself that since all is God and all is therefore perfection, then it is illusory to engage in any spiritual practice because we are already perfect spirit. This is the folly propagated by the book The Impersonal Life that has supplied a lot of spiritual layabouts with the excuse to pursue everything in the world but enlightenment. As Yogananda said: Humans are so skilled in their ignorance. Empty philosophy can be one of the most harmful factors in a person's life. In my early life as a yogi I always knew someone was about to abandon yoga and spiritual life when I saw them reading either *The Impersonal Life* or *Commentaries On Living.*

In St. Thomas Christianity is there any purpose beyond Lila proposed?

The idea of "all is lila" is the rationalization behind acceptance of foolish, negative and destructive behavior on the part of gurus and religious authorities–and the excuser himself. Right along with it is the "crazy wisdom" cant of contemporary Western spiritual frauds about their own ignorance and evil. Nothing in the cosmos is just for fun, everything is for the attainment of jnana–of liberated consciousness. It all means something except to those who themselves are meaningless because they identify with illusion and do not know the reality behind everything.

In reply to a sadhaka living in an area where there were no others of her practice or philosophy. She asked which meditation groups I would recommend to a person looking for some spiritual association.

The problem with meditation groups is that they are often for propaganda and keeping people followers of whatever philosophy or guru they have. And frankly, most of such meditation groups put out negative or confused vibrations. It is better to meditate alone than with such people.

Satsang is so important, but what kind of satsang can you have with people who believe things contrary to dharma? Sincerity counts for very little as a substitute for true understanding.

Also, when these groups find you do not follow their ideas or ways they are not really accepting of you, only waiting to "bring you around" to their ideas and ways.

Unity and the Church of Religious Science can be positive, but they are tending more and more to be whatever the current New Age fads dictate. So you would need to visit them and see their actual character, which can vary from center to center.

Are there no Hindu temples in your area? Even when our ashram was in California where there are so many groups, we confined our association to orthodox Hindu temples and devotees' homes and Mahayana Buddhist temples of the Pure Land (Amitabha) or Kuan Yin traditions. We always found an instant spiritual affinity with them.

I am afraid I am not being much help, but outside India it is a real problem to find true, spiritually helpful satsang. It is better to be alone than to be in worthless or detrimental company.

To an Indian Methodist bishop who wanted to visit us because: "Here in India I am deeply concerned about reaching Hindus with the Christian gospel, in a way acceptable to them in the language and form they understand. After a lot of research and browsing I have found your way of understanding and presentation of the Christian faith may be the answer to lead the majority community in India and diaspora to the TRUTH."

Please look more carefully at our website, especially the article and book: *The Christ of India*. There you will see that our sole purpose is to demonstrate that Jesus of Nazareth travelled to India and became an orthodox Sanatana Dharmi. Then after living half of his life in India he returned to Israel as a teacher of Dharma and after three years returned to India where he lived the rest of his life in the Himalayas as a master yogi.

Those who would truly follow Jesus have only one option: the adoption and following of Sanatana Dharma—not that which is today called Christianity, but is only Churchianity.

Since the teachings of Jesus were pure Sanatana Dharma, they can be learned from the eleven principal Upanishads (Isha, Kena, Katha, Prashna, Mundaka, Mandukya, Taittiriya, Aitareya, Chandogya, Brihadaranyaka, and Shvetashvatara), the Bhagavad Gita and the Yoga Darshan (Yoga Sutras) of Patanjali. Anything that contradicts or adds to them is contrary to Dharma, and therefore contradictory to the original teachings of Jesus.

Hindus do not need "the Christian gospel," which is a corruption of Jesus' teachings, but they need to become more deeply aware of and grounded in traditional, authentic Sanatana Dharma. One of my friends in Delhi for some reason (perhaps from past life samskaras) became interested in converting to Christianity, so he went to consult with some Catholic priests. They asked him to first carefully study the scriptures of Sanatana Dharma and then decide what he felt was right to do. He did so, and did the right thing: he did not convert, but began following the Brahminical traditions of his ancestors. He kept a picture of Jesus in his puja room along with the pictures and images of the Hindu deities, understanding that Jesus was a worshipper of them as was he.

We certainly do hope that our website and publications will help seekers in America to find the eternal truths revealed to the ancient rishis of India, and will confirm those of India in the faith and practice of their divine, ancestral heritage: Sanatana Dharma.

Satyam Eva Jayate: "Truth alone prevails, not falsehood. By truth the path is laid out, the Way of the Gods, on which the seers, whose every desire is satisfied, proceed to the Highest Abode of the True" (Mundaka Upanishad 3:1:6).

May you find that path.

A blogpost in reference to the previous question and answer.

Dear friends,

There are two reasons for this blogpost besides the fact that I received the letter from India quoted previously.

The first is the need to make clear to all visitors to our website and readers of my books that the purpose of the website and my writings is to demonstrate that Jesus of Nazareth travelled to India in his so-called "lost years" and was a convert to Sanatana Dharma (Hinduism). He returned to Israel as a messenger of that Dharma and was persecuted and executed for teaching Dharma. He returned to India where he lived the remainder of his life in the Himalayas. Therefore those who feel a spiritual affinity for Jesus become his true disciples by following his example and adopting Sanatana Dharma.

A Saint Thomas Christian priest once told me: "You cannot understand the teachings of Jesus if you do not know the scriptures of India." That is because Jesus taught those scriptures! What is today popularly considered Christianity (Churchianity) is an insult and defamation of both Jesus and his teachings. The purpose of our website is to help Christians of both East and West to find the true religion of Jesus: Sanatana Dharma, and follow it as he did. They will be Sanatana Dharmis who have devotion to Jesus, just as there are Sanatana Dharmis who have devotion to Rama, Krishna, Vishnu, Shiva, Durga, Ganesha and the other forms of God. They will no longer be Churchians and need not even call themselves Christians.

The second is to explain that in India there are missionaries and their adherents that incorporate token elements of Hinduism into their churches in the hope that they will attract Indian converts. For example, they will read passages from the Upanishads or Gita and follow them with passages from the Bible to pretend that the Vedic rishis were seeking truth and that the Bible and Christianity are the fulfillment of that search.

When the writer of the letter I answered got my reply he wrote a long letter of semi-defense which was really an admission of such underhanded and brazen deceptions on his part. He even said that his desire was to help those that pray: Asato ma sad gamaya, Lead me from the unreal to the Real (which he rendered, Lead me from the untrue to the Truth) to "the Truth that is Jesus." And of course he expressed indignation at my reference to Brahmins—and therefore caste—in my answer to him. In other words, the man aspires to destroy dharma and usher people into profound ignorance and blasphemy. These may be strong words, but one of my first Indian friends told me what he and his Hindu classmates endured day after day in a Christian school in Gujerat. Every day there was a session of sneering at them and Dharma. They were told they were stupid, fools and going to hell. Often pictures and images of the deities were brought in and mocked and disrespected. The teachers also read out passages from the scriptures and mocked them. (Now their successors read them in church, as I have mentioned.) As a result he detested Jesus personally. That is the evil of the missionaries who came to "dark India" to bring the false "light" of lies. Of course their version of Jesus is detestable.

For thirty-two years Paramhansa Yogananda lived in the West and explained the real teachings of Jesus and Jesus himself as a yogi and disciple of the masters of India. All of his writings present the truth, especially *The Second Coming of Christ*. If you have not already done so, I hope that you will read *The Christ of India* and the other related articles on our website.

Yours in the Light of the Spirit, the Atma Jyoti,

Abbot George Burke
(Swami Nirmalananda Giri)

I am a student preparing for my civil service examinations next year. Eating meat has greatly decreased my concentration level. Every year for at least a month I eat only vegetarian food before I make a pilgrimage to the Sabarimala Temple. I can feel the difference in my intellectual level during that time. Now I would like to become a vegetarian. But I am confused as to whether I can eat eggs or not.

I know there are those who say that eating non-fertile eggs is acceptable because it does not violate the principle of ahimsa. That is so, but it does violate the principle of shaucha–purity. Eggs are animal flesh, a dead embryo, and as such are unclean, often being contaminated by elements such as salmonella which are detrimental–even dangerous–to health. As you have seen for yourself, the food you eat affects your mental abilities. Here is what the Chandogya Upanishad tells us about food and the mind:

"Food when eaten becomes threefold. What is coarsest in it becomes faeces, what is medium becomes flesh and what is subtlest becomes mind. Water when drunk becomes threefold. What is coarsest in it becomes urine, what is medium becomes blood and what is subtlest becomes prana....The mind consists of food, [and] the prana of water..." (Chandogya Upanishad 6.5.1, 2, 4).

"That which is the subtlest part of curds rises, when they are churned and becomes butter. In the same manner that which is the subtlest part of the food that is eaten rises and becomes mind. Thus the mind consists of food" (Chandogya Upanishad 6.6.1, 2,5; the same is confirmed in 6.7.1-6).

"Now is described the discipline for inner purification by which self-knowledge is attained: When the food is pure, the mind becomes pure. When the mind is pure the memory [smriti–memory of our eternal spirit-Self] becomes firm. When the memory is firm all ties are loosened" (Chandogya Upanishad 7.26.2).

No intelligent person wants to absorb the mental energies of a chicken into his mind!

To a friend who wrote concerned about derogatory things being spoken about some people who, being departed from this world, had no defence.

Not only are falsehoods spread, but so are faults in understanding. I want to tell you about one I myself encountered.

Before I went to see the great Master Shivananda, a very serious and good sadhaka, Brahmachari Haridas who was living at the Yogoda Math in Dakshineswar, told me that letters were being sent from Sivanandashram with the signature of Sivananda that he did not really write. This was told to me in all sincerity and as a caution for me to not think everyone in Sivanandashram was fully honest.

Here is the actual situation I found out.

Sivananda was incredibly busy with people coming day and night seeking his blessing, help and advice. His very advanced disciple, Swami Venkateshananda, would sit in his room with a typewriter and as Sivananda spoke with people in another part of the ashram he would at the same time psychically dictate letters to Venkateshananda who would type them out and bring them to Sivananda who would sign them. The situation showed the yogic capacities of both guru and disciple. But it can easily be understood that people might not understand the truth of it.

As Swami Brahmananda, the great disciple of Sri Ramakrishna used to say: "Just see the fun!"

This we know: God is true. It is Him that we must seek.

What is your perspective on the possible correspondences between the Holy Trinity and the human trinity of body, soul and spirit?

Our eternal spirit which is one with the Father "is" the father in our trinity. The higher bodies which reflect the spirit correspond to the Son, and the lower bodies correspond to the Holy Spirit, the Energy of creation.

However, the analogy is more symbolic than accurate. The Father aspect of us is our spirit's transcendental nature, the Son is our spirit's immanent, incarnate nature, and the energy bodies, our evolving energies in which our spirit is incarnate, are the Holy Spirit.

And all are one. As we move toward perfection, our bodies become increasingly refined until they are assumed into our spirit. For nothing but spirit has ever really existed.

This assumption is symbolized by the Assumption of the Virgin Mary, but all the mythologies and superstitions concerning that event have obscured its meaning.

What exactly is the blasphemy against the Holy Spirit which cannot be forgiven?

First we should look at the Bible references to the blasphemy against the Holy Spirit: "All manner of sin and blasphemy shall be forgiven unto men: but the blasphemy against the Holy Ghost shall not be forgiven unto men. And whosoever speaketh a word against the Son of man, it shall be forgiven him: but whosoever speaketh against the Holy Ghost, it shall not be forgiven him, neither in this world, neither in the world to come" (Matthew 12:31-32, Luke 12:10).

The word translated "blasphemy" is *blasfemia*, which means to villify and rave against someone—even to curse and defame them. Intense hatred of the target is implied, also. The word translated "forgive" is *afiemi*, which means to banish, leave behind, omit, remit. It implies separation from, cessation or reversal. So this means to hate and work or speak against something and for the slate not to ever be wiped clean or the penalty cancelled.

In a nutshell: whoever actively and intentionally defames or denounces the action of the Holy Spirit will suffer the consequences, the negative karma—not that they will be damned forever, but that they will absolutely pay off the karmic debt they created by their negativity. All other karma can be neutralized by positive words and deeds, but not that karma, for it is self-destruction.

How do we blaspheme the Holy Spirit? It is not doing or speaking evil of a saint or master, because Jesus says: "Whosoever speaketh a word against the Son of man, it shall be forgiven him." Those who lied about Jesus and claimed he was demon-possessed, born of fornication, a liar and a fraud, and even those who engineered his death, could have that karma dissolved by future positive words and acts. The same is true of those who have injured and even killed saints and masters.

Now we should turn to the *Aquarian Gospel* where, as usual, Jesus' words in the Bible are made clear and comprehensible in a spiritually sensible manner.

"If you sin against a son of man, you may be pardoned and your guilt be cleansed by acts of kindness and of love; but if you sin against the Holy Breath [Pneuma–Spirit] by disregarding her when she would open up the doors of life for you; by closing up the windows of the soul when she would pour the light of love into your hearts, and cleanse them with the fires of God; your guilt shall not be blotted out in this, nor in the life to come.

"An opportunity has gone to come no more, and you must wait until the ages roll again. Then will the Holy Breath again breathe on your fires of life, and fan them to a living flame. Then she will open up the doors again, and you may let her in to sup with you for evermore, or you may slight her once again, and then again" (105:32-38).

So we see that the basic "blasphemy" against the Holy Spirit is to ignore or actively turn against the inner awakening She seeks to bring about in us. It is not insulting and rejecting Her messengers, but our refusal to act according to what our now-evolving consciousness reveals to us is the truth about higher consciousness and its requisite: higher life. People do this all time, not wanting to change their life to conform to the spiritual insight they have gained. I have watched this tragic drama unfold in the lives of people over and over again. They consider the "price" is too high for them to pay. This is the saddest thing anyone can witness. Physical death is small compared to seeing a person condemn themselves to inner death and future suffering when the way to peace and freedom is disdained and considered not worth the trouble.

Sometimes the call from On High comes several times and is rejected, but mostly it comes only once. Please understand that this unhappy fate is not decreed by God/the Holy Spirit, but is the simple principle of karma. The magnitude of a situation determines the magnitude of the karma. And when the Holy Spirit Mother is involved, it is tremendous, indeed. Yet, as Jesus says, in time She will awaken us again and we can choose again—wisely or foolishly. But it is usually a very long time before that "again" occurs. And I know of instances in which the habit of rejection manifested in many lives in succession. But it is always our choice.

Letter To A Spiritual Codependent

Quite a few years ago a man who was living in a spiritual com-munity wrote to me about some of his problems. But he really only had one problem: he could not be himself. He had to be a part of

something; he had to draw his identity from association, not his per-
sonality or even his ideas. He was a Pinocchio looking for someone
to make him "a real boy." It was not going to happen, but I tried to
help him at least think of the possibility of being real in his own right.

"And Jesus saith unto him, The foxes have holes, and the birds of
the air have nests; but the Son of man hath not where to lay his head"
(Matthew 8:20). There are many interpretation of these words, all viable
since the words spoken by a person of infinite consciousness can have
infinite meanings. One I feel is legitimate is the idea that those of lesser
evolution ("foxes" and "birds") can find a home on earth, but a true,
awakened human being cannot.

Please do not look for a spiritual home or a place where you belong
on this earth—and that includes churches, spiritual groups, or ashrams.
You are not even a human being—you are a god within God. And only
God is your home. Disappointment and frustration, not to mention pain
and grief, can only result from trying to find a resting place anywhere
but in Infinity. That is a tough thing to face, but if we are to be spiritual
adults the bullet must be faced and bitten.

Many people's lives are a chain of "home at last," none of which
really are home at all, as they eventually discover. At the time they were
spiritually beneficial and worthy of gratitude and respect, necessary
steps—but that is just it: steps leading to something higher. If we come
to rest on any of them we will stagnate and die.

Growth is change—keep on changing! The spiritual stick-in-the-
muds will look at you and cluck and shake their heads and talk about
instability and (in the group you are involved in now) being "out of
tune with Master" and other tripe. They like stagnancy and, as Jesus
said, they have their reward. But you be different.

Sri Ramakrishna told the parable of a woodcutter that met a sadhu
in the forest who told him: "Go forward." He did, and discovered a
sandalwood grove. He started to cut it but remembered he had been

told Go Further, so he went on. He found an iron deposit, then a copper deposit, then a silver deposit, then a gold deposit, and finally a diamond field–all because he kept on going further.

All teachings and teachers are finite and limited by human boundaries. Eventually they must all be grown beyond. Truth is another matter altogether. Discovery of Truth should be the purpose of teachings and teachers, but is it? Aren't most of them meant to "answer all questions," "give comfort," or "bring peace"? Are there any real answers, comfort, or peace in this world? I do not think so. But it can certainly be found within.

However, all rungs of the ladder are worthy of regard. Without the rungs of a ladder or the steps of a stair we do not ascend, but we ascend by leaving them behind, not stopping on them and calling all the world to come stand still with us. It is the willingness to keep moving onward, leaving everything behind, that is the highest renunciation. Years ago I came to realize that the journey was never going to end as long as I was moving from point to point rather than stepping off into eternity.

Someone asked Shankara: "What is truth [satya]?" Shankara replied: "There is no 'truth.' There is only The True [Sat]." As Yogananda's most advanced disciple, Sister Gyanamata, said: God Alone.

Like the egoic children we are, we hate admitting that we were wrong in thinking we had "found it." The ego keeps people "loyal" from life to life. "God and Guru" my foot. In God there is no "and." Remember: Sri Ramakrishna did not attain liberation until he mentally cut the living image of Kali in half with the sword of discrimination.

Does this all sound like I am one of those cynical, warped, and dried up souls like X—— that denounce everyone but themselves and all ideas but theirs? I hope not, for you cannot progress without any of these things I have mentioned, but you must also get (grow) beyond them. Every time you sit to do math, do you call up your first math teacher and ask her to come do it for you? Or when you get the right answer, do you say: "I have done nothing. It is all my first grade arithmetic teacher.

I just surrender to her and she does it all through me. All credit goes to her"? Of course not, because you are not nuts. So why be spiritually crazy?

People talk about "walking the Path," but the whole idea of the path is to come to its end and leave it behind. All books, however wise, have an ending, as do the discourses of even avatars. And then the Real Thing begins. We will not reach the Real without the paths, the books, or the discourses, but we must use them, not make idols or security blankets of them. A few years ago I figured out the unspoken universal motto of all religions is: Adore The Messenger And Ignore The Message. The message is always: Move on until you reach the place where there is no more "on."

The problem is not with the masters but with the ignorant and deluded "disciples." The masters liberate, the groupies bind. Do you have the recording: *Self-Realization: the Inner and the Outer Path*? Dr. Lewis' talk presents the right perspective: it is not an organization but an attainment.

I say all this because I know how a seeker can suffer from continual disillusionment if he keeps conscious and keeps his eyes open. But you will not suffer, only benefit, if you understand the way things are. Learn. Apply. Move on. It is all between you and God. And since when does God need any vows or promises? Either you seek him or you do not. And he can tell the difference.

My chief interest for some years has been how people can break all dependencies and find God on their own. Nearly all religious and "spiritual" situations involve manipulation and dependence. Religion is the number one field for victimizers and victims, though with sacred labels instead of the true ones. Coercion and submission is the order of the day. It is evil.

There is deep significance in the fact that the word "monk" comes from the Greek word *monachos*—one who lives alone. In a real monastery there many be dozens or hundreds of monks, but each one is truly a solitary in spirit. Not isolated, but alone—with God. An institution that does not provide for that is a soul trap.

There are many things that people need at a certain level of development, but a time comes when external input no longer is what we need. Rather, we must open up the inner life and live on that alone. "Man shall not live by bread alone…" implies this. The "…word that proceedeth out of the mouth of God" (Matthew 4:40) is purely internal. God speaks in the depths of our spirit, the core of our consciousness. And not as a cosmic rumble as we sit with our thumbs stuck in our ears. That, too, is outward-turned. Rather, he speaks as "a still small voice" (I Kings 19:12) in the inner silence.

The absolute essential is the procedure by which our entire being is transmuted into the Life Divine. Just this morning I was reading Dr. I. K. Taimni's statement that the purpose of following and seeking the Truth is to *be* the Truth. Ultimately, though not prematurely, we must come to say with Jesus: "I am the way, the truth, and the life" (John 14:6). We need to pass from feeding on the Bread of Life to becoming the Bread of Life. This is real yoga–nothing else.

I have declaimed enough. Thank you for your letters. I hope you find some things that I have written useful–if only to disagree with.

Did you enjoy reading this book?

Thank you for taking the time to read *Satsang with the Abbot*. If you enjoyed it, please consider telling your friends or posting a short review at Amazon.com, Goodreads, or the online site of your choice.

Word of mouth is an author's best friend and much appreciated.

Get your FREE Meditation Guide

Sign up for the Light of the Spirit Newsletter and get
Ten Simple Tips to Improve Your Meditation Today.

Get free updates: newsletters, blog posts, and podcasts, plus exclusive
content from Light of the Spirit Monastery.

Visit: http://ocoy.org/newsletter-registration

GLOSSARY

Abhaya(m): "Without fear;" fearlessness; a state of steadfastness in which one is not swayed by fear of any kind.

Acharya: Preceptor; teacher; spiritual teacher; guide; guru.

Adharma: Unrighteousness; demerit, failure to perform one's proper duty; unrighteous action; lawlessness; absence of virtue; all that is contrary to righteousness (dharma).

Adhyatma: The individual Self; the supreme Self; spirit.

Adhyatmika: Adhyatmic; pertaining to the Self (Atman or Jivatman), individual and Supreme (Paramatman).

Advaita: Non-dualism; non-duality; literally: not [a] two [dvaita].

Advaita Vedanta: The teaching that there is only One Reality (Brahman-Atman), as found in the Upanishads. Non-dualistic philosophy, especially that of Shankara.

Advaitic: Non-dual; having to do with the philosophy of Advaita (Non-Dualism).

Agni: Fire; Vedic god of fire.

Ahimsa: Non-injury in thought, word, and deed; non-violence; non-killing; harmlessness.

Ajna chakra: "Command Wheel." Energy center located at the point between the eyebrows, the "third eye." The seat of the mind. The medulla center opposite the point between the eyebrows, having two "petals" or rays.

Akasha: Ether; space; sky; literally: "not visible." The subtlest of the five elements (panchabhuta), from which the other four arise. It is all-pervading, and is sometimes identified with consciousness–chidakasha. It is the basis of sound (shabda), which is its particular property.

Anahata: "Unstruck;" "unbeaten." Continuous bell-like inner resonance; the heart; the heart chakra; the inner divine melody (mystic sounds heard by the Yogis); supernatural sound; Soham.

Anahata chakra: "Unstruck." Energy center located in the spine at the point opposite the center of the chest (sternum bone). Seat of the Air element.

Anandamayi Ma: One of the major spiritual figures in twentieth-century India, first made known to the West by Paramhansa Yogananda in his *Autobiography of a Yogi*.

Annapurna: "Full of Food." A title of the Goddess (Shakti) depicted as the Goddess of Food and Abundance. The consort of Shiva.

Anushthana: Observance; religious exercise; repetition of a mantra for a set number of times during a given period; systematic performance of religious practices, usually undertaken for some definite period of time.

Apa(h): Water.

Aparigraha: Non-possessiveness, non-greed, non-selfishness, non-acquisitive-ness; freedom from covetousness; non-receiving of gifts conducive to luxury.

Apsara: A celestial damsel, nymph, and dancer.

Arjuna: The great disciple of Krishna, who imparted to him the teachings found in the Bhagavad Gita. The third of the Pandava brothers who were major figures in the Mahabharata War. His name literally means "bright," "white," or "clear."

Arya(n): One who is an Arya–literally, "one who strives upward." Both Arya and Aryan are exclusively psychological terms having nothing whatsoever to do with birth, race, or nationality. In his teachings Buddha habitually referred to spiritually qualified people as "the Aryas." Although in English translations we find the expressions: "The Four Noble Truths," and "The Noble Eightfold Path," Buddha actually said: "The Four Aryan Truths," and "The Eightfold Aryan Path."

Ashram(a): A place for spiritual discipline and study, usually a monastic residence.

Ashtanga Yoga: The "eight-limbed" Yoga of Patanjali consisting of yama, niyama, asana, pranayama, pratyahara, dharana, dhyana, and samadhi (see separate entries for each "limb").

Asteya: Non-stealing; honesty; non-misappropriativeness.

Asura: Demon; evil being (a-sura: without the light).

Atman-darshan: The seeing or sight of the Self (atman); the vision of the Self; knowledge of the Self through direct vision or knowing; the vision of seeing everything as the Self.

Atmajnana: Direct knowledge of the Self; Brahma-Jnana.

Atman(n): The individual spirit or Self that is one with Brahman. The true nature or identity.

Avatar(a): A fully liberated spirit (jiva) who is born into a world below Satya Loka to help others attain liberation. Though commonly referred to as a divine incarnation, an avatar actually is totally one with God, and therefore an incarnation of God-Consciousness.

Bhagavad Gita: "The Song of God." The sacred philosophical text often called "the Hindu Bible," part of the epic Mahabharata by Vyasa; the most popular sacred text in Hinduism.

Bhava: Subjective state of being (existence); attitude of mind; mental attitude or feeling; state of realization in the heart or mind.

Bhumi: The earth; ground; region; place.

Brahma: The Creator (Prajapati) of the three worlds of men, angels, and archangels (Bhur, Bhuwah, and Swah); the first of the created beings; Hiranyagarbha or cosmic intelligence.

Brahma Sutras: A treatise by Vyasa on Vedanta philosophy in the form of aphorisms. Also called the Vedanta Sutras or Vedanta Darshana.

Brahmachari(n): One who observes continence; a celibate student in the first stage of life (ashrama); a junior monk.

Brahmacharya: Continence; self-restraint on all levels; discipline; dwelling in Brahman.

Brahmajnana: Direct, transcendental knowledge of Brahman; Self-realization.

Brahmamuhurta: "The muhurta of Brahman." The period of one and a half hours before sunrise (sometime between 3:00 a.m. and 6:00 a.m.), which is said to be the best time for meditation and worship.

Brahman: The Absolute Reality; the Truth proclaimed in the Upanishads; the Supreme Reality that is one and indivisible, infinite, and eternal; all-pervading, changeless Existence; Existence-knowledge-bliss Absolute (Satchidananda); Absolute Consciousness; it is not only all-powerful but all-power itself; not only all-knowing and blissful but all-knowledge and all-bliss itself.

Brahmavadin: Literally "one who walks the path of Brahman." One who advocates that there is one existence alone–Parabrahman.

Brindaban: The place where Krishna was born and where he lived until the age of twelve. Today it is a city of devotees and temples. Many agree with my friend who once said to me in a very matter-of-fact way: "Brindaban is my life." Its actual name is Vrindavan, but so many Bengali devotees and saints for centuries have called it "Brindaban" in their dialect, it has become common usage throughout India.

Buddhi: Intellect; intelligence; understanding; reason; the thinking mind; the higher mind, which is the seat of wisdom; the discriminating faculty.

Chaitanya: Consciousness; intelligence; awareness; the consciousness that knows itself and knows others; Pure Consciousness.

Chakra: Plexus; center of psychic energy in the human system, particularly in the spine or head.

Chitta: The subtle energy that is the substance of the mind, and therefore the mind itself; mind in all its aspects; the field of the mind; the field of consciousness; consciousness itself; the subconscious mind.

Darshan: Literally "sight" or "seeing;" vision, literal and metaphysical; a system of philosophy (see Sad-darshanas). Darshan is the seeing of a holy being as well as the blessing received by seeing such a one.

Deva: "A shining one," a god–greater or lesser in the evolutionary hierarchy; a semi-divine or celestial being with great powers, and therefore a "god." Sometimes called a demi-god. Devas are the demigods presiding over various powers of material and psychic nature. In many instances "devas" refer to the powers of the senses or the sense organs themselves.

Devi: Goddess; the Supreme Shakti (Divine Power) or Divine Mother, or a demigoddess.

Dharma: The righteous way of living, as enjoined by the sacred scriptures and the spiritually illumined; characteristics; law; lawfulness; virtue; righteousness; norm.

Durga: "Incomprehensible One;" "Difficult to reach;" the Universal Mother; she rides a lion (or tiger) and carries a weapon in each of her eight arms symbolizing the powers of the Self against ignorance and evil. She is invoked against all forms of evil–physical and metaphysical. Considered the consort, the shakti, of Shiva.

Dvaita: Dual; duality; dualism.

Dwandwa(s): The pairs of opposites inherent in nature (prakriti) such as pleasure and pain, hot and cold, light and darkness, gain and loss, victory and defeat, love and hatred.

Dwapara Yuga: See Yuga.

Eka(m): One.

Ekam-evam-advitiyam: "One, only, without a second." A description of Brahman.

Gandharva: A demigod–a celestial musician and singer.

Ganesha: The elephant-headed son of Shiva and Parvati; the remover of obstacles; lord (pati) of the ganas (spirits that always accompany Shiva); god of wisdom; god of beginnings; the granter of success in spiritual and material life; in ritual worship he is worshipped first, and is therefore known as Adi-deva, the First God.

Ganga: See Ganges.

Ganges (Ganga): The sacred river–believed to be of divine origin–that flows from high up in the Himalayas, through the plains of Northern India, and empties into the Bay of Bengal. Hindus consider that bathing in the Ganges profoundly purifies both body and mind.

Gayatri Mantra: A Rig Vedic mantra in the gayatri meter invoking the solar powers of evolution and enlightenment, recited at sunrise and sunset.

Gorakhnath/Gorakshanath: A master yogi of the Nath Yogi (Siddha Yogi) tradition. His dates are not positively known, but he seems to have lived for many centuries and travelled throughout all of India, Bhutan, Tibet, and Ladakh teaching philosophy and yoga.

Guna: Quality, attribute, or characteristic arising from nature (Prakriti) itself; a mode of energy behavior. As a rule, when "guna" is used it is in reference to the three qualities of Prakriti, the three modes of energy behavior that are the basic qualities of nature, and which determine the inherent characteristics of all created things. They are: 1) sattwa–purity, light, harmony; 2) rajas–activity, passion; and 3) tamas–dullness, inertia, and ignorance.

Hardwar: "The Gateway to Hari," a holy city in north-central India where the Ganges river flows into the plains.

Ichcha shakti: The power of desire; the power of the will; Shakti in the aspect of omnipotent Divine Will.

Ida: The subtle channel that extends from the base of the spine to the medulla on the left side of the spine.

Indra: King of the lesser "gods" (demigods); the ruler of heaven (Surendra Loka); the rain-god.

Isha: The Lord; Ishwara.

Isha Nath: The monastic name of Jesus in India as a member of the Nath Yogi Sampradaya.

Ishta-devata: Beloved deity. The deity preferred above all others by an individual. "Chosen ideal" is the usual English translation.

Ishwara: "God" or "Lord" in the sense of the Supreme Power, Ruler, Master, or Controller of the cosmos. "Ishwara" implies the powers of omnipotence, omnipresence, and omniscience.

Ishwarapranidhana: Offering of one's life to God (Ishwara).

Jada Bharata: A king of ancient India who became so fond of a deer that he was thinking of it intently at the time of death and was reborn as a deer though with full awareness of his previous life.

Jagannath Puri: A pilgrim city on the east coast of India in Orissa State where multitudes come daily to worship Krishna in the temple of Jagannath (Lord of the World).

Jagrat: The waking state.

Janaka: The royal sage (raja rishi) who was the king of Mithila and a liberated yogi, a highly sought-after teacher of philosophy in ancient India. Sita, the wife of Rama, was his adopted daughter.

Japa: Repetition of a mantra.

Jivanmukta: One who is liberated here and now in this present life.

Jivatma(n): Individual spirit; individual consciousness.

Jnana: Knowledge; knowledge of Reality–of Brahman, the Absolute; also denotes the process of reasoning by which the Ultimate Truth is attained. The word is generally used to denote the knowledge by which one is aware of one's identity with Brahman.

Kali: "The Black One;" the black-skinned goddess who emerged from the body of Goddess Durga to defeat the demons that were attacking her. She wears a garland of skulls (or severed heads) around her neck and a skirt of severed arms–both symbolizing the sense of egotism. In one hand she wields the sword of spiritual wisdom (prajna) and in the other carries a severed head (ego). Despite her fearsome appearance, her two other hands are held in the gestures (mudras) that indicate: "Fear not" and "Draw near."

Kali Yuga: The dark age of spiritual and moral decline, said to be current now. See Yuga.

Kalpa: A Day of Brahma–4,320,000,000 years. It alternates with a Night of Brahma of the same length. He lives hundred such years. Brahma's life is known as Para, being of a longer duration than the life of any other being, and a half of it is called Parardha. He has now completed the first Parardha and is in the first day of the second Parardha. This day or Kalpa is known as Svetavarahakalpa. In the Day of Brahma creation is manifest and in the Night of Brahma is it resolved into its causal state.

Kama: Desire; passion; lust.

Kamadhenu: Wish-fulfilling cow produced at the churning of the milk ocean.

Karma: Karma, derived from the Sanskrit root *kri*, which means to act, do, or make, means any kind of action, including thought and feeling. It also means the effects of action. Karma is both action and reaction, the metaphysical equivalent of the principle: "For every action there is an equal and opposite reaction." "Whatsoever a man soweth, that shall he also reap" (Galatians 6:7). It is karma operating through the law of cause and effect that binds the jiva or the individual soul to the wheel of birth and death. There are three forms of karma: sanchita, agami, and prarabdha. Sanchita karma is the vast store of accumulated actions done in the past, the fruits of which have not yet been reaped. Agami karma is the action that will be done by the individual in the future. Prarabdha karma is the action that has begun to fructify, the fruit of which is being reaped in this life.

Karmakanda: The ritual portion of the Veda. The philosophy that Vedic ritual is the only path to perfection.

Kinnara: A celestial musician.

Kirtan: Singing the names and praises of God; devotional chanting.

Kosha: Sheath; bag; scabbard; a sheath enclosing the soul; body. There are five such concentric sheaths or bodies: the sheaths of bliss, intellect, mind, life-force and the physical body–the anandamaya, jnanamaya, manomaya, pranamaya and annamaya bodies respectively.

Krishna: An avatar born in India about three thousand years ago, Whose teachings to His disciple Arjuna on the eve of the Great India (Mahabharata) War comprise the Bhagavad Gita.

Kriya Yoga: The Yoga of Purification: "Austerity (tapasya), self-study (swadhyaya), and offering of the life to God (Ishwara pranidhana) are Kriya Yoga" (Yoga Sutras 2:1).

Krodha: Anger, wrath; fury.

Kshatriya: A member of the ruler/warrior caste.

Kundalini: The primordial cosmic conscious/energy located in the individual; it is usually thought of as lying coiled up like a serpent at the base of the spine.

Kutastha: Immutable; absolutely changeless; not subject to change; literally: "summit abiding" or "on the summit." He who is found without exception in all creatures from Brahma or the creator down to ants and Who is shining as the Self and dwells as witness to the intellect of all creatures; rock-seated; unchanging; another name for Brahman.

Lahiri Mahasaya: Shyama Charan Lahiri, one of the greatest yogis of nineteenth-century India, written about extensively in *Autobiography of a Yogi* by Paramhansa Yogananda.

Lakshmi: The consort of Vishnu; the goddess of wealth and prosperity.

Lila: Play; sport; divine play; the cosmic play. The concept that creation is a play of the divine, existing for no other reason than for the mere joy of it. The life of an avatar is often spoken of as lila.

Linga: Mark; gender; sign; symbol. Usually a reference to a column-like or egg-shaped symbol of Shiva.

Loka: World or realm; sphere, level, or plane of existence, whether physical, astral, or causal.

Madhvacharya: The thirteenth century Vaishnava founder and expounder of the Dvaita (Dualist) Vedanta philosophy.

Mahabharata: The world's longest epic poem (110,00 verses) about the Mahabharata (Great Indian) War that took place about three thousand years ago. The Mahabharata also includes the Bhagavad Gita, the most popular sacred text of Hinduism.

Mahabhutas: The Five Elements (Panchabhuta): ether (akasha), air (vayu), fire (agni), water(ap), and earth (prithvi).

Mahashakti: The Great Power; the divine creative energy.

Manas(a): The sensory mind; the perceiving faculty that receives the messages of the senses.

Mandir(a): Temple; abode.

Manipura chakra: Energy center located in the spine at the point opposite the navel. Seat of the Fire element.

Mantra(m): Sacred syllable or word or set of words through the repetition and reflection of which one attains perfection or realization of the Self. Literally, "a transforming thought" (manat trayate). A mantra, then is a sound formula that transforms the consciousness.

Maya: The illusive power of Brahman; the veiling and the projecting power of the universe, the power of Cosmic Illusion. "The Measurer"–a reference to the two delusive "measures," Time and Space.

Mleccha: Foreigner; an alien; barbarian; non-Aryan.

Moksha: Release; liberation; the term is particularly applied to the liberation from the bondage of karma and the wheel of birth and death; Absolute Experience.

Mrityunjaya: Conquerer of death; one of the names of Lord Siva.

Mukti: Moksha; liberation.

Muladhara chakra: "Seat of the root." Energy center located at the base of the spine. Seat of the Earth element.

Mulamantra: Root Mantra; the powerful and the most important of the Mantras of any deity.

Murti: Image; statue; idol; figure; embodiment.

Naraka: Hell. In Sanatana Dharma's cosmology there are many hells according to the karma of those dwelling in them before being reincarnated.

Nasikagram: The origin of the nose (nasik). *Agram* means beginning, top, tip and the nearest end. Although in translations of texts such as the Bhagavad Gita (6:13), "tip [end] of the nose" is often the translation of nasikagram, some yogis insist that the top of the nose is meant and that the eyes must be turned upward in meditation. This is in harmony with Bhagavad Gita 5:27 where the yogi is told to turn up the eyes toward the two eyebrows.

Nath Yogi: A member of the Nath Yogi Sampradaya.

Nath Yogi Sampradaya: An ancient order of yogis, sometimes called Siddha Yogis, claiming Patanjali, Gorakhnath, Jnaneshwar and Jesus (Isha Nath) among their master teachers.

Nityananda (Paramhansa): A great Master of the nineteenth and twentieth centuries, and the most renowned Nath Yogi of our times. His *Chidakasha Gita* contains some of the most profound statements on philosophy and yoga.

Neti-neti: "Not this, not this." The way of describing the indescribable Brahman by enumerating what It is not; the analytical process of progressively negating all names and forms, in order to arrive at the eternal underlying Truth.

Nirakara: Without form.

Nirguna: Without attributes or qualities (gunas).

Nirguna Brahman: The impersonal, attributeless Absolute beyond all description or designation.

Nirodha: Restraint; restriction; suppression; dissolving/dissolution; cessation; disappearance; control inhibition; annihilation; process of ending.

Nirvana: Liberation; final emancipation; the term is particularly applied to the liberation from the bondage of karma and the wheel of birth and death that comes from knowing Brahman; Absolute Experience. See Moksha.

Niyama: Observance; the five Do's of Yoga: 1) shaucha–purity, cleanliness; 2) santosha–contentment, peacefulness; 3) tapas–austerity, practical (i.e., result-producing) spiritual discipline; 4) swadhyaya–self-study, spiritual study; 5) Ishwarapranidhana–offering of one's life to God.

Om: The Pranava or the sacred syllable symbolizing and embodying Brahman.

Omkara: Om.

Panchabhuta: The Five Elements (Mahabhuta): ether (akasha), air (vayu), fire (agni), water (ap), and earth (prithvi).

Parabrahman: Supreme Brahman.

Paramatman(n): The Supreme Self, God.

Parameshwara: The Supreme (Param) Lord (eshwara; Ishwara).

Paramhansa Yogananda: See Yogananda.

Patanjali: A yogi of ancient India, a Nath Yogi and the author of the Yoga Sutras.

Pingala: The subtle channel that extends from the base of the spine to the medulla on the right side of the spine.

Prajapati: Progenitor; the Creator; a title of Brahma the Creator.

Prakriti: Causal matter; the fundamental power (shakti) of God from which the entire cosmos is formed; the root base of all elements; undifferentiated matter; the material cause of the world. Also known as Pradhana. Prakriti can also mean the entire range of vibratory existence (energy).

Prana: Life; vital energy; life-breath; life-force; inhalation. In the human body the prana is divided into five forms: 1) Prana, the prana that moves upward; 2) Apana: The prana that moves downward, producing the excretory functions in general. 3) Vyana: The prana that holds prana and apana together and produces circulation in the body. 4) Samana: The prana that carries the grosser material of food to the apana and brings the subtler material to each limb; the general force of digestion. 5) Udana: The prana which brings up or carries down what has been drunk or eaten; the general force of assimilation.

Pranamaya kosha: "The sheath of vital air (prana)." The sheath consisting of vital forces and the (psychic) nervous system, including the karmendriyas.

Pranava: A title of Om, meaning "Life-ness" or "Life-Giver." Om is the expression or controller of prana–the life force within the individual being and the cosmos.

Pranayama: Control of the subtle life forces, often by means of special modes of breathing. Therefore breath control or breathing exercises are usually mistaken for pranayama. It also means the refining (making subtle) of the breath, and its lengthening through spontaneous slowing down of the respiratory rate.

Prithivi: The element of earth with density and fragrance as its characteristic features.

Punya: Merit; virtue; meritorious acts; virtuous deeds.

Purana: Literally "The Ancient." The Puranas are a number of scriptures attributed to the sage Vyasa that teach spiritual principles and practices through stories about sacred historical personages which often include their teachings given in conversations.

Purna: Full; complete; infinite; absolute; Brahman.

Purusha: "Person" in the sense of a conscious spirit. Both God and the individual spirits are purushas, but God is the Adi (Original, Archetypal) Purusha, Parama (Highest) Purusha, and the Purushottama (Highest or Best of the Purushas).

Radha: The beloved of Sri Krishna during his early life in Brindaban; an incarnation of the divine feminine as Krishna is an incarnation of the divine masculine. Though her role (lila) was highly symbolic, nevertheless she was not a myth but a very real person. Furthermore, since she and Krishna were both children, their love for one another and their interaction was thoroughly spiritual and sacred. Any other depiction or interpretation is erroneous.

Raja Yoga: See Ashtanga Yoga.

Rajas: Activity, passion, desire for an object or goal.

Rama: An incarnation of God—the king of ancient Ayodhya in north-central India. His life is recorded in the ancient epic Ramayana.

Rama Tirtha: One the key spiritual figures in late nineteenth and early twentieth century India. A former university professor of mathematics in the Punjab, Swami Rama Tirtha traveled throughout India and even to Japan and America, preaching the truths of Advaita Vedanta and vigorously teaching the practice of Om Yoga.

Ramakrishna, Sri: Sri Ramakrishna lived in India in the second half of the nineteenth century, and is regarded by all India as a perfectly enlightened person—and by many as an Incarnation of God.

Ramana: Enjoyer; one who enjoys or delights in something.

Ramana Maharshi: A great sage of the twentieth century who lived in Arunachala in South India. He taught the path of Self-Inquiry (Atman Vichara) wherein the person simply turns his awareness within with the unspoken question—the attitude—of "Who am I?" until the self (atman) is revealed.

Ramanuja (Sri): The great Vaishnava teacher of the eleventh century who formulated the philosophy known as Vishishtadvaita Vedanta (Qualified Non-Dualism).

Ramayana: The great Sanskrit epic poem by the sage Valmiki describing the life of Rama, the king of ancient Ayodhya in north-central India, who is regarded as an incarnation of God. The renowned Hindi devotional poem by the saint Tulsidas, also on the life of Rama.

Rishi: Sage; seer of the Truth.

Sadhaka: One who practices spiritual discipline—sadhana—particularly meditation.

Sadhana: Spiritual practice.

Saguna: Possessing attributes or qualities (gunas).

Saguna Brahman: Brahman with attributes, such as mercy, omnipotence, omniscience, etc.; the Absolute conceived as the Creator, Preserver, and Destroyer of the universe; also the Personal God according to the Vedanta.

Sahasrara: The "thousand-petalled lotus" of the brain. The highest center of consciousness, the point at which the spirit (atman) and the bodies (koshas) are integrated and from which they are disengaged.

Sakara: With form.

Samadhi: The state of superconsciousness where Absoluteness is experienced attended with all-knowledge and joy; Oneness; here the mind becomes identified with the object of meditation; the meditator and the meditated, thinker and thought become one in perfect absorption of the mind.

Sampradaya: Tradition; philosophical school; literally: "handed-down instruction;" also a line of initiatic empowerment.

Samsara: Life through repeated births and deaths; the wheel of birth and death; the process of earthly life.

Samskara (1): Impression in the mind, either conscious or subconscious, produced by action or experience in this or previous lives; propensities of the mental residue of impressions; subliminal activators; prenatal tendency.

Samskara (2): A ritual that makes an impression or change in the individual for whom it is done. There are sixteen samskaras prescribed by the dharma shastras, beginning with conception (garbhadan) and concluding with the rite for the departed soul (antyshthi). The major ones besides these two are the birth rite (jatakarman), naming ceremony (namakaranam), the first eating of solid food (annaprasannam), the first cutting of the hair (chudakaraman), bestowal of the sacred thread and instruction in the Gayatri mantra (upanayanam), marriage (vivahanam), taking up of the retired life (vanaprastha), and taking up the monastic life (sannyasa). They are all done at points in the person's life when significant changes in the subtle energy bodies are going to take place. Thus the samskara protects and strengthens the individual at those times and also prepares him for those changes, making actual alterations in his subtle bodies. Although they are often made social occasions, they are very real instruments of change to facilitate and further the person's personal evolution. They are the linchpins of dharmic life, and essentially spiritual events.

Sanatana Dharma: "The Eternal Religion," also known as "Arya Dharma," "the religion of those who strive upward [Aryas]." Hinduism.

Sanatana Dharmi: One who follows Sanatana Dharma.

Sankalpa: A life-changing wish, desire, volition, resolution, will, determination, or intention—not a mere momentary aspiration, but an empowering act of will that persists until the intention is fully realized. It is an act of spiritual, divine creative will inherent in each person as a power of the Atman.

Sankhya: One of the six orthodox systems of Hindu philosophy whose originator was the sage Kapila, Sankhya is the original Vedic philosophy, endorsed by Krishna in the Bhagavad Gita (Gita 2:39; 3:3, 5; 18:13, 19), the second chapter of which is entitled "Sankhya Yoga." *A Ramakrishna-Vedanta Wordbook* says: "Sankhya postulates two ultimate realities, Purusha and Prakriti. Declaring that the cause of suffering is man's identification of Purusha with Prakriti and its products, Sankhya teaches that liberation and true knowledge are attained in the supreme consciousness, where such identification ceases and Purusha is realized as existing independently in its transcendental nature." Not surprisingly, then, Yoga is based on the Sankhya philosophy.

Sannyas(a): Renunciation; monastic life. Sannyasa literally means "total throwing away," in the sense of absolute rejection of worldly life, ways and attitudes. True sannyas is based on viveka and vairagya. It is not just a mode of external life, but a profound insight and indifference to the things of the world and the world itself—not the world of God's creation, but the world of human ignorance, illusion, folly and suffering which binds all sentient beings to the wheel of continual birth and death. The sannyasi's one goal is liberation through total purification and enlightenment. His creed is Shankara's renowned Vedanta in Half a Verse: "Brahman is real. The world is illusion. The jiva is none other than Brahman."

Sannyasi(n): A renunciate; a monk.

Sanskrit: The language of the ancient sages of India and therefore of the Indian scriptures and yoga treatises.

Santosha: Contentment; joy; happiness; peacefulness.

Sarada Devi ("Holy Mother"): The virgin-wife of Sri Ramakrishna, and a great teacher in her own right, considered by many to be an incarnation of the Mother aspect of God.

Saraswati: The goddess of speech, wisdom, learning and the arts—particularly music.

Sat: Existence; reality; truth; being; a title of Brahman, the Absolute or Pure Being.

Satchidananda: Existence-Knowledge-Bliss Absolute; Brahman.

Satsang(a): Literally: "company with Truth." Association with godly-minded persons. The company of saints and devotees.

Sattwa Guna: Quality of light, purity, harmony, and **Satya(m):** Truth; the Real; Brahman, or the Absolute; truthfulness; honesty.

Satya Yuga: See Yuga.

Shakti: Power; energy; force; the Divine Power of becoming; the apparent dynamic aspect of Eternal Being; the Absolute Power or Cosmic Energy; the Divine Feminine.

Shaktipata: Descent of power (through Upasana).

Shankara(charya): Shankaracharya; Adi (the first) Shankaracharya: The great reformer and re-establisher of Vedic Religion in India around 500 B.C. He is the unparalleled exponent of Advaita (Non-Dual) Vedanta. He also reformed the mode of monastic life and founded (or regenerated) the ancient Swami Order.

Shankara Shankaracharya Adi Shankaracharya

Sharanagati: One who has taken refuge or shelter, or **Sharanam:** Refuge; protection, shelter.

Shastra: Scripture; spiritual treatise.

Shaucha: Purity; cleanliness.

Shiva: A name of God meaning "One Who is all Bliss and the giver of happiness to all." Although classically applied to the Absolute Brahman, Shiva can also refer to God (Ishwara) in His aspect of Dissolver and Liberator (often mistakenly thought of as "destroyer").

Siddha: A perfected—liberated—being, an adept, a seer, a perfect yogi.

Siddhi: Spiritual perfection; psychic power; power; modes of success;

attainment; accomplishment; achievement; mastery; supernatural power attained through mantra, meditation, or other yogic practices. From the verb root sidh–to attain.

Sita: The consort of Rama, an avatara of the Divine Mother aspect of God.

Sri: Holy; sacred; excellent; venerated (venerable); revered; a term of respect similar to "Reverend." Also: prosperity, glory, and success–and therefore an epithet for Lakshmi, the goddess of wealth and abundance, the consort of Vishnu. It is often used as an honorific prefix to the name of deities and holy persons to indicate holiness (Sri Krishna, Sri Swami N., etc.). Also used as the equivalent of the English "Mr." (Srimati would be the equivalent of "Mrs.")

Sukhadeva: The son of Vyasa who was liberated before coming into incarnation. He is considered a supreme renunciate, a perfect avadhuta.

Surya: The sun; the presiding deity of the sun, sometimes identified with Vishnu (Surya-Narayana) or the Absolute Brahman.

Sushumna: A subtle passage in the midst of the spinal column, corresponding to the spinal cord, that extends from the base of the spine to the medulla oblongata in the head.

Sushupti: The dreamless sleep state.

Sutra: Literally: a thread; an aphorism with minimum words and maximum sense; a terse sentence; in Buddhism, an entire scripture.

Swadharma: One's own natural (innate) duty (dharma, based on their karma and samskara. One's own prescribed duty in life according to the eternal law (ritam).

Swadhishthana chakra: Energy center located in the spine a little less than midway between the base of the spine and the area opposite the navel. Seat of the Water element.

Swadhyaya: Introspective self-study or self-analysis leading to self-understanding. Study of spiritual texts regarding the Self.

Sivananda (Swami): A great twentieth-century Master, founder of the worldwide Divine Life Society, whose books on spiritual life and religion are widely circulated in the West as well as in India.

Swapna: The dream state; a dream.

Tantra: A manual of, or a particular path of, sadhana laying great stress upon japa of a mantra and other esoteric practices relating to the powers latent in the human complex of physical, astral, and causal bodies in relation to the cosmic Power usually thought as the Divine Feminine.

Tapas: See tapasya.

Tapasya: Austerity; practical (i.e., result-producing) spiritual discipline; spiritual force. Literally it means the generation of heat or energy, but is always used in a symbolic manner, referring to spiritual practice and its effect, especially the roasting of karmic seeds, the burning up of karma.

Tapaswi(n): Ascetic; one who is practising Tapas.

Trailanga Swami: One of the most renowned and miraculous yogis of the nineteenth century, who was over three hundred and fifty years old. He lived during the latter years of his life in Varanasi (Benares).

Treta Yuga: See Yuga.

Trimurti: "The three forms"–Brahma, Vishnu, and Shiva, the Hindu "Trinity."

Triveni: The confluence of the three sacred rivers Ganges, Jumna (Yamuna), and Saraswati, located outside the sacred city of Rudraprayag (called Allahabad in modern times). Considered the most auspicious place for purificatory bathing. The space between the eyebrows.

Turiya: The state of pure consciousness. *A Ramakrishna-Vedanta Wordbook* defines it as: "The superconscious; lit., 'the Fourth,' in relation to the three ordinary states of consciousness–waking, dreaming, and dreamless sleep–which it transcends."

Upadhi: Adjunct; association; superimposed thing or attribute that veils and gives a colored view of the substance beneath it; limiting adjunct; instrument; vehicle; body; a technical term used in Vedanta philosophy for any superimposition that gives a limited view of the Absolute and makes It appear as the relative.

Upanishads: Books (of varying lengths) of the philosophical teachings of the ancient sages of India on the knowledge of Absolute Reality. The

Upanishads contain two major themes: (1) the individual self (atman) and the Supreme Self (Paramatman) are one in essence, and (2) the goal of life is the realization/manifestation of this unity, the realization of God (Brahman). There are eleven principal Upanishads: Isha, Kena, Katha, Prashna, Mundaka, Mandukya, Taittiriya, Aitareya, Chandogya, Brihadaranyaka, and Shvetashvatara, all of which were commented on by Shankara, Ramanuja and Madhvacharya, thus setting the seal of authenticity on them.

Upasana: "Sitting near" or "drawing near;" worship; adoration; contemplation of God or deity; devout meditation; both teaching and learning.

Urdhvareta yogi: A yogi in whom the subtle (including sexual) energies flow upwards.

Vaikuntha: The celestial abode (loka) of Vishnu and His devotees.

Vaishnava: A devotee of Vishnu.

Vaishya: A member of the merchant, farmer, artisan, businessman caste.

Varanasi: The most holy city of India, called by Yogananda "the Hindu Jerusalem." Located on the Ganges and dedicated to Shiva (Vishwanatha), it is believed that anyone who dies there will be liberated.

Varuna: A Vedic deity considered the sustainer of the universe and also the presiding deity of the oceans and water. Often identified with the conscience.

Vayu: The Vedic god of the wind; air; vital breath; Prana.

Veda: Knowledge, wisdom, revealed scripture. See Vedas.

Vedanta: Literally, "the end of the Vedas;" the Upanishads; the school of Hindu thought, based primarily on the Upanishads, upholding the doctrine of either pure non-dualism or conditional non-dualism. The original text of this school is Vedanta-darshana, the Brahma Sutras compiled by the sage Vyasa.

Vedas: The oldest scriptures of India, considered the oldest scriptures of the world, that were revealed in meditation to the Vedic Rishis (seers). Although in modern times there are said to be four Vedas (Rig, Sama, Yajur, and Atharva), in the Upanishads only three are listed (Rig, Sama, and Yajur). In actuality, there is only one Veda: the Rig Veda. The Sama Veda is only a collection of Rig Veda hymns that are marked (pointed) for singing. The

Yajur Veda is a small book giving directions on just one form of Vedic sacrifice. The Atharva Veda is only a collection of theurgical mantras to be recited for the cure of various afflictions or to be recited over the herbs to be taken as medicine for those afflictions.

Vipra: Inspired; wise, gifted with superior insight; sage; seer; priest; Brahmin.

Vishishtadvaita Vedanta: The philosophy of Qualified Non-Dualism formulated by Sri Ramanuja.

Vishnu: "The all-pervading;" God as the Preserver.

Vishuddha chakra: "Supreme purity." Energy center located in the spine opposite the hollow of the throat. Seat of the Ether element.

Vishwanatha: "Lord of the Universe;" a title of Shiva, often applied to his temple in Varanasi (Benares).

Viveka: Discrimination between the Real and the unreal, between the Self and the non-Self, between the permanent and the impermanent; right intuitive discrimination.

Viveki(n): One who possesses discrimination (viveka).

Vivekananda (Swami): The chief disciple of Sri Ramakrishna, who brought the message of Vedanta to the West at the end of the nineteenth century.

Vritti: Thought-wave; mental modification; mental whirlpool; a ripple in the chitta (mind substance).

Vyasa: One of the greatest sages of India, commentator on the Yoga Sutras, author of the Mahabharata (which includes the Bhagavad Gita), the Brahma Sutras, and the codifier of the Vedas.

Yajnavalkya: A great sage whose teachings are recorded in the Brihadaranyaka Upanishad; the guru of King Janaka.

Yajnopavita: Sacred thread. A triple thread worn by the twice-born (dwijas) that represents the threefold Brahman. It is essential for the performance of all the rites of the twice-born. Usually worn only by Brahmins, originally it was worn by Kshatriyas and Vaishyas as well.

Yama (1): Restraint; the five Don'ts of Yoga: 1) ahimsa–non-violence, non-injury, harmlessness; 2) satya–truthfulness, honesty; 3) asteya–non-stealing, honesty, non-misappropriativeness; 4) brahmacharya–continence; 5) aparigraha–non-possessiveness, non-greed, non-selfishness, non-acquisitiveness. These five are called the Great Vow (Observance, Mahavrata) in the Yoga Sutras.

Yama (2): Yamaraja; the Lord of Death, controller of who dies and what happens to them after death.

Yoga Darshana: See Yoga Sutras.

Yoga Sutras: The oldest known writing on the subject of yoga, written by the sage Patanjali, a yogi of ancient India, and considered the most authoritative text on yoga. Also known as Yoga Darshana, it is the basis of the Yoga Philosophy which is based on the philosophical system known as Sankhya.

Yogamaya: The power of Maya, of divine illusion. It is Maya in operation, the operation/movement rising from the presence (union–yoga) of God (Ishwara) within it, and therefore possessing delusive power.

Yogananda (Paramhansa): The most influential yogi of the twentieth century in the West, author of *Autobiography of a Yogi* and founder of Self-Realization Fellowship in America.

Yogeshwara: Lord of Yoga; a name of Lord Krishna.

Yogi(n): One who practices Yoga; one who strives earnestly for union with God; an aspirant going through any course of spiritual discipline.

Yuga: Age or cycle; aeon; world era. Hindus believe that there are four yugas: the Golden Age (Satya or Krita Yuga), the Silver age (Treta Yuga), The Bronze Age (Dwapara Yuga), and the Iron Age (Kali Yuga). Satya Yuga is four times as long as the Kali Yuga; Treta Yuga is three times as long; and Dwapara Yuga is twice as long. In the Satya Yuga the majority of humans use the total potential–four-fourths–of their minds; in the Treta Yuga, three-fourths; in the Dwapara Yuga, one half; and in the Kali Yuga, one fourth. (In each Yuga there are those who are using either more or less of their minds than the general populace.) The Yugas move in a perpetual circle: Ascending Kali Yuga, ascending Dwapara Yuga, ascending Treta Yuga, ascending Satya Yuga, descending Satya Yuga, descending, Treta Yuga, descending Dwapara Yuga, and descending Kali Yuga–over and over. Furthermore, there are yuga cycles within yuga cycles. For example, there are yuga cycles that affect the entire cosmos, and smaller yuga cycles within those greater cycles that affect a solar system. The cosmic yuga cycle takes 8,640,000,000 years, whereas the solar yuga cycle only takes 24,000 years. At the present time our solar system is in the ascending Dwapara Yuga, but the cosmos is in the descending Kali Yuga. Consequently, the more the general mind of humanity develops, the more folly and evil it becomes able to accomplish.

Yukteswar Giri, Swami Sri: The guru of Paramhansa Yogananda.

INDEX

A

Adam 379
Advaita 2, 28, 85-87, 119-120, 167,
    174, 187, 260, 318, 328, 348,
    360, 363
Afterlife 58, 88, 202
Age of Aquarius 116
Akshaya Kumar Banerjea 108, 115
Amitabha Buddha 332
Anandamayi Ma vii, 5, 44, 130, 142
    147, 182, 184, 208, 212, 218 244,
    349
Angels 6, 40, 57, 187-190, 209, 222,
    350
Animals 14-15, 75, 81, 106-107, 142,
    193-195, 205-208, 237-238, 307
Animal sacrifice 117, 142-143
Anna Catharine Emmerich 117
Antichrist 71, 74
Aquarian Gospel 13, 66, 102, 109, 144,
    161, 248, 253, 268, 287, 288,
    326, 339, 371
Astral worlds, astral plane 40, 58, 67,
    84, 98, 185, 186, 193, 217, 272,
    273, 320, 356
Astral experiences 34, 222, 297
Astral travel 171-72, 215-216, 220
Astral bodies 40, 131, 145, 173, 175,
    188, 249, 272, 365
Astrology 58, 196, 197
Asuras 39-40
Atman(n) 4, 20, 21, 26, 33, 35, 42, 51,
    106, 119, 132, 137, 160, 162-163,
    165, 242, 283, 320, 348, 350,
    360, 361, 366
Autobiography of a Yogi 14, 31, 50, 51,
    52, 62, 63, 100, 108, 127, 209,
    247, 264, 266, 288, 289, 290,
    301, 304, 306, 349, 356, 368
Avatar 45, 46, 66, 113, 118, 144, 148,
    201, 251, 306, 328, 350, 355,
    356

B

Bhagavad Gita viii, 2, 4-5, 7, 16-17, 27,
    30-33, 36, 39, 45, 48, 51, 55, 62,
    69-70, 77-78, 80, 106, 108-109,
    114, 117-120, 125, 127, 137-138,
    141-144, 152, 159, 167, 174, 176,
    179, 187, 204, 246, 254, 257,
    262, 281, 288, 293, 303, 323,
    325, 328, 333, 349, 350, 355-357,
    362, 367
Bhakti 120, 158, 252
Bharati Krishna Tirtha vii, 12, 124,
    153. *See also* Shankaracharya
Bhavishya Mahapurana 326
Bhrigu Samhita 183
Blasphemy 335, 338-340
Brahmacharya 16, 23, 30, 52, 54, 150,
    151, 300, 367
Brahmins 29, 159, 335, 367
Buddha 5, 16, 25, 31, 36, 45, 56, 105,
    123, 130, 142, 144, 167, 186,

246, 271, 295, 323, 349

Buddhism 1, 10, 24, 25, 73, 167, 229, 289, 364

Buddhist 31, 101, 124, 128, 129, 203, 204, 228, 332, 376

C

Catholic vii

Chakra 121, 131-132, 175, 254-257, 297, 348-349, 356-357, 364, 367

Channeling 198, 216

Charles W. Leadbeater 128, 244

Chetan Natha 248

Chitta 26-27, 44, 163, 168, 367

Christ Consciousness 268, 327

Christian vii, 6, 9-10, 13-14, 73-74, 82, 86, 98, 102, 105, 110, 112-113, 124, 127-128, 130-131, 153, 161, 195, 202-204, 228-231, 237, 240-241, 243-245, 265, 278, 280, 288, 315, 318-321, 328-329, 332-335

Christianity 6, 10, 13, 24-25, 73, 82, 98, 102, 113, 123, 125, 127, 129, 131, 152-153, 187, 189, 202-203, 228-229, 231, 239-241, 245, 267, 278, 285, 287-289, 318-320, 322, 325, 328, 331, 333-335

Church of Religious Science 332

Cosmic Consciousness 132

Cremation 217

D

Dakshineswar 123, 337

Death 9, 22, 34, 42, 46, 51, 58, 69, 76, 84-85, 88, 91, 106, 124, 131, 145, 158, 162, 170, 186, 193-194, 208, 216-218, 220, 247, 249, 253, 261, 267, 272-273, 280, 286, 289-291, 298, 301, 339-340, 353, 355, 357, 358, 361-362, 368

Demons 40-42, 106, 110, 189, 190, 192, 207, 317, 321, 323, 354

Departed spirits 180

Deva 5, 39-40, 181, 187-189, 351, 352

Devil 39, 41, 146, 318-319 259

Devotion 27, 31, 55, 124, 156, 158, 178, 252, 256, 281, 283, 334

Dharma 226

Dion Fortune 8, 22, 59, 233

Divine incarnation 46, 202-203, 350

Divine Life Society 30, 55, 125, 152, 364

Divine Name 147-150

Dogma 231

Dreams 47, 48, 57, 84, 166, 167

Durga 181, 251, 334, 352, 354

Dvaita 85, 86, 87, 352, 356

Dwelling In The Mirror viii

E

Eastern Orthodox Church 54, 71, 84, 102, 112, 239

Edgar Cayce 184, 228

Enlightenment 4, 28, 56, 118, 132, 143-144, 148, 176, 225, 250, 330, 352, 362

Esoteric view 84, 87-88, 105, 131, 133, 155, 233, 234, 241, 327, 365

Evolution of consciousness 21-22, 63, 72, 75-76, 81-82, 87-89, 91, 93, 95, 97, 100, 109, 129, 132, 142, 155, 188, 192-195, 204, 208, 210-211, 216, 219, 221, 227, 231, 249, 259, 272, 316-317, 319, 321, 325, 341, 352, 361

Exoteric view 87-88, 90, 92, 98, 155, 233

F

Free will 20-22, 64-65, 76, 122, 191, 223-224, 226

G

Gajanana Maharaj 115

Ganesha 187, 251, 302, 303, 334, 352
Gayatri 29, 284, 352, 361
Ghosts 180, 191
Goddesses 180, 181
Gods 27, 63, 88, 93, 114, 141, 178, 180,
        181, 187, 189, 190, 191, 194,
        203, 248, 251, 294, 321, 353
Gospel of Sri Ramakrishna 7, 154, 300,
        304, 305, 320, 323
Guru 5, 7, 12, 19, 104, 117, 124, 134,
        136, 142, 148, 153, 158, 169,
        215, 221, 235, 263, 290-291, 297,
        300, 310, 313, 330-331, 337, 348,
        367, 369

H

Hariakhan Baba 247, 289-290
Heaven 23, 25, 66, 70, 84, 88, 90, 131,
        182, 186, 239, 241, 243, 322, 353
Hell 9-10, 19, 23, 81-82, 84, 88, 90,
        145-146, 186, 202, 319-320, 322,
        335
Higher worlds 13, 89, 201, 215, 217,
        219, 316, 318
Hinduism 5, 10, 24, 25, 64, 69, 73, 113,
        119, 123-129, 131, 142-143, 152,
        178, 181, 202-204, 228-229, 231,
        243, 248, 289, 302-303, 320, 332,
        333-335, 350, 356, 362, 365, 366
Holy Spirit 86, 112, 130, 141, 200, 203,
        338-340
Homosexual 54
Householder 4, 299-301, 329

I

I. K. Taimni 112, 168, 185, 344
Incarnations of God 201, 203
India vii, viii, 5, 7, 11, 14, 18, 24, 28-29,
        34-36, 46-47, 53, 68, 72, 94, 100,
        102-104, 108, 110, 113, 118-
        119, 123-127, 130, 132, 136-137,
        140-144, 152-154, 158-159, 161,
        167, 170-173, 175-176, 183-187,

195, 204, 208-209, 219, 231-232,
        241-248, 252, 254, 256, 258-259,
        264, 266, 268, 274, 278-279,
        281, 283, 286-288, 290-295, 300,
        302-304, 306, 309, 313, 318-319,
        322, 326, 328-330, 332-335, 349,
        351-356, 358, 360, 362-363, 365,
        366, 367, 368-
Initiate 136, 204
Initiation 136, 204, 380
Ishwara 46, 130, 136, 186, 258-259,
        268, 324, 353, 355, 358, 363,
        368
Islam 24

J

James the Just 241
Japa 7, 16, 43-44, 47, 50, 52, 79, 132,
        148-151, 168, 226, 253, 260-261,
        264, 269, 283-285, 296, 365
Jesus vii, 5, 9-14, 25-26, 28, 31, 34,
        36, 43, 45, 64, 66, 71, 73-74, 83,
        98, 102, 109, 112-113, 116-117,
        123-127, 129-130, 138, 141,
        144, 152-154, 158-159, 161,
        165, 176-177, 184, 186, 190-
        191, 200-201, 203-208, 218-219,
        238-239, 241, 243-248, 253-254,
        261, 263, 268, 270-271, 274-275,
        278-280, 285-292, 294-295, 297,
        318, 320-323, 326-329, 332-335,
        339-341, 344, 353, 357
Jesus lived in India vii
Jiva (individual spirit) 118, 120, 132,
        165, 278, 282, 284, 285, 350,
        355, 362
Judaism 9, 82, 152, 189, 228, 243, 287,
        320

K

Kali 63, 100-101, 123, 142, 181, 267,
        291, 300, 303, 342, 354, 368,
        369

Karma 7, 16, 20-21, 27, 34, 40, 49, 58,
  59-60, 66-67, 69, 76, 83, 88-89,
  99, 104, 106-107, 111-123, 129,
  135, 139-140, 145-146, 155, 159,
  162, 177-178, 180, 184, 186,
  209, 215-218, 222-227, 264, 272,
  274-276, 278-280, 320-322, 325,
  339-340, 355, 357-358, 364-365
Kasmir Shaivism 185
Krishna vii, 7, 11-13, 17, 25, 27, 30-31,
  36, 51, 59, 70-71, 77-78, 106,
  108-109, 117-118, 124, 128-129,
  138-139, 142, 144, 153, 167, 174,
  178, 181, 186, 246, 249, 251,
  263, 271, 282, 295, 303, 305,
  323, 328, 334, 349, 351, 353,
  355, 359, 362, 364, 368
Kriya Yoga 46, 305, 355
Kuan Yin 332
Kundalini 115, 134, 156, 157, 158, 171,
  256-257, 284, 355

L

Lahiri Mahasaya 50, 289, 295, 299,
  300-301, 304-305, 307, 314, 355
Liberal Catholic Church vii, 128, 244
Liberation 27, 30, 35, 42, 45-46, 56, 60,
  90, 112, 118, 130, 136, 138, 167,
  184, 250-252, 257, 268, 271, 278,
  284, 319, 322, 324, 342, 350,
  357-358, 362
Lucifer 41, 189-193, 317, 379

M

Mahabharata 68, 117, 118, 290, 349,
  350, 355, 356, 367
Mahayana Buddhism 332
Mahendranath Gupta 2
Mantra 2, 7, 29, 43, 47, 50, 147, 149,
  151, 156, 172, 252, 260, 264,
  284, 285, 306, 349, 352, 354,
  356, 361, 364, 365, 374, 380
Maria Montessori 93

Marriage 7, 239, 361
Masters 19, 43, 46, 49, 50, 52, 57, 78,
  80, 124, 130, 186, 192, 215, 221,
  250, 258, 265, 271, 274-276, 288,
  297, 299, 308, 310, 313-315, 337,
  341, 353, 357, 364
Meditation iv, v, viii, 1, 3-4, 6-8, 11,
  14, 16-17, 23, 26-27, 37, 43-44,
  46-47, 50, 52-53, 55-57, 60, 63,
  71, 72, 79, 85, 105, 108, 110-111,
  114-115, 120, 122, 132, 134-
  136, 149-151, 160, 162, 164-165,
  168-170, 175-178, 203, 213,
  219-221, 226, 233-234, 236, 248,
  252-253, 260-264, 266, 269, 275,
  283, 295-296, 298, 301, 302, 303,
  306, 311, 313, 316, 331, 347,
  350, 357, 360, 361, 364, 366
Mentally ill 67, 70
Messiah 144
Miracles 39, 135, 182-183, 264, 328
Moksha. *See also* liberation
Monastic(s)s 4-6, 20, 30, 51, 183, 237-
  239, 300, 327, 349, 353, 361-363
Monism 28, 211, 213

N

Names of God 129
Nathanamavali 247, 290
Neem Karoli Baba 49, 142, 306
Negative entities or spirits 8, 198
Negative forces 3, 189
Negative thoughts 78, 168
New Age 222, 332
Nicene Creed 243
Nicholas Notovitch 124
Niyama 104, 108, 164, 349
Non-dualism 28, 86, 211, 213, 260,
  366

O

Om viii, 8, 50, 110, 148, 172, 269, 358-
  360, 374

Om Yoga Meditation viii
Orthodox Church *See Eastern Orthodox Church*

P

Padre Pio 229
Paramhansa Nityananda 118, 169, 324
Paramhansa Yogananda vii, 14, 41,
    48, 50, 71, 78, 98, 102, 108, 118,
    123-124, 127-128, 131, 134, 153,
    178, 183, 195, 221, 254, 259,
    263, 278, 288-289, 296, 301, 310,
    322, 335, 349, 356, 358, 369
Past lives 99, 105, 182, 272, 276-277,
    333
Patanjali 377, 383
Pilgrimage 18, 141, 244, 247, 289, 306,
    309, 329, 330, 336
Prana 52, 75, 163, 336, 358, 359
Prayer(s) 12, 27, 33-34, 36, 84, 135,
    139, 178, 191, 217, 253, 261-264,
    324
Prayers for the departed 217
Prophecies 183-184
Pure Land 332

R

Rama 7, 123, 128, 181, 246, 251, 282,
    295, 303, 305-306, 323, 334, 354,
    360, 364
Ramakrishna Mission 8, 30, 108, 125,
    319
Ramana Maharshi 5, 37, 57, 175, 330,
    360
Ramanashram 330
Ramanuja 28, 152, 159, 175, 360, 366,
    367
Ramayana 68, 328, 360
Rebirth *See Reincarnation*
Reincarnation 9, 20-22, 46, 60, 76, 82,
    89, 93, 138, 145-146, 159, 162,
    169, 184, 205, 222-225, 228-231,
    249-251, 275, 280, 321

Repenting 227-228
Resurrection of the body 231
Rishikesh vii
Ritualistic worship 27
Roman Catholic Church 71, 93, 229,
    239, 244

S

Sadhana 3-5, 7, 46-47, 148, 152, 174,
    182, 244-245, 250-252, 258, 263,
    360, 365
Sahasrara 157, 175, 361
Saint Bartholomew 172
Saint Gregory Palamas 202
Saint John Maximovitch 112
Saint John of Kronstadt 112
Saint Philaret Voznesensky vii
Saint Seraphim of Sarov 112
Saint Thomas 373, 378
Saint Thomas Christian 14, 161, 245,
    328, 329, 334
Saint Thomas Christian Creed 245
Saint Thomas Christian Church 158,
    159, 293
Salvation 46, 89-90, 112, 201-202, 205,
    271, 284, 292
Samadhi 1, 2, 115, 157-158, 248, 298,
    300, 349
Samskaras 99, 333, 361
Sanatana Dharma vii, viii, 5, 28, 34-35,
    44-45, 91-92, 95-96, 102, 112-
    113, 123-127, 129-130, 141, 145,
    152-154, 159, 184, 231, 241-245,
    278, 302, 318-320, 322-323,
    325-326, 328, 333-334, 357,
    361-362
Sankhya 61, 74, 117-118, 120, 132,
    144, 174, 187, 259, 362, 368
Sannyasa 7, 12, 330, 361
Sarada Devi 7, 18, 114, 124, 142, 292,
    300, 322, 362
Satan 41-42, 78-79, 189-190, 192, 317
Satanism 23

Satsang i, iii, v, 1, 47, 52, 104, 125, 128, 247, 304, 329, 331-332, 346, 363
Savior 91, 159, 248, 272, 287, 292
Scriptures viii, 14, 31, 79, 80, 116, 118, 254, 364, 366
Second Coming 14, 52, 98, 109, 125, 204, 254, 288, 322, 326, 335
Self-realization 42, 52, 109, 251, 269, 350
Sex 18, 19, 30, 53, 54, 151, 255, 314
Shakti 137, 163, 244, 250, 352, 353, 358
Shankara 26-28, 43, 124, 136, 152-153, 159, 168, 174-175, 182, 242-243, 252, 258, 295-296, 342, 348, 362-363, 366
Shankaracharya vii, 12, 48, 124, 153, 363
Shiva (Siva) 11, 115, 127-128, 132, 158, 181, 185, 251, 261, 266, 278, 283-284, 302, 304, 334, 349, 352, 356-357, 363, 365-367
Siddhis 35, 328
Sins 30, 55, 89, 202, 262, 267-268, 280, 284-285, 287, 290
Sivanandashram 20, 126, 309, 337
Soham 4, 6, 8, 52, 64, 132, 156, 160, 169, 252-253, 269-270, 283-285, 349
Soham Yoga 4, 6, 8, 52, 64, 132, 156, 160, 169, 252-253, 269-270, 285
Spiritual music 53
Spiritual name 68, 186
Spiritual practice 42, 157, 236, 251, 316, 330, 365
Spiritual reading 55
Spiritual routine 6
Sri Ma Anandamayi. See Anandamayi Ma
Sri Ramakrishna 2, 4, 7, 18, 25, 30, 36, 46, 56, 123-124, 126-127, 129, 154, 156, 180, 184, 253, 291-292, 296, 299-300, 304-305, 318-320, 323-324, 326, 337, 341-342, 360,

362, 367
Sri Yukteswar 16, 19, 31, 63, 124, 209, 263, 289, 295, 297
Suicide 34, 67
Swadharma 72, 364
Swami Abhedananda 124
Swami Akhilananda 125
Swami Brahmananda 30, 123, 337
Swami Prabhavananda 4, 39, 48, 108, 125
Swami Rama Tirtha 123, 360
Swami (Papa) Ramdas 30, 110, 123, 126
Swami Saradananda 124, 323
Swami Sivananda vii, 17, 30, 35, 48, 55, 125-126, 142, 152, 169, 252
Swami Swarupananda 48, 183
Swami Trigunatitananda 124
Swami Vidyananda Giri vii, 7
Swami Vivekananda 2, 56, 140, 195, 252, 300, 324, 367
Swami Yatiswarananda 8, 23, 52, 55-56, 108

T

Tantra 157-158, 177, 285, 365
The Christ of India viii
Theology 82, 86, 91, 96, 98, 202, 230, 267, 285, 287, 318
Theosophical Society 93, 244
Tomb of Jesus 329
Trinity 86, 130, 141, 200, 245, 293, 324, 338, 365

U

UFOs 221, 222
Universes 192, 209
Unknown Life of Jesus Christ 25, 124, 326
Upanishads 5, 28, 44, 45, 48, 59, 62, 69, 85, 96, 114, 118, 119, 152, 159, 176, 294, 366

V

Vaishnava 119, 305, 356, 360, 366
Vashishtha Guha 11, 123
Vedas 10-11, 29, 35, 328, 355, 366-367
Vedanta 8, 85-87, 108, 119, 124-125,
174, 187, 259, 318-323, 348, 350,
356, 360, 362-363, 365-367, 375
Vedanta Society 8, 108, 125, 319
Vedas 70, 80, 85, 157, 366, 367
Vegetarian 14, 54, 74, 107, 113, 151,
156, 170-171, 173, 236-237, 336-
Vegetarianism 142, 173, 238
Virgin birth 45
Virgin Mary 72-73, 109, 125, 141, 161,
203, 338
Vishishtadvaita 85, 360, 367
Vishnu 117, 181, 283, 334, 356, 364-
367
Visions 37-38, 57, 123-124, 134, 183,
311-312
Vrittis 26, 44
Vyasa 27, 43, 85, 118, 136, 142, 182,
187, 258, 296, 350, 359, 364,
366, 367

W

Warren Vickerman 221, 296
Western Christian monastics 6
William Branham 183

Y

Yama 104, 108, 164, 349
Yama and Niyama 69, 383
Yoga vii, viii, 4, 5, 6, 8, 26-27, 31, 37,
39, 43-46, 52, 60-62, 64, 69-70,
75, 78, 95, 97, 105, 108-109,
111-112, 114, 116, 118, 120,
122-123, 125, 130, 132, 134-137,
143, 144, 152, 155-156, 158,
159-161, 167-170, 174, 176, 178,
182, 184-185, 187, 219, 244-246,
248, 251-253, 258-259, 265, 266,
269-270, 281-282, 284-285, 288,
296, 302, 305, 310, 330, 331,
333, 344, 349, 353, 355, 357-358,
360, 362, 367-368
Yogananda *See Paramhansa Yogananda*
Yoga Sutras 5, 26, 43-45, 69, 111, 114,
120, 136, 152, 176, 182, 187,
288, 296, 333, 355, 358, 367-368
Yuga 63, 100, 101, 352, 354, 363, 365,
368, 369

Z

Zen 96

Light of the Spirit Monastery

Light of the Spirit Monastery is an esoteric Christian monastic community for those men who seek direct experience of the Spirit through meditation, sacramental worship, discipline and dedicated communal life, emphasizing the inner reality of "Christ in you the hope of glory," as taught by the illumined mystics of East and West.

The public outreach of the monastery is through its website, OCOY.org (Original Christianity and Original Yoga). There you will find many articles on Original Christianity and Original Yoga, including *Esoteric Christian Beliefs*. *Foundations of Yoga* and *How to Be a Yogi* are practical guides for anyone seriously interested in living the Yoga Life.

You will also discover many other articles on leading an effective spiritual life, including *The Yoga of the Sacraments* and *Spiritual Benefits of a Vegetarian Diet*, as well as the "Dharma for Awakening" series—in-depth commentaries on these spiritual classics: the Upanishads, the Bhagavad Gita, the Dhammapada, and the Tao Teh King.

You can listen to podcasts by Abbot George on meditation, the Yoga Life, and remarkable spiritual people he has met in India and elsewhere, at http://ocoy.org/podcasts/

Reading for Awakening

Light of the Spirit Press presents books on spiritual wisdom and Original Christianity and Original Yoga. From our "Dharma for Awakening" series (practical commentaries on the world's scriptures) to books on how to meditate and live a successful spiritual life, you will find books that are informative, helpful, and even entertaining.

Light of the Spirit Press is the publishing house of Light of the Spirit Monastery (Atma Jyoti Ashram) in Cedar Crest, New Mexico, USA. Our books feature the writings of the founder and director of the monastery, Abbot George Burke (Swami Nirmalananda Giri) which are also found on the monastery's website, OCOY.org.

We invite you to explore our publications in the following pages.

Find out more about our publications at
lightofthespiritpress.com

Soham Yoga
The Yoga of the Self

An in-depth guide to the practice of Soham sadhana.

Soham (which is pronounced like "Sohum") means: I Am That. It is the natural vibration of the Self, which occurs spontaneously with each incoming and outgoing breath. By becoming aware of it on the conscious level by mentally repeating it in time with the breath (*So* when inhaling and *Ham* when exhaling), a yogi experiences the identity between his individual Self and the Supreme Self.

The practice is very simple, and the results very profound. Truly wondrous is the fact that Soham Yoga can go on all the time, not just during meditation, if we apply ourselves to it. The whole life can become a continuous stream of liberating sadhana. "By the mantra 'Soham' separate the jivatma from the Paramatma and locate the jivatma in the heart" (Devi Bhagavatam 11.8.15). When we repeat Soham in time with the breath we are invoking our eternal being. This is why we need only listen to our inner mental intonations of Soham in time with the breath which itself is Soham.

What Readers say:

"The more I read this book, study it and practice Soham meditation and japa, the more thrilled I am to find this book. It is a complete spiritual path of Yoga."—*Arnold Van Wie*

Visit sohamyogameditation.com to read online or to download a free PDF.
Also available online in paperback and ebook versions.

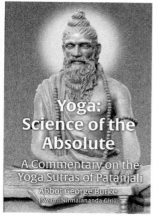

Yoga: Science of the Absolute
A Commentary on the Yoga Sutras of Patanjali

In *Yoga: Science of the Absolute*, Abbot George Burke draws on the age-long tradition regarding this essential text, including the commentaries of Vyasa and Shankara, the most highly regarded writers on Indian philosophy and practice, as well as I. K. Taimni and other authoritative commentators, and adds his own ideas based on half a century of study and practice.Serious students of yoga will find this an essential addition to their spiritual studies.

What Readers say:

"Abbot George has provided a commentary that is not only deeply informative, making brilliant connections across multiple traditions, but eminently practical. More importantly he describes how they can help one empower their own practice, their own sadhana." —*Michael Sabani*

The Bhagavad Gita for Awakening

A Practical Commentary for Leading a Successful Spiritual Life

With penetrating insight, Abbot George Burke illumines the Bhagavad Gita's practical value for spiritual seekers. With a unique perspective from a lifetime of study and practice of both Eastern and Western spirituality, Abbot George presents the treasures of the Gita in an easily intelligible fashion.

Drawing from the teachings of Sri Ramakrishna, Jesus, Paramhansa Yogananda, Ramana Maharshi, Swami Vivekananda, Swami Sivananda of Rishikesh, Papa Ramdas, and other spiritual masters and teachers, as well as his own experiences, Abbot Burke illustrates the teachings of the Gita with stories which make the teachings of Krishna in the Gita vibrant and living.

What Readers say:

"This is not a book for only "Hindus" or "Christians." Anyone desiring to better their lives mentally, emotionally, and spiritually would benefit greatly by reading this book." — *Sailaja Kuruvadi*

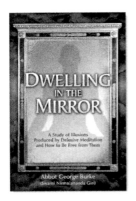

Dwelling in the Mirror

A Study of Illusions Produced by Delusive Meditation and How to Be Free from Them

"There are those who can have an experience and realize that it really cannot be real, but a vagary of their mind. Some may not understand that on their own, but can be shown by others the truth about it. For them and those that may one day be in danger of meditation-produced delusions I have written this brief study." –Abbot George Burke

In *Dwelling in the Mirror* you will learn:
  • different types of meditation and the experiences they produce, and the problems and delusions which can arise from them.
  • how to get rid of negative initiation energies and mantras.
  • what are authentic, positive meditation practices and their effects and aspects.
  • an ancient, universal method of meditation which is both proven and effective.

What Readers say:

"I totally loved this book! After running across many spiritual and self-help books filled with unrealistic promises, this little jewel had the impact of a triple Espresso."—Sandra Carrington-Smith, author of *Housekeeping for the Soul*

The Christ of India
The Story of Original Christianity

"Original Christianity" is the teaching of both Jesus of Nazareth and his Apostle Saint Thomas in India. Although it was new to the Mediterranean world, it was really the classical, traditional teachings of the ancient rishis of India that even today comprise Sanatana Dharma, the Eternal Dharma, that goes far beyond religion into realization.

In The Christ of India Abbot George Burke presents what those ancient teachings are, as well as the growing evidence that Jesus spent much of his "Lost Years" in India and Tibet. This is also the story of how the original teachings of Jesus and Saint Thomas thrived in India for centuries before the coming of the European colonialists.

What Readers say:

"Interpreting the teachings of Jesus from the perspective of Santana Dharma, The Christ of India is a knowledgeable yet engaging collection of authentic details and evident manuscripts about the Essene roots of Jesus and his 'Lost years'. ...delightful to read and a work of substance, vividly written and rich in historical analysis, this is an excellent work written by a masterful teacher and a storyteller." —*Enas Reviews*

The Dhammapada for Awakening
A Commentary on Buddha's Practical Wisdom

The Dhammapada for Awakening brings a refreshing and timely perspective to ancient wisdom and shows seekers of inner peace practical ways to improve their inner lives today.

It explores the Buddha's answers to the urgent questions, such as "How can I find find lasting peace, happiness and fulfillment that seems so elusive?" and "What can I do to avoid many of the miseries big and small that afflict all of us?".

Drawing on the proven wisdom of different ancient traditions, and the contemporary masters of spiritual life, as well as his own studies and first-hand knowledge of the mystical traditions of East and West, Abbot George illumines the practical wisdom of Buddha in the Dhammapada, and more importantly, and make that makes that teaching relevant to present day spiritual seekers.

What Readers say:

"In this compelling book, Abbot George Burke brings his considerable knowledge and background in Christian teachings and the Vedic tradition of India to convey a practical understanding of the teachings of the Buddha. ...This is a book you'll want to take your time to read and keep as reference to reread. Highly recommended for earnest spiritual aspirants" —*Anna Hourihan, author, editor, and publisher at Vedanta Shores Press*

May a Christian Believe in Reincarnation?

Discover the real and surprising history of reincarnation and Christianity.

A growing number of people are open to the subject of past lives, and the belief in rebirth–reincarnation, metempsychosis, or transmigration–is becoming commonplace. It often thought that belief in reincarnation and Christianity are incompatible. But is this really true? May a Christian believe in reincarnation? The answer may surprise you.

Reincarnation-also known as the transmigration of souls-is not just some exotic idea of non-Christian mysticism. Nor is it an exclusively Hindu-Buddhist teaching.

In orthodox Jewish and early Christian writings, as well as the Holy Scriptures, we find reincarnation as a fully developed belief, although today it is commonly ignored. But from the beginning it has been an integral part of Orthodox Judaism, and therefore as Orthodox Jews, Jesus and his Apostles would have believed in rebirth.

What Readers say:

"Those needing evidence that a belief in reincarnation is in accordance with teachings of the Christ need look no further: Plainly laid out and explained in an intelligent manner from one who has spent his life on a Christ-like path of renunciation and prayer/meditation."
—*Christopher T. Cook*

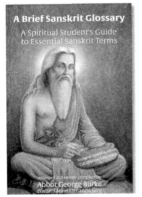

A Brief Sanskrit Glossary
A Spiritual Student's Guide to Essential Sanskrit Terms

This Sanskrit glossary contains full translations and explanations of many of the most commonly used spiritual Sanskrit terms, and will help students of the Bhagavad Gita, the Upanishads, the Yoga Sutras of Patanjali, and other Indian scriptures and philosophical works to expand their vocabularies to include the Sanskrit terms contained in them, and gain a fuller understanding in their studies.

What Readers say:

"If you are reading the writings of Swami Sivananda you will find a basketful of untranslated Sanskrit words which often have no explanation, as he assumes his readers have a background in Hindu philosophy. For writings like his, this book is invaluable, as it lists frequently used Sanskrit terms used in writings on yoga and Hindu philosophical thought.

"As the title says, this is a spiritual students' guidebook, listing not only commonly used spiritual terms, but also giving brief information about spiritual teachers and writers, both modern and ancient.

"Abbot George's collection is just long enough to give the meanings of useful terms without overwhelming the reader with an overabundance of extraneous words. This is a book that the spiritual student will use frequently."—*Simeon Davis*

The Gospel of Thomas for Awakening

A Commentary on Jesus' Sayings as Recorded by the Apostle Thomas

"From the very beginning there were two Christianities." So begins this remarkable work. While the rest of the Apostles dispersed to various areas of the Mediterranean world, the apostle Thomas travelled to India, where growing evidence shows that Jesus spent his "Lost Years," and which had been the source of the wisdom which he had brought to the "West."

In *The Gospel of Thomas for Awakening*, Abbot George shines the "Light of the East" on the sometimes enigmatic sayings of Jesus recorded by his apostle Saint Thomas, revealing their unique and rich practical nature for modern day seekers for spiritual life.

Ideal for daily study or group discussion.

What Readers say:

"An extraordinary work of theological commentary, *The Gospel of Thomas for Awakening* is as informed and informative as it is inspired and inspiring".—*James A. Cox, Editor-in-Chief, Midwest Book Review*

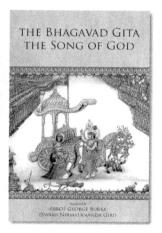

The Bhagavad Gita–The Song of God

A new translation of the most important spiritual classic which India has produced.

Often called the "Bible" of Hinduism, the Bhagavad Gita is found in households throughout India and has been translated into every major language of the world. Literally billions of copies have been handwritten and printed.

The clarity of this translation by Abbot George Burke makes for easy reading, while the rich content makes this the ideal "study" Gita. As the original Sanskrit language is so rich, often there are several accurate translations for the same word, which are noted in the text, giving the spiritual student the needed understanding of the fullness of the Gita.

For those unable to make a spiritual journey to India, a greater pilgrimage can be made by anyone anywhere in the world by simply reading The Holy Song of God, the Srimad Bhagavad Gita. It will be a holy pilgrimage of mind and spirit.

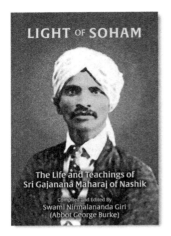

Light of Soham
The Life and Teachings of Sri Gajanana Maharaj of Nashik

At the beginning of the twentieth century, a young crippled boy in North India met a spiritual teacher in the Nath tradition of the great teachers Matsyendranath and Gorakhnath, who imparted to him the precious knowledge of yoga meditation. The boy began to apply himself to this meditation practice and became a very unusual saint indeed.

Gajanana Maharaj taught the ajapa-japa of the Soham mantra with the breath. In Light of Soham his teachings for success in Soham sadhana and spiritual life in general have been collected from the writings of himself and his disciples.

What Readers say:

"This book cuts straight to the problem of life - our separation from the Godhead - and without dwelling too much on this immediately cuts to the solution: Meditation." —Dylan Grant

---

Robe of Light
An Esoteric Christian Cosmology

In *Robe of Light* Abbot George Burke explores the whys and wherefores of the mystery of creation. From the emanation of the worlds from the very Being of God, to the evolution of the souls to their ultimate destiny as perfected Sons of God, the ideal progression of creation is described. Since the rebellion of Lucifer and the fall of Adam and Eve from Paradise flawed the normal plan of evolution, a restoration was necessary. How this came about is the prime subject of this insightful study.

Moreover, what this means to aspirants for spiritual perfection is expounded, with a compelling knowledge of the scriptures and of the mystical traditions of East and West.

What Readers say:

"Having previously read several offerings from the pen of Abbot George Burke I was anticipating this work to be well written and an enjoyable read. However, Robe of Light actually exceeded my expectations. Abbot Burke explicates the subject perfectly, making a difficult and complex subject like Christian cosmology accessible to those of us who are not great theologians."—*Russ Thomas*

384

Foundations of Yoga
Ten Important Principles Every Meditator Should Know

An in-depth examination of the important foundation principles of Patanjali's Yoga, Yama & Niyama.

Yama and Niyama are often called the Ten Commandments of Yoga, but they have nothing to do with the ideas of sin and virtue or good and evil as dictated by some cosmic potentate. Rather they are determined on a thoroughly practical, pragmatic basis: that which strengthens and facilitates our yoga practice should be observed and that which weakens or hinders it should be avoided.

It is not a matter of being good or bad, but of being wise or foolish. Each one of these Five Don'ts (Yama) and Five Do's (Niyama) is a supporting, liberating foundation of Yoga. An introduction to the important foundation principles of Patanjali's Yoga: Yama & Niyama

Available as a free Kindle ebook download at Amazon.com, as well as in paperback

---

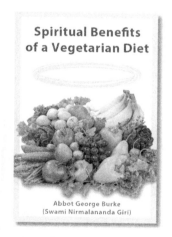

Spiritual Benefits of a Vegetarian Diet

The health benefits of a vegetarian diet are well known, as are the ethical aspects. But the spiritual advantages should be studied by anyone involved in meditation, yoga, or any type of spiritual practice.

Although diet is commonly considered a matter of physical health alone, since the Hermetic principle "as above, so below" is a fundamental truth of the cosmos, diet is a crucial aspect of emotional, intellectual, and spiritual development as well. For diet and consciousness are interrelated, and purity of diet is an effective aid to purity and clarity of consciousness.

The major thing to keep in mind when considering the subject of vegetarianism is its relevancy in relation to our explorations of consciousness. We need only ask: Does it facilitate my spiritual growth–the development and expansion of my consciousness? The answer is Yes.

A second essay, *Christian Vegetarianism,* continues with a consideration of the esoteric side of diet, the vegetarian roots of early Christianity, and an insightful exploration of vegetarianism in the Old and New Testaments.

Available as a free Kindle ebook download at Amazon.com..

385

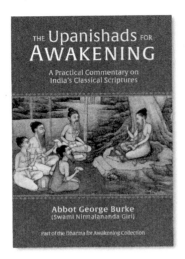

The Upanishads for Awakening
A Practical Commentary on India's Classical Scriptures

With penetrating insight, Abbot George Burke illumines the Upanishads' practical value for spiritual seekers, and the timelessness of India's most beloved scriptures. With a unique perspective of a lifetime of study and practice of both Eastern and Western spirituality, Abbot George mines the treasures of the Upanishads and presents them in an easily intelligible fashion for those wishing to put these priceless teachings into practice..

Notes